THE ARCHITECTURE
OF SCOTTISH CITIES

The Architecture
of Scottish Cities

Essays in Honour of David Walker

EDITED BY

Deborah Mays

FOREWORD BY

Sir Howard Colvin

TUCKWELL PRESS
EAST LINTON, SCOTLAND

First published in Great Britain by
Tuckwell Press
The Mill House
Phantassie
East Linton
East Lothian EH40 3DG
Scotland

ISBN 1 86232 028 4

The publishers gratefully acknowledge financial support towards this volume
from the Bank of Scotland, the University of St Andrews, and an anonymous donor

British Library Cataloguing-in-Publication Data
A catalogue record for this book is available
on request from the British Library

Typeset and originated by Carnegie Publishing Ltd, Preston
Printed in Spain by GraphyCems

Table of Contents

List of Illustrations

Picture Credits

Mr I. Adams: 6.4
Aerofilms: 1.2
The Carnegie Library, Ayr: 8.6
The British Library: 13.3
The Clydesdale Bank plc: 5.3
Dundee Central Library: 16.3–16.4
Dundee City Archives: 16.1–16.2
Department of Fine Art, the University of Edinburgh: 5.5
Glasgow City Archives: 6.2
The Mitchell Library, Glasgow: 4.2; 6.5
The Trustees of the Late John Hope: 10.3
The National Galleries of Scotland: 5.1

The National Library of Scotland: 13.2; 13.4
Paisley Central Library and Museum: 6.3
Joe Rock, Photographer: 5.2; 5.3 ; 10.6
The Royal Commission on the Ancient and Historical Monuments of Scotland: 2.3–2.6; 4.3–4.5; 8.2; 9.1–9.11; 10.1–10.2; 10.4–10.5; 11.4–11.6; 12.1; 14.2; 14.5
St Andrews Preservation Trust: 1.1
St Andrews University Library: 1.3–1.7; 16.8
Sir John Soane's Museum, London: 8.1; 8.5
The Society of Antiquaries: 4.1
Mrs Laura Wilson: 13.5

Abbreviations

GD	:	Gift Deposit
GHT	:	George Heriot Trust
NMRS	:	National Monuments Record of Scotland
RCAHMS	:	Royal Commission on the Ancient and Historical Monuments of Scotland
SRO	:	Scottish Record Office
V & A	:	Victoria and Albert Museum

Acknowledgements

THIS collection of essays, conceived by many separately and collectively, was first advanced by a committee of four, John Hume, Aonghus MacKechnie, Ranald MacInnes and Deborah Mays. It would not have reached fruition without the contributions and advice of the authors and many more, a handful of whom may here be given particular mention.

In the early stages Jill Lever, Professor Sir James Dunbar-Nasmith and Ian Gow generously gave the benefits of experience in the search for funding. The University of St Andrews, the Bank of Scotland and a particularly generous donor – who modestly prefers to remain anonymous – provided the financial injection which enabled the translation of ideas into reality. David Breeze and Hugh Andrew helpfully and wisely steered the editor to a willing publisher, John Tuckwell, who, with his wife Valerie, also kindly undertook the compilation of the index.

Anne Riches, John Frew, Peter Willis, Ian Gow and Kitty Cruft all gave welcome pointers on diverse issues from copyright and editorial policy to sponsorship. The Royal Commission on the Ancient and Historical Monuments of Scotland assisted invaluably with illustrations, and Iain Gordon Brown offered advice on the thorny matter of reproduction fees. Dawn Waddell acted with customary ingenuity and professionalism in advancing David's bibliography. Historic Scotland, most notably in the persons of Frank Lawrie and John Hume, generously gave organisational support and editorial advice, and unqualified permission to use David's fine montage for the cover.

The authors have given their own personal acknowledgements at the foot of their respective chapters. Those cited in these closing paragraphs belong here too: they have the combined thanks of the body of authors, and make their own contribution to this *festschrift*. It must be emphasised also that the tribute and thanks to David made by the authors in this volume stand for those of a wider majority whom it was not possible to include but whose wishes are equally embodied here.

Each contributor stayed loyal to an unexpectedly protracted project. They share with the editor the sadness that it was not completed in time for Averil Walker to witness the presentation and enjoy the intended honour.

David Walker

Foreword

FOR THIRTY YEARS David Walker has been a central figure in Scottish architectural studies. As Chief Inspector of Historic Buildings his authority and judgement have been crucial in implementing the legislation for the preservation of Scotland's architectural heritage. As a scholar his knowledge of Scottish architectural history is immense, and his generosity in sharing it with fellow scholars and students is widely appreciated. His observation of architectural form and detail (often recorded in his own elegant sketches) is as accurate and as perceptive as his use of historical records. His writings have done much to make the nineteenth century better understood, and his surveys of the principal Scottish towns and cities, undertaken in the 1960s for the Scottish Development Department, provided a foundation both for conservation and for research such as no other part of the British Isles then enjoyed. No one in fact knows the architecture of Scottish cities better than David Walker, and it is with a collection of essays on that subject that the contributors to this volume pay tribute to his achievement as artist, architectural historian and civil servant.

Sir Howard Colvin

Preface

As a young student in vernacular architecture I first encountered the Dundee-based Investigator of Historic Buildings, David Walker, during 1968. The disbelief and awe which I experienced as I left our first meeting is as strong now as it was twenty-eight years ago.

In the interim I have been extremely fortunate to have had the privilege to work closely with David Walker as a professional colleague in Historic Scotland and its predecessor Departments. Over that time I have never ceased to be amazed by the encyclopaedic knowledge, his ability to give chapter and verse on the mere sight of a chimney through the trees, and the instant recall of a vast fund of architectural information which freely flowed in response to any question on Scotland's architectural heritage.

I also had the unenviable challenge of having to act with him as 'tour guide' on a number of Historic Buildings Council for Scotland annual tours around the country. It was always a daunting task to be put 'up front' with him and to prepare my notes in such a way that our contributions complemented each other. Not infrequently the question crossed my mind: how could I put myself in such a situation!

To friends and colleagues his generosity knows no bounds and I shall be forever grateful for the times I shared his company, magnanimity and benevolence.

In that regard I am not alone. It is therefore my special delight to preface this volume on *The Architecture of Scottish Cities* as a tribute to David Walker and to offer these words in recognition of what many others may feel in having had the good fortune to meet and work with him.

Ingval Maxwell

Notes on the Contributors

DR IAN CAMPBELL worked as a Historic Buildings Inspector under David Walker from 1981 to 1986. He returned to Edinburgh in 1992 to teach architectural history at the College of Art. In 1996–7 he held a Leverhulme Research Fellowship cataloguing architectural drawings at Windsor Castle.

DR RONALD GORDON CANT is of Angus and Renfrewshire descent, and received his schooling in Aberdeen and Edinburgh and his university education at St Andrews and Oxford. From 1936 to 1974, he was successively a lecturer in Medieval History and Reader in Scottish History at St Andrews, also serving as President of the Society of Antiquaries of Scotland. His published work has been mainly in Constitutional, Ecclesiastical and Architectural History.

KITTY CRUFT retired as Curator of the National Monuments Record of Scotland in 1991. She is currently researching and writing the forthcoming volume on the *Borders* in the *Buildings of Scotland* series published by Penguin Books. She is an Honorary Fellow of the Royal Incorporation of Architects in Scotland and a Vice-President of the Architectural Heritage Society of Edinburgh.

DR RICHARD FAWCETT is a Principal Inspector of Ancient Monuments with Historic Scotland and is author of a number of works on medieval ecclesiastical architecture, notably *Scottish Architecture from the Accession of the Stewarts to the Reformation* (1994).

DR JOHN FREW is a senior lecturer in the University of St Andrews' School of Art History. He is a member of the Historic Buildings Council for Scotland and joint editor of *St Andrews Studies in Scottish Architecture and Design*.

DR MILES GLENDINNING works at the Royal Commission on the Ancient and Historical Monuments of Scotland in the Buildings Survey. He is an Honorary Fellow of the Social Policy Department, Edinburgh University. He is co-author with Stefan Muthesius of *Tower Block* (1994), and editor with Ranald MacInnes and Aonghus MacKechnie of *A History of Scottish Architecture* (1996).

ANDOR GOMME is Emeritus Professor of English Literature and Architectural History at Keele University and currently honorary editor to the Society of Architectural Historians of Great Britain. He is the author of many papers and several books in both his main fields of study, including *The Architecture of Glasgow* in collaboration with David Walker. He has also produced a performing edition of Bach's *St Mark's Passion*, recently professionally recorded.

IAN GOW was born in Edinburgh and is now Curator of Collections in the National Monuments Record of Scotland and Hon Curator of the Royal Incorporation of Architects in Scotland. He has published extensively on the decorative arts and architecture in Scotland.

JOHN ROBERT HUME is Chief Inspector of Historic Buildings at Historic Scotland. He attended Glasgow University and was until 1984 a Senior Lecturer in Economic History at Strathclyde University. He is Honorary President of the Seagull

Trust and a Trustee of the Scottish Maritime Museum. Among his many publications are *The Making of Scottish Whisky* and the two-volume *The Industrial Archaeology of Scotland*.

JOHN KNIGHT works as an architect with Historic Scotland. In his spare time he has sketched much of Edinburgh – where he has lived since 1970 – and also cities as far afield as New York, Prague and Colombo. His work has been exhibited in group exhibitions at the Talbot Rice Gallery and the Fine Art Society. He has illustrated several books, including in 1974 a commission to draw Robert Louis Stevenson's Edinburgh houses for James Pope-Hennessy's biography of the author.

DR JAMES MACAULAY is a former senior lecturer in architectural history in the Mackintosh School of Architecture, Glasgow. He is author of *The Gothic Revival, 1745–1845, The Classical Country House in Scotland, 1660–1800, Glasgow School of Art* and *Hill House*. He is co-editor of the *MacJournal*.

RANALD MACINNES was born in Arran and educated in Glasgow. After a spell with English Heritage he joined David Walker's Resurvey Team in 1985. He has written various articles on Scottish architecture and has recently produced an extensive history with Miles Glendinning and Aonghus MacKechnie, *A History of Scottish Architecture* (1996).

DUNCAN MACMILLAN is Professor of History of Scottish Art at Edinburgh University and Curator of the Talbot Rice Gallery and the University's Collections. He attended St Andrews, London and Edinburgh Universities and has served at the latter as Senior Lecturer and Reader in previous years. He is the author of leading texts on Scottish art.

DR DEBORAH MAYS is a Principal Inspector of Historic Buildings. She took her PhD at St Andrews University before joining Historic Scotland. She has written on several late nineteenth-century Scottish architects and worked with Angus and Pat Macdonald on *Above Edinburgh and South East Scotland*. She is currently Honorary Secretary of the Society of Architectural Historians of Great Britain.

ANNE RICHES moved from the Greater London Council's Historic Buildings Division to work under David Walker from 1978 to 1989, taking responsibility for the Resurvey of listed buildings. She now serves on building preservation trusts north and south of the border and sits on both the Scottish and English Royal Commissions on historical monuments. She is a co-author of the *Buildings of Scotland, Glasgow* and is currently working on Ayrshire.

PROFESSOR ALISTAIR ROWAN trained as an architect and architectural historian in Edinburgh, Cambridge and Padua. He is editor and author for the *Buildings of Ireland* series and has published extensively on the work of Robert Adam. He is currently Principal of the Edinburgh College of Art, Chairman of the Paxton Trust and a Past President of the Society of Architectural Historians of Great Britain.

RONALD CANT

Burgh Planning and early Domestic Architecture: the Example of St Andrews (*c.* 1130–1730)

A MONG the historic burghs of Scotland, St Andrews holds a place of unique significance. Not only was it one of the earliest to be established (between 1124 and 1144) but, in addition, the circumstances in which this came about, and how these affected its subsequent form and function, were recorded in a remarkable *memorandum* issued at the time. Furthermore, the medieval burgh, as planned and developed on its spacious headland in the four centuries following its inception, survives in recognisable form, with a remarkably high proportion of the distinctive domestic architecture of these and the two succeeding centuries (see Figures 1 and 2).

The *memorandum* issued by Bishop Robert, in whose episcopate (1124–59) the character of medieval St Andrews was mainly determined, was associated with his reorganisation of the ancient monastic community of Kinrimund or Kilrimund as a priory of Augustinian canons in 1144.[1] It states that by leave of King David (I) he had founded a 'burgh at St Andrews' and appointed Mainard a Fleming as its provost, he having been the king's own burgess of Berwick assigned to the bishop, together with the *vill* or township of St Andrews at some anterior date. From now on, accordingly, 'St Andrews' would replace 'Kilrimund' as a place-name for the entire locality, and although not impinging on the latter's traditional autonomy, would comprehend it within a unified townscape of outstanding distinction.

Through recent research by Professor and Mrs Alcock the character of 'pre-urban Kinrimund' is now reasonably well established.[2] In plan it comprised a 'double *cashel*' or defensive perimeter, its inner element enclosing the early monastic buildings and in due course the medieval cathedral and priory, its outer (on the lines of Castle Street, Abbey Street, and Abbey Walk) four distinct areas providing space for activities often associated with monastic centres.[3] Of these the first, between the east end of North Street and the cliff-top site of the later castle (itself quite possibly succeeding an earlier royal stronghold), provided space for both a Celtic *clachan* or market settlement and a Norman-Flemish *vill* – from the fusion and extension of which the medieval burgh of St Andrews would emerge.

While the foundation of the burgh is explicitly mentioned in Bishop Robert's *memorandum*, its extension is also implied – in his grant, to its provost, of three *tofts* or plots of land 'in the street of the burgesses'.[4] As these were said to extend to 'the Prior's stream' (the newly completed Priory lade) they were clearly located on the south side of what would come to be called South Street, somewhere between Abbey Street and West Burn Lane. This, like North Street, may well have been on the line of an older trackway, both now to be given a more dignified form worthy of the intended ecclesiastical metropolis of Scotland as twin processional avenues converging uninterrupted eastwards in an open space before the great new cathedral and priory church planned by Bishop Robert but not begun until the episcopate of his successor Arnold, 1160–62.[5]

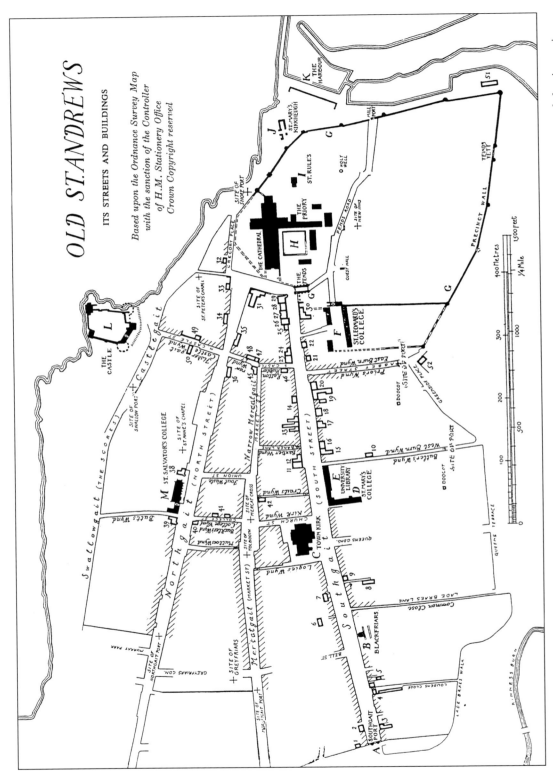

Figure 1. Plan of 'Old St Andrews', as published in its most complete form under that title by St Andrews Preservation Trust in 1955 and showing major historic buildings (solid) and 'domestic items' (in outline) as at that date but somewhat altered by the widening of Abbey Street (on its east side) in 1969–70.

Figure 2. Aerial view of St Andrews from the east. (Aerofilms)

The churches and chapels of 'Kilrimund–St Andrews' would seem to have been constructed from the outset in stone (in the case of St Rule's of high quality ashlar). As in other early burghs, however, virtually all the residential buildings (of the twelfth, thirteenth, and fourteenth centuries) that can be identified here were of timber, wattle-and-daub, and thatch.[6] This might even have been the case with the royal stronghold assigned to Bishop Robert by King David but not 'founded' (in durable stone) until circa 1200 by Bishop Roger. By this time, however, there might have been at least one stone structure of domestic character in the Archdeacon's Manse (for some time now misnamed 'Dean's Court') across the square to the west of the definitive cathedral.[7]

As now to be seen, this derives most of its historic character from an enlargement and remodelling of the later sixteenth century. But the ground floor of its eastmost section, comprising a barrel vault 8.8 by 5.8m within walls of ashlar masonry some 1.3m thick and indications of a floor level identical with that of the cathedral, might date from the twelfth century.[8] The crown of the vault has, however, been renewed (or perhaps completed) less skilfully at a later period, and in its original form the structure would have had an upper storey probably approached from North Street by an outside stair.

In the secondary and subsequent development of the burgh the most desirable building sites were clearly in North Street and South Street, the latter in particular. Nevertheless, such archaeological investigation as has proved possible hitherto, as on the east side of its junction with Abbey Street in 1970 and at 'St John's House' (Nos 67–69 on its north side) in 1972–73, while revealing structures of the twelfth and thirteenth centuries, showed that these were of timber and wattle and set at right angles to the street.[9] Around 1450, however, St John's seems to have been re-built in stone, the street frontage to a height of three storeys with a

Figure 3. 36–46 South Street, St Andrews. (St Andrews University Library, G M Cowie Photographic Collection)

pend leading through to a *close* behind where the wing was now provided with a barrel-vaulted lower storey supporting an upper hall with a large fireplace. Aperture surrounds here are mainly of later date but the pend and blocked windows in the rear wall have chamfered margins perhaps contemperaneous.[10]

Alongside St John's, No 71 has vaults of similar character and in its repeatedly altered frontage vestiges of chamfered margins that might place its origins in the same general period. Across the street, Nos 44, 46, 52 and 58 (see Figure 3) have comparable vaults, though their design is otherwise of the succeeding century and the closest analogies to St John's would seem to be in North Street, on either side of Butts Wynd. These formed part of the second major extension of the burgh, completed in the thirteenth century and involving the prolongation of South Street westwards as far as Lade Braes Lane and of North Street to an equivalent distance. In the intervening space their divergent alignment allowed for the creation of a new market-place and civic centre linked by short wynds to the major thoroughfares on each side.[11]

In 1410–12, furthermore, a new parish church of the Holy Trinity, more appropriate in size and location than that within the Priory precinct designated at the foundation of the burgh, was constructed on the north side of South Street to the west of what would now be known as Kirk Wynd (Church Street).[12] And at the very same time the first university in Scotland was founded by Bishop Wardlaw and before long provided with buildings of some architectural distinction in both main streets.

The most impressive of these was St Salvator's College founded by Bishop Kennedy in 1450 on the north side of North Street to the east of Butts Wynd (a continuation of the northern outlet from the market place that would now become College Wynd). Its site comprised six tenements, four of them acquired from 1426 onwards by Henry Dryden, canon of Holyrood, and donated by him to the founder.[13] Remarkably, the westmost seems to have been already occupied by a stone house of three storeys and an attic, the ground floor being

vaulted and at a level attributable to the early fifteenth century, though the ashlar frontage might have been added when the building was (apparently) incorporated in the college.

Across Butts Wynd to the west (No 75) is another stone house of even more complex character.[14] Its most striking feature is a cylindrical tower of three storeys at the west end of the façade but perhaps originating as the central feature of a two-storeyed design and clearly housing a turnpike or access staircase to the upper quarters over a more prolonged period. To the rear is a vaulted wing with details attributable to the mid-fifteenth century – from which period forward its ownership can be traced continuously and related to subsequent changes in its design.

Completing this group, to the east of the college, is a three-storeyed house (No 71) much altered and extended but with a west gable of large gableted crowsteps associated with a cylindrical tower with a conical roof, all of exemplary ashlar and providing the original main entry to the house by a newel stair with defensive gun-loops. The remarkable Geddie plan of St Andrews (circa 1580) [15] shows this with that at 75 North Street and another surviving example at 1 South Street with others of larger scale at the north-east corner of Abbey Street and the south-west corner of Baker Lane (on South Street) no longer extant (see Figure 4).

By 1500 the medieval burgh had reached the limits of its expansion in that the west port of South Street can be identified in the location (if not the precise architectural form) [16] it was to retain thereafter. In the ensuing period the first signs of what might be described as renaissance influences can be detected in the domestic architecture of the community, less in any complete design that in the disposition of living space and the details of doors and windows. In the Geddie plan a high proportion of the houses in both sections of South Street to the east of Church Street appear to be of three storeys. Many of them, indeed, may be seen to this day, making this area of special importance to the study of urban domestic architecture of the period.

Figure 4. 1–3 South Street, St Andrews. (St Andrews University Library, G M Cowie Photographic Collection)

In detail, doors and windows now tended to be of greater size, the latter at first floor level in particular, as in the superseded example in the frontage of 3 South Street and others formerly at 100–108 North Street – so large as to involve the insertion of mullions and transoms (even if none survive complete). In place of the plain chamfer hitherto in vogue such apertures now tended to have roll-moulded or roll and hollow margins, the former sometimes with a medieval ridge derived from the construction of groined vaults.[17] Such vaults were, of course, predominantly of ecclesiastical provenance but in St Andrews one might well expect the influence of architects and craftsmen so

engaged to extend beyond this area. Many of them, indeed, were themselves concerned with buildings of a residential character, like the Castle and colleges of the university, both under the control of the bishop – from 1472, at long last, archbishop and primate of the Scottish church.

It is, in fact, in such structures that the new architectural influences first appear. In 1538 a new college of St Mary was founded in place of an earlier 'pedagogy', its initial building a three-storey design with elegant oriels in its South Street frontage by Archbishop James Beaton's master of works, Walter Mar.[18] In 1541 French masons were brought from Falkland Palace to inspect and advise on the work – by this time principally concerned with details of the chapel. When (circa 1555) Archbishop Hamilton completed the college and a new frontage to his castle, Mar was still alive and might perhaps be credited with the segmental arched entry and advanced renaissance detail of the latter.[19]

Of comparable designs elsewhere in St Andrews there are at least two extant examples and representations of some others. The first is the enlargement of the Archdeacon's Manse by Sir George Douglas circa 1580 – with well-moulded window margins of two different forms – and an arched entry not unlike that at the Castle though on a smaller scale.[20] The second is the wing, surmounted by a remarkable corner oriel, added circa 1575 to the mansion at 4 South Street known (erroneously) as Queen Mary's House.[21]

The third – recorded in 1799 and 1805 – was on the west side of the Blackfriars chapel in South Street (see Figure 5).[22] It comprised two three-storeyed houses, the eastern with twin crowstepped gables and a pend that seems to have formed part of a two-arched *piazza* as first designed. The windows have richly moulded surrounds, the sills of those on the first floor extended into continuous cornices. The location suggests a date subsequent to the Reformation of 1560 when Blackfriars passed to the fifth Lord Seton who might have built the group circa 1580.

More representative than these – in the context of urban design – is the sequence of houses on the south side of South Street between Abbey Street and West Burn Lane, seven of the twelve embodying features of some age and distinction. Among them 'South Court' (Nos 40–42) is especially interesting (see Figures 6 and 7).[23]. Of three storeys, it is entered by a pend framed in a roll and rib moulding and surmounted by a panel with the Martine arms, suggesting a date of circa 1565. Within the court the somewhat altered east range has indications of a hall on the upper level, perhaps

Figure 5. Blackfriars 'Palace', South Street, St Andrews. (St Andrews University Library)

Figure 6. 4 South Street, St Andrews, garden view. (St Andrews University Library, G M Cowie Photographic Collection)

Figure 7. South Court, 40–42 South Street, St Andrews, garden view (St Andrews University Library, G M Cowie Photographic Collection)

earlier than the long gallery in the front building, though the adjoining stair-tower is of circa 1590. On the south side of the court, a *piazza* of three segmental arches (of slightly later date) was discovered in the course of the renovations of 1968–72.

While South Court and its neighbours constitute so important a part of the urban domestic architecture of this period, the fact that the buildings have been in continuous occupation – and to a great extent in the possession of residents of some means – have led to numerous alterations and a loss of earlier features. Thus, regrettably, no example is now to be seen here of the carved dormer windows so characteristic of most historic Scottish burghs and only one of the comparable surrounds of other windows – at South Court and probably not in its original location. On the other

hand there are numerous examples of heraldic panels (without and within) and several of painted wall decoration (at South Court) and ceilings (at 49 South Street), also early panelling (at 71 North Street and 4 and 71 South Street).

In addition to these major designs, by the beginning of the seventeenth century the domestic architecture of St Andrews had come to include a wide range of smaller structures for artisans and others of comparable status in the narrower wynds and private closes. It also comprised almost the entire area of the early burgh on Castle Street and the eastern part of North Street, one consideration being its proximity to the landing-place (for smaller boats) below the Castle which continued to be used by the fishing community in preference to the larger harbour at the mouth of the Kinness Burn.[24]

Figure 8. 19–21 North Street, St Andrews. (St Andrews University Library, G M Cowie Photographic Collection)

The most interesting building here is undoubtedly that at 19–21 North Street (see Figure 8). Of two storeys, the traces of plain chamfered surrounds to replaced apertures and the depth of the ground floor beneath street level suggest a fifteenth-century origin. At a later date, however, probably in the seventeenth century to judge by the narrow roll-moulded margins, it was reconstructed as four units, two on the ground floor and two above reached by separate forestairs (the existing pillared example a replacement of circa 1800). Across the street, Nos 12–18 provide a later and more compact alternative, its moulded doorway (like that inserted at No 75, circa 1690) set between ones with plain checked margins (as a stop for harling) and giving access to single end units while itself leading up to two more above.

At 13–15 South Castle Street is a more typical forestaired house with a marriage lintel of 1735 and another (with both features) at 22–24 College Street (1722). An alternative location for a date was on the lowest stone or skewputt of a crow-stepped gable, as at 68 Market Street (1728).[25] Sometimes a marriage lintel is all that has survived of a wynd or close after the clearances of the 1930s, like the fine example of 1735 from Baker Lane built into the garden wall of 24 South Street, itself of much the same period and fortunately saved from demolition in the widening of Abbey Street in 1970.

Among former wynds Castle Street and College Street retain something of their pristine character even if the number of buildings of earlier date than circa 1730 is relatively small and some of these of perplexing design, 17–19 College Street in particular. Although featuring an arched doorway and moulded window surrounds, these might well have come from grander structures elsewhere in the later sixteenth century. The same might be true of comparable details at 36 North Castle Street, otherwise of the mid-seventeenth century. Of the older closes those at 122, 141 and 144 South Street have features of interest but the most complete example is at 146–148, latterly associated with the Louden family, its two-storeyed buildings (like the others) mainly of the early eighteenth century.

These developments suggest that however much the fall of the medieval church order in 1560 – and the subsequent abandonment and ruin of its greatest buildings – may have affected the appearance and standing of St Andrews among the urban centres of Scotland, its domestic architecture was maintained at a creditable level. And if there were losses in this category also – and few major additions – its street frontages almost certainly contained a higher proportion of stone structures than before.

In this context an important part continued to be played by the residential buildings of the university. While their requirements differed somewhat from those of the individual householder, their architectural form provided models for such features as doorways, windows, chimneys and staircases. In the course of the seventeenth century, as it so happened, important alterations and additions were made to all three colleges, though in the case of St Salvator's it is difficult to relate the extensive building accounts of the 1680s to particular features.[26] At St Mary's, however, despite the demolition in 1829 of the north buildings of circa 1620 – two storeys above a six-arched *piazza* akin to that of South Court – it was recorded in some detail and its entry-porch from South Street re-built in its replacement. And at St Leonard's, the ranges of student *chalmers* of 1616 and 1655, albeit no longer used for their original purpose, survive largely intact.[27]

Among more characteristic examples of seventeenth-century domestic architecture the most prominent is 'The Roundel' (1 South Street). While much of the structure dates – like No 3 – from the preceding century, the ornamental lugged

surround of the main entry, the regular five-window disposition of the two upper storeys, and the balustraded summit of the projecting angle-tower are all of this later period. The same is true of the garden front of No 5, its twin crowstepped wings enclosing a fine *scale and platt* stair – parallel flights separated by a solid wall with pilastered ends on the landings and in St Andrews mainly of the period 1680–1730, and of which others are to be seen at 71 and 75 North Street and 52 and 58 South Street (as also in the colleges of St Salvator and St Leonard, the former with suggestions of classical design).

At South Court the garden frontage added by George Martine, circa 1670, has a single large three-storeyed gable reflecting the fine panelled interior. Elsewhere in this part of South Street – as in the frontages of Nos 58 and 71 – are vestiges of large-scale alterations of this same period, themselves superseded in turn by others of still later date, awaiting investigation and interpretation.

It will be noted that the grandest of these designs continued to be predominantly on the more southerly of the two main streets of the burgh. But the more northerly, especially on its north side eastwards of St Salvator's College, offered sites nearly as spacious and attractive. Here, until the Reformation, the Abbots of Scone had a stately *ludging*, though nothing is known of its design. Eastwards of it, to the corner of the Fishergate, two large mansions were built in the seventeenth century with a third to the north (Castle Wynd House) still extant. That on the corner survived long enough to be recorded in an early photograph circa 1840 which shows it as having a single three-storeyed crowstepped gable to North Street. The adjacent house to the west, though reduced in height and otherwise altered, persisted until 1882 and seems to have had a three-arched *piazza* on the ground floor.[28]

As the seventeenth century gave way to the eighteenth the architectural tradition, robustly indigenous yet open to external influences, that had served the burghs of Scotland so long and so well, yielded to the classical modes by now predominant in most parts of Europe. In St Andrews the situation is well summarised in three buildings of the early eighteenth century. The first is 203–205 South Street, a large two-storeyed crowstepped structure of 1734, the upper floor and attic arranged as two houses, one with a panelled room.[29] The second is 42 South Street, incorporating vaults and other features of earlier date but reconstructed in a classical idiom about 1723 as a private residence for Principal Hadow of St Mary's College. It is entered through a pillared and pedimented portico and contains a fine wooden staircase and several panelled rooms on the two upper floors, those facing south commanding a large formal garden with a dovecot as its focal point and beyond that other amenities extending to the line of the old Priory lade.

The third building is 86 Market Street constructed circa 1713 for Patrick Haldane (then a professor at St Mary's, later laird of Gleneagles). Towards the street the curvilinear gable[30] originally surmounting its severe three-storeyed façade has been replaced by a plain pediment but the formal garden frontage retains a handsome Venetian window proclaiming the arrival of a new epoch in the domestic architecture of St Andrews.

NOTES

1. Sir Archibald C Lawrie, *Early Scottish Charters* (1905), pp 124–6, 132–3.

2. I am much indebted for permission to refer to this research, which forms a continuation of 'Reconnaissance Excavations on Historic Fortifications and other royal sites in Scotland', as published in *Proceedings of the Society of Antiquaries of Scotland*, (1986–92), vols 116–22.

3. The *clachan* is likely to have been located on the north side of the eastmost part of North Street, with associated market place occupying the open space to the south, and the *vill* on North Castle Street and fronting the Castle site.

   The second element in the 'outer casbel', between the east ends of North Street and South Street, pertained to the *scolocs* or 'scholars' of the early monastic foundation, and after 1144 to the Archdeacon. The third element, south of South Street and east of Abbey Street, was associated with a pilgrim hospice of St Leonard, subsequently a college of the University. Eastward of this and south of Pends Road (and the 'inner cashel' latterly occupied by the Cathedral and Priory) was a fourth 'outer area' mainly associated with the 'economy' of the monastic community.

   After the organisation of the burgh the first or northmost section of the outer cashel passed under its jurisdiction, but 'frontagers' of the second and third sections, though answerable to separate regality courts, seem to have shared in the economic activities of the burgh community unobstructed by walls or *ports* on their jurisdictional boundaries.

4. Lawrie, *In vico burgensium* (1905), 132, *recte*. These intraburghal *tofts* or *rigs* came to be known, more formally, as *tenements* or *burgages*.

5. On the origin and extension of the burgh, see R G Cant, 'The Development of the Burgh of St Andrews in the Middle Ages' in Mary M Innes and Joan A Whelan (eds), *Three Decades of Historical Notes* (1991), pp 44–9 (reprinted from *Yearbooks* of the St Andrews Preservation Trust, 1964–89); R G Cant, 'The Medieval City of St Andrews' in N P G Pounds (ed), *The St Andrews Area*, supplement to *Archaeological Journal*, (1991), vol 148, pp 7–12; also N P Brooks and G Whittington, 'Planning and growth in the medieval Scottish burgh: the example of St Andrews', *Transactions of the Institute of British Geographers*, 2, No 3, pp 278–95.

6. Anne Turner Simpson and Sylvia Stevenson, *Historic St Andrews* Scottish Burgh Survey (1981), especially p 26. See also Note 9 below.

7. R N Smart, 'Deans Court' in D M G Lloyd (ed), *St Leonard's College and Deans Court* (1977), [17]-[28].

8. It is mentioned in a sequence of documents consequent upon the foundation of the Augustinian Priory of St Andrews by Bishop Robert in 1144 (*St Andrews Liber*, p 124).

9. Simpson and Stevenson, *Historic St Andrews*, pp 25–6.

10. N P Brooks, 'St John's House: its History and Archaeology' in Innes and Whelan, *Three Decades*, pp 89–95.

11. Cant 'Medieval City' in Pounds, *The St Andrews Area*, pp 10–11. The earlier location of the cross was apparently at the old *clachan* in North Street where it may have served a purpose as the Fish Cross – latterly sited on the boundary of the fishing quarter somewhat to the west of Castle Street as shown in the 'Geddie plan'.

The 'definitive location' of the principal cross was now (and until 1768) in the centre of the new Market Place, opposite the Kirk and College Wynds. The Tolbooth or Town Hall, previously unidentifiable, was on an island site to the west though nothing is known of its design until the sixteenth century. See below Note 23.

12. W E K Rankin, *The Parish Church of the Holy Trinity, St Andrews, Pre-Reformation* (1954).

13. R G Cant, *The College of St Salvator* (1950), especially pp 94–101 and 104.

14. R G Cant, '75 North Street: its Associations and Architecture', in Innes and Whelan, *Three Decades*, pp 81–7.

15. R N Smart, 'The Sixteenth Century Bird's Eye View Plan of St Andrews' in Innes and Whelan, *Three Decades*, pp 81–7.

16. R G Cant, 'The West Port of St Andrews' in Innes and Whelan, *Three Decades*, pp 33–6.

17. For this identification – and much more of the kind – credit is due to Dr J S Richardson, for many years Inspector of Ancient Monuments for Scotland.

18. The prefix 'Sir', included in reference to him, was no more than a mark of respect customarily assigned to clergy of his status. He was recorded as a chantry chaplain of Holy Trinity Church between 1508 and 1560 and was master of works there as well as for the last three medieval Archbishops (Rankin, *Holy Trinity*, pp 36, 87).

19. RCAHMS *Inventory for Fife* (1933), Figure 416.

20. Smart, 'Deans Court' in Lloyd, *St Leonard's*.

21. Aylwin Clark, *Queen Mary's House* (1977).

22. The first (reproduced here) was by Professor John Cook (circa 1790s) in a volume of water-colour paintings of the later eighteenth century in St Andrews University Library, and the second (dated 1805) in a series of pen and ink sketches by John Sime in the NMRS.

23. R G Cant, 'South Court, St Andrews and its Renovation' in Innes and Whelan, *Three Decades*, pp

66–73. The *piazza* is now the only survivor of several St Andrews examples, the most ambitious being a covered market of nine lateral and five (eastern) terminal arches forming the ground floor of the Tolbooth removed from the Market Place in 1862 – though by then obscured by later alterations and additions.

24. Following the disastrous losses sustained by the St Andrew fishing fleet in 1763, there was an almost complete suspension of activities until the early 1800s. When resumed, moreover, they were conducted from the 'commercial harbour' at the mouth of the Kinness Burn, although most of those engaged continued to live in the old 'fishing quarter'.

25. Its style of building was repeated in several others of this same period and locality, as recorded by John Oliphant in his view of the west end of the Market Place in his *St Andrews Delineated*, 1767 (MS, St Andrews University Library).

26. D Hay Fleming, 'The Accounts of Dr Alexander Skene, Provost of St Salvator's College, St Andrews, relating to the ... Repairs of the College Buildings 1683–1690', *Proceedings of the Society of Antiquaries of Scotland*, liv (1920), pp 216–48.

27. R G Cant, 'St Leonard's College' in Lloyd, *St Leonard's College* (1977), [3]-[16].

28. D Hay Fleming, *St Andrews Cathedral Museum* (1931), pp 138–9. The description of the building is undoubtedly accurate, but the quotation from Lamont's *Diary* attributing the property to 'the vicars of St Andrews of old' would seem to be erroneous, their manse being in the corresponding position one 'block' to the east.

29. This building, although the latest in date of those discussed here, is also the most conservative in its architectural design, its main innovation being that it was a 'double house' with ranges of rooms to the back as well as to the front.

30. Recorded by John Oliphant in his *St Andrews Delineated*, 1767.

2

RICHARD FAWCETT

The Churches of the Greater Medieval Cities

EXCEPT where there was a cathedral, a monastery or a castle, the most ambitious building in a medieval city was likely to be its parish church. This was particularly so in the later Middle Ages, when several of the major burghs rebuilt their churches on a magnificent scale. The main purpose of this short piece is to consider the range of architectural forms that were given to such places of worship, but before doing so it is necessary briefly to rehearse some of the factors which lay behind this outburst of architectural activity.

Although medieval Scotland was an essentially rural society, the urban settlements came to have an importance out of proportion to their size and numbers through their wealth-generating rôle as centres for trade both with the surrounding hinterland and with the continent.[1] It was in the interests of the king and land-holders to give encouragement to the activities of these settlements through the granting of privileges. Naturally enough, it tended to be the established centres of royal administration that were initially the best-placed trading centres, and many of these received formal recognition as royal burghs around the first half of the twelfth century.[2] But other burghs grew up under the protection of a local magnate or prelate, and rose to similar prominence.

Also from the twelfth century onwards, the parochial network of the church was being more systematically organised and, since the burghs were almost invariably treated as single parishes, there was one focus of lay spiritual life in each.[3] As the pride of the burghs in their own achievements increased in the later Middle Ages, and as the desire for an architectural and ritual focus for this

pride emerged, the parish churches therefore tended to be the chief beneficiaries. This was especially the case since, although disenchantment with the older forms of religious life as represented by the monks, canons and (to a lesser extent) the friars was increasing, the church still attracted deep loyalty and layfolk were looking for forms of religious expression in which they could themselves participate. Within many burghs it is additionally significant that the main powers of corporate patronage had come to be concentrated in the hands of the oligarchies of the merchant gilds, the members of which were best-placed to be aware of architectural developments in the wider world as a result of their trading activities. There was thus not only the will to create fine architecture, but some awareness of what was being achieved elsewhere.

From the customs returns we know that by the later Middle Ages it was the burghs of the east coast, and particularly those in the counties to either side of the Firth of Forth, that were prospering best, and it was in those same burghs that the urge to rebuild the parish churches seems to have been strongest. However, while the evidence is not as straightforward as it might seem, the customs returns also suggest that a period of economic decline may have begun around the very time that many of the burghs started rebuilding their churches. Though it is clear that surplus funds must still have been available for such major projects to be instigated, this may explain why some projects were never completed.

Declining revenues were not the only difficulty faced by the burghs when rebuilding their churches; another factor was the divided responsibility for the architectural fabric. Established practice dictated that it was the principal priest of a parish, the rector or parson, who had to maintain his church's chancel or choir – the part which was used by the clergy – while the nave was the responsibility of the layfolk. However, the majority of parishes were appropriated to some other religious institution – usually a monastery or cathedral – with which went responsibility for the choir, though such institutions did not always share the eagerness of the burgh to take part in costly re-building. In view of this, it is perhaps the clearest indication of the importance of their parish church to many burghs that in several cases those burghs were prepared to shoulder the burden of building both choir and nave. This was certainly the case at Dundee, Haddington, Linlithgow, Perth and Stirling, and perhaps at others as well, including St Andrews.

The degree of effort invested in these operations is also clear from the way that leading masons and

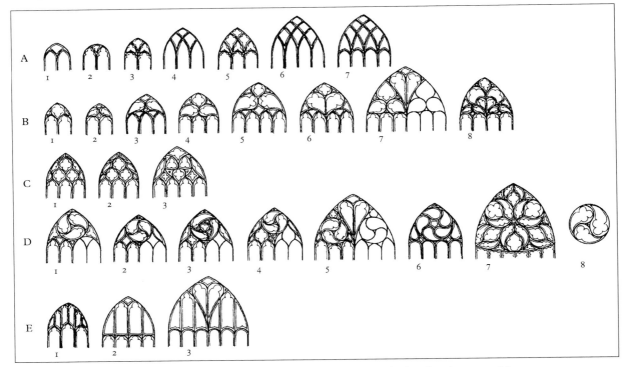

Figure 1. Diagrammatic sketches of examples of window tracery in the burgh churches (not to scale).
A. 1. Linlithgow St Michael, nave triforium; 2. Linlithgow St Michael, clearstorey; 3. Stirling Holy Rude, nave; 4. Stirling Holy Rude, St Andrews Chapel; 5. Stirling Holy Rude, nave; 6. Perth St John, south transept; 7. Perth St John, choir; (Aberdeen St Nicholas, north transept, but with different arcs, and with a transom instead of sub-arches at the light heads).
B. 1. Haddington St Mary, choir (with differences); Perth St John, choir clearstorey; 2. Haddington St Mary, nave (with differences); 3. Stirling Holy Rude, apse; 4. Haddington St Mary, nave; Linlithgow St Michael, choir; Stirling Holy Rude, apse; 5. Linlithgow St Michael, choir; Stirling Holy Rude, choir; 6. Linlithgow St Michael, choir; 7. Haddington St Mary, west window; 8. Linlithgow St Michael, nave.
C. 1. Perth St John, choir; 2. Edinburgh St Giles, south transept; 3. Linlithgow St Michael, nave.
D. 1. Stirling Holy Rude, choir; 2. Linlithgow St Michael, nave; 3. Linlithgow St Michael, nave; 4. Perth St John, choir; 5. Dundee St Mary, tower; 6. Linlithgow St Michael, apse; 7. Linlithgow St Michael, south chapel; 8. Linlithgow St Michael. tower.
E. 1. Linlithgow St Michael, tower; 2. Linlithgow St Michael, apse; 3. Stirling Holy Rude, apse.
(Author)

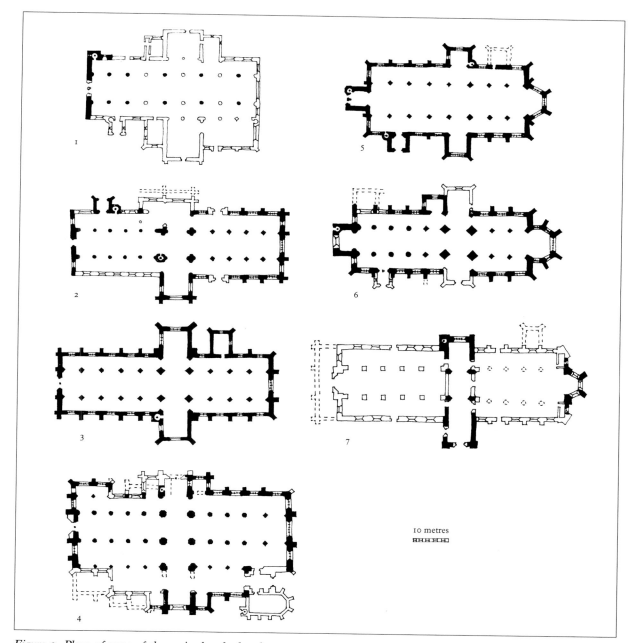

Figure 2. Plans of some of the major burgh churches.
1. St Andrews Holy Trinity; 2. Perth St John; 3. Haddington St Mary; 4. Edinburgh St Giles; 5. Linlithgow St Michael; 6. Stirling Holy Rude; 7. Aberdeen St Nicholas.
(Author)

wrights might be engaged. At Linlithgow two members of the French family may have been involved, who were also at work on the adjacent royal palace. At Perth work on the nave was apparently under the direction of Walter Merlioun, who designed a number of the most prestigious royal projects, including the king's own residence within Stirling Castle. At Aberdeen the wright was John Fendour, who is known to have been supplying materials to the royal works, while at Edinburgh the king's French wright, Andrew Mansioun, was engaged. This suggests that the architectural opportunities offered by the burgh churches had come to rival those of the cathedrals, and it is clear that the same craftsmen might be at work on both, as is seen from the similarity of particularly ambitious windows at Dunkeld Cathedral and Linlithgow Church, for example (see Figure 1, D7). It is also of interest that Bishop William Elphinstone of Aberdeen cited the central steeple of Perth Parish Church as the model for the new tower at his cathedral in 1511, rather than that of some other cathedral.[4]

The vast size of the rebuilt churches was partly to accommodate large-scale gatherings at the great events in the life of the burgh, and partly to make a grand architectural statement. But there was also a need to accommodate increasing numbers of side altars founded by individuals or groups as the late medieval craving for soul masses continued to expand, and Edinburgh, for example, may eventually have had nearly fifty altars. Some of these were simply placed against arcade piers or within the aisles, but for others specially designed chapels were required, which added to the scale and architectural complexity of the buildings. With the additional altars went endowments for more clergy, and at a number of churches it was decided that it would be appropriate for at least some of them to be incorporated within a body known as a college. By this means the lives of the clergy could be more fully regulated, and forms of religious observance emulating those of the cathedrals could be achieved at a time when the rituals associated with worship were becoming ever more elaborate.[5] At Edinburgh the first attempt to found such a college was made as early as 1419, though it was not eventually established until the 1460s. Other colleges within burgh churches were founded at Aberdeen, Haddington, Peebles and Stirling, and attempts to found them were made at Linlithgow and St Andrews.[6] But even where this was not done it may be assumed that the burgh churches would be the setting for a highly enriched daily round of services.

Well before the great period of late medieval rebuilding, some churches of the wealthier burghs had attained considerable size. The late twelfth-century transepts at Aberdeen belonged to a large aisled cruciform church, and there were substantial twelfth-century aisled churches at Ayr and Ruther-glen, for example. In addition, apart from periods in the fourteenth century when the wars with England meant that ecclesiastical building could be afforded only with difficulty, there is continuing evidence of work on several of the burgh churches. Rebuilding was underway at Perth in 1328[7] and at Aberdeen in 1355,[8] while Edinburgh had already grown to be a large building by 1385. In the fifteenth and early sixteenth centuries, however, the scale of burgh church building changed dramatically. In some cases, and most notably at Edinburgh and Aberdeen, earlier work was retained as a nucleus around which the new building was progessively added, and at Edinburgh the external appearance was consequently strikingly irregular. But more often the aim was complete rebuilding to a more-or-less unified scheme.

At St Giles' Church in Edinburgh the campaign of rebuilding began in the 1380s, with ribbed tunnel vaults being built over the choir and transepts after the English attack of 1385, and five chapels were built against the south flank of the nave in 1387.[9] The first campaigns to have a major impact on Edinburgh as we now see it, however, were the addition of the Albany Aisle on the north side of the nave after 1400, followed at some uncertain date by the rebuilding of the aisles and chapels on the south side of the nave. The rebuilding of the two eastern bays of the choir, and the addition of a vaulted clerestorey over the whole choir came around the 1450s.[10] These were followed by the Preston Aisle on the south side of the choir in 1454, the Chepman Aisle to its west in 1507, and the Holy Blood Aisle finished in 1518.[11]

At St John's Church in Perth rebuilding was started with the choir, after an agreement was reached with Dunfermline Abbey in 1440.[12] Work was in progress on the nave there in 1489 and 1496, when royal contributions were made, and Walter Merlioun was apparently the architect,[13] although that part of the work was probably never finished.

At Haddington the only date for the rebuilding is an agreement of 1462 with St Andrews Priory over the choir,[14] but the church is likely to have been complete well before the college was founded in 1540.

St Michael's Church at Linlithgow is said to have been started after a fire of 1424, although all of the evidence points to the work being later. The nave was sufficiently complete for the mason John French to be buried there in 1489, and the tower was presumably complete by the time a bell was cast in 1490. An agreement was reached with St Andrews over the building of the choir in 1497, there were royal gifts to the work in 1506, and in 1532 an agreement was reached on the design of the wall-head with the mason Thomas French;[15] the arms of Bishop Crichton of Dunkeld (1526–44), a former vicar of the parish, are said to have been on the choir roof. At Holy Rude Church at Stirling the most likely spur to rebuilding was the destruction caused by the Douglas riots of 1452. The nave was the first part to be rebuilt, and was nearing completion when altars were founded in 1471 and 1473; the chapel of St Mary was being built against the nave flank by 1481. An agreement with Dunfermline Abbey in 1507 marked the start of work on Stirling's choir, and the mason John Coutts is know to have been still at work in 1529.[16] Stirling was never completed, but construction is likely to have been at a halt before 1546, when a college was founded.

Of the less complete buildings to be considered here, Holy Trinity Church at St Andrews was founded in 1412, on a new site, and St Michael's Church at Cupar was also founded on a fresh site in 1415.[17] Prior Bissett of St Andrews Priory is said to have played a rôle in both projects, though there is evidence of the burgesses being active at Cupar around 1429, and at St Andrews a leading part was taken by the Lindsay family, while responsibility for that choir was transferred to the burgh in 1494.[18] At St Mary's Church at Dundee the tower, which is the only medieval part to survive, was probably one of the last parts of a campaign which began after an agreement had been reached with Lindores Abbey in 1442–43.[19] It was probably

started after the choir was nearing completion around 1461, and is likely to have been substantially finished by 1495, when a bell was donated. At St Nicholas' Church at Aberdeen only the transepts and the eastern crypt survive from the medieval church, but the choir is partly known from illustrations.[20] The master mason of the choir from 1483 was apparently John Gray, but much of the impact of the interior was created by John Fendour's woodwork. He was paid for this in 1495, though inscriptions on the ceiling included the dates 1510 and 1515. By then Fendour had also undertaken to carve the choir stalls in 1507,[21] fragments of which survive in the National Museums of Scotland, and the college was formally established in 1540.

The ideal plan for the more ambitious burgh churches seems to have included aisles running the full length of both nave and choir (see Figure 2), as at Edinburgh, Haddington, Linlithgow, Perth, St Andrews and Stirling. With the exception of St Andrews, where there was no structural demarcation between nave and choir, all of those had naves of five bays. Linlithgow and Stirling had choirs of three bays, Haddington's was of four bays, while those of Aberdeen, Edinburgh and Perth were of five bays. At three churches, Aberdeen, Linlithgow (see Figure 3) and Stirling, an eastern apse was built as the setting of the high altar. At the junction of nave and choir, Aberdeen, Edinburgh, Haddington (see Figure 4), Perth and Stirling were all designed to have transepts, with defined crossings. But at Stirling these were only planned at a later stage and were never completed in the Middle Ages, while at Edinburgh the transepts were almost lost to sight as a result of later additions. Both Linlithgow and St Andrews had transeptal chapels, rather than full transepts, and these were not acknowledged in the arcades.

Aberdeen, Edinburgh, Haddington (see Figure 4) and Perth all had central towers, and one was presumably planned for Stirling. Linlithgow, Dundee and Stirling had axial western towers, with a processional doorway in their lowest storey; if built according to the later proposals, Stirling would thus have been unique in having both a

Figure 3.
Linlithgow, Church of St
Michael. The interior
looking eastwards from the
nave into the choir.
(RCAHMS)

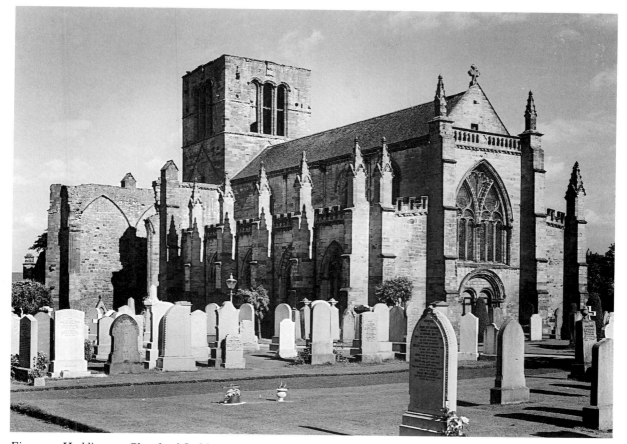

Figure 4. Haddington, Church of St Mary. The exterior from the north-west, before the restoration of the choir and transepts. (RCAHMS)

western and a central tower. Cupar and St Andrews each had a tower above the western bay of the north nave aisle. At Perth and St Andrews, and eventually at Cupar and possibly Stirling, the towers were capped by spires; at Edinburgh, Dundee, Haddington and Linlithgow openwork crown steeples were planned, though they were definitely only built at the first and last of those.

Of the various other possible projections from the body of a church, there were rectangular sacristies on the north side of the choir at Haddington and Linlithgow. Linlithgow and Stirling had porches on the south side of the nave, while Edinburgh and Perth had porches on both north and south sides. The greatest variety of treatment resulted from the progressive addition of chapels

to house chantries against the flanks of the churches. St Andrews apparently had a number of these, while Stirling had at least three against its nave. The largest number, however, was at Edinburgh, where the almost random process of accretion largely hid the core of the nave and much of the south flank of the choir.

The majority of the greater churches were of basilican section, with a clearstorey rising above the flanking aisles. In its late fourteenth-century state, however, the choir of Edinburgh had been a hall church, with vaults over the central aisle and transepts that were little higher than those over the flanking aisles. It is possible that the late fifteenth-century nave of Perth was also planned as a hall church – on a particularly grand scale.[22] On a

Figure 5. Stirling, Church of the Holy Rude. The interior of the nave looking westwards. (RCAHMS)

Figure 6. Perth, Church of St John. The interior of the choir looking eastwards.
(RCAHMS)

slightly less exalted scale, Cupar was designed without a clearstorey. A rather surprising feature of a number of churches is the way in which the clearstoreys are asymmetrical: Stirling nave has windows only in the south clearstorey wall (see Figure 5), and the same may have been true in Edinburgh's nave, while at Perth the choir clearstorey has twin-light windows on the north and single-light windows in the south clearstorey (see Figure 6).

The most ambitious elevation is that of the nave at Linlithgow, which is of three full storeys, with triforium openings into the space above the aisle roofs (see Figure 3). However, it seems that there may have been an unfulfilled intention to have a similar arrangement in the later phase of the works at Stirling since, in the choir, what is now the clearstorey was originally a series of openings into the aisle roof spaces like those in the middle stage at Linlithgow. There may also have been an intention to repeat this in the nave at Stirling, since the heightened west tower made provision for the roof of the central aisle to be raised to a higher level. Such three-storeyed arrangements were perhaps an attempt to mimic the elevations which had previously been a particular feature of the greater cathedral and monastic churches.

In most of the burgh churches where stone vaulting was provided it was limited to the aisles and towers. But some of the more ambitious churches were also partly vaulted at the higher levels. Edinburgh, which had already had a choir vault in its earlier state was given a handsome tierceron vault over the heightened choir as part of the mid-fifteenth-century works, while Haddington has quadripartite vaulting over the choir and north transept and, curiously enough, more elaborate tierceron vaulting over the south transept. Other fine tierceron vaults are to be found within the north porch at Perth, over the Preston Aisle at Edinburgh and in the tower at Dundee. In the nave at Stirling and the choir at Perth (see Figures 2 and 6) there are still medieval open-timber roofs, though the latter has been very heavily restored. Aberdeen had a handsome ribbed wagon ceiling

over its choir, which was very like that which survives in King's College Chapel.

Although each of the burgh churches has its own pronounced character, there are many points in common between them which together demonstrate the coherence of the emerging Scottish approach to ecclesiastical architecture in the later Middle Ages. In pier design, for example, we find a strong taste for stocky cylindrical piers, with examples at St Andrews and in the naves of Stirling (see Figure 5) and Cupar.[23] Elsewhere the piers are usually of the multiple-shafted type. At Haddington the piers have three-quarter shafts in the four cardinal directions, with angled faces between. The piers in the choir of Linlithgow are similar, except that the shafts have fillets (see Figure 3).[24] Most of the other piers in these churches are variants on the octofoil type. Those in the nave of Linlithgow have fillets to the cardinal shafts,[25] while the choir piers at Stirling have fillets to all eight shafts. The piers in the choir at Perth are rather more complex, with keeled shafts on the diagonal axes and filleted shafts in the cardinal directions, separated by deep hollows.

The most elaborate pier type is one of those at the east end of Stirling's nave (see Figure 5), which perhaps gave added prominence to the position of the nave altars; that on the south has filleted shafts flanked by smaller rolls to the cardinal axes, and filleted shafts in hollows on the diagonal faces. Its northern counterpart is simpler, having four filleted shafts separated by quadrant hollows. Additional enrichment of piers and arcades in the vicinity of major altars is also to be seen in the presbyteries of Edinburgh and Perth.

Perhaps most interesting of all the pier types is that used at Edinburgh where, despite the wide date range of the additions, great efforts were made to achieve internal homogeneity by using essentially the same form. These piers are basically of octofoil section, with spurs between the shafts, and in most cases the main shafts are filleted, with keeled shafts on the diagonal axes; in the Albany Aisle, however the diagonally-directed shafts are also filleted. It is a fascinating pointer to the aesthetic attitudes of the time that, despite the apparently random growth of Edinburgh, such great pains should have been taken over so long a period to attain at least internal unity of treatment.

Apart from the pier types, it is in the window tracery that we see the clearest signs of the inter-relationships between this group of churches (see Figure 1). Two churches have windows with pairs of curved daggers as a main motif: the choir clear-storey at Haddington has a two-light version,[26] while there is a three-light version in the apse at Stirling. Even more common are variants with a third vertical dagger rising between the two curved ones: three-light examples are found in Hadding-ton nave, Linlithgow choir and the apse of Stirling;[27] a four-light version is to be seen in the choirs of Linlithgow and Stirling. A permutation on this same theme provides the basis for the six-light design of Haddington's west window (see Figure 4). Spiralling daggers within circlets were another common motif, with examples in the nave of Linlithgow, the tower of Dundee and the choirs of Perth and Stirling.[28] For a short period which possibly opened around the time of James IV's marriage to Margaret Tudor in 1503, there was a vogue for simplified English Perpendicular types, as seen particularly in the apses of Linlithgow and Stirling, and in the west window of the former.

Few of these windows show any particular in-ventiveness, and it is perhaps only in the nave of Linlithgow that we find tracery design of real flare.[29] Three types there, in particular, show such sophisticated combinations of restrained curvi-linear forms that it is tempting to speculate they were the work of John French, the mason who was buried there in 1489, and beyond that to suspect that he was of the French origin that his name suggests. This is especially true of the window of the south transeptal chapel, with a complex pattern of intersecting dagger shapes within larger contain-ing forms. It had a close counterpart in the window inserted in the west front of Dunkeld Cathedral, presumably after work was started on the adjacent tower there in 1469.

In conclusion, the burgh churches, which were largely largely rebuilt in the fifteenth and the first half of the sixteenth centuries, magnificently demonstrate the synthesis of architectural ideas that was emerging at this period, and that perhaps repre-sents the most identifiably 'Scottish' phase of our architectural history. This synthesis emerged at a period when patrons and masons were strongly receptive to new ideas from beyond our borders, and the trading links of the major burghs meant they were among the most important channels for the importation of ideas from abroad. It has already been suggested that there could be French inspir-ation behind some of the tracery designs of Linlithgow, and the eastern apses of Aberdeen, Linlithgow and Stirling could also represent an idea of ultimately French origin. At the same time, English influences are detectable in the apse tracery at Linlithgow and Stirling. But Scotland's closest trading links were with the Low Countries, and it was almost certainly from there that the extraordi-nary telescoped design of the tower at Dundee must have been taken. Other borrowings from the Netherlands could be evident in the stocky cylind-rical arcade piers at Cupar, St Andrews and Stirling (see Figure 5), in the lateral gables of chapels at Edinburgh and Stirling, and in aspects of the facade design at Haddington (see Figure 4).[30]

Such borrowings must not be interpreted as a sign of poverty of inspiration within the native tradition of architectural design, however, but rather as evidence for a phase of great creative vitality in which new ideas were being constantly investigated and re-interpreted. Despite the fact that medieval Scotland was towards the northern fringes of Europe and less wealthy than many of its continental European counterparts, in its greater burgh churches we see an impressive at-tempt to create buildings that were worthy of the pride that their burgesses felt in them. It must also be remembered that these buildings were the ve-hicles for a lavish display of art and music to enrich the liturgy that was their raison d'être, and it can-not be without significance that the first reference we have to an organ in Scotland is at the burgh church of Aberdeen in 1437.[31] Little has survived of the furnishings of these churches, and it would be invaluable to know more about the stalls carved for Edinburgh by the French wright

Andrew Mansioun between 1552 and 1554, for example, with which the council was so pleased that it granted him a pension for ten years.[32] Nevertheless, the fragments of Fendour's stall canopies from Aberdeen, together with damaged stalls at St Andrews, still give us some idea of the quality of work that could be obtained, as do some pieces of what may have been a carved stone altar reredos at Linlithgow. Even without their furnishings, however, as a group the burgh churches are probably the most important contribution that Scotland made to the art of the later Middle Ages, and certainly they were the greatest artistic contribution of the period to the burghs.

NOTES

1. For fuller information on the burghs see A A M Duncan, *Scotland, the making of the kingdom* (Edinburgh, 1975), ch 5; Michael Lynch, Michael Spearman and Geoffrey Stell (eds), *The Scottish medieval town* (Edinburgh, 1988); and Elizabeth Ewan, *Townlife in fourteenth-century Scotland* (Edinburgh, 1990).

2. For the foundation dates of the burghs see George Smith Pryde, *The burghs of Scotland, a critical list* (Oxford, 1965).

3. For the origins of the parishes see Ian Cowan, 'The development of the parochial system in medieval Scotland', *Scottish Historical Review*, vol 44 (1961), pp 43–55 and *The parishes of medieval Scotland*, Scottish Record Society (1967).

4. *Records of the Sheriff Court of Aberdeenshire*, New Spalding Club, vol 1 (1904–7), p 102.

5. R N Swanson, *Religion and devotion in Europe circa 1215–circa 1515* (Cambridge, 1995), p 102.

6. For the foundation of the burgh colleges see Ian Cowan and David Easson, *Medieval religious houses, Scotland*, 2nd edn (London, 1976), pp 213–30.

7. In that year Robert I asked Scone Abbey to allow stone to be taken from its quarries for work on Perth Church, see A A M Duncan (ed), *Regesta Regum Scottorum, Acts of Robert I* (Edinburgh, 1988), no 350.

8. James Cooper (ed), *Cartularium ecclesiae Sancti Nicholai Aberdonensis*, Spalding Club (1881–92), IX, 14.

9. The contract for these chapels is in *Registrum cartarum ecclesie Sancti Egidii de Edinburgh*, Bannatyne Club (1859), p 24.

10. These campaigns are approximately datable on heraldic evidence. I am grateful to Mr Nicholas Holmes for discussing his 1981 excavations with me, which indicated that the eastern limb had been only slightly lengthened in the operations of circa 1450.

11. *Registrum cartarum ecclesie Sancti Egidii*, pp 106–7 and pp 203–7; J C Lees, *St Giles' Edinburgh, church, college and cathedral* (Edinburgh, 1889), p 80.

12. *Registrum de Dunfermlyn*, Bannatyne Club (1842), 291–3, no 413.

13. *Accounts of the Lord High Treasurer of Scotland*, vol 1, pp 121, 323.

14. *Illustrations of Scottish history*, Maitland Club, (1834), pp 75–6.

15. *Registrum prioratus Sancti Andree*, Bannatyne Club (1841), pxxxviii, no 47; *Accounts of the Lord High Treasurer*, vol 3, p 205; *Liber curiae capitalis burgi de Linlithgw*.

16. Thomas Ross, 'Stirling Parish Church', *Transactions of the Stirling Natural History and Archaeological Society* (1913–14), pp 115–36; R. Renwick (ed), *Charters and other records relating to the royal burgh of Stirling*, Scottish Burgh Records Society (1884), no xxxvii; R Renwick (ed), *Extracts from the records of the royal burgh of Stirling*, Scottish Burgh Records Society, vol 1 (1887), p 38.

17. *Scotichronicon* (ed D E R Watt), vol 8 (Aberdeen, 1987), pp 83 and 85.

18. Ian Cowan and Annie Dunlop, *Calendar of Scottish supplications to Rome*, Scottish History Society, vol 3 (1970), pp 27, 140 and 176; W E K Rankin, *The parish church of the Holy Trinity, St Andrews* (Edinburgh, 1955), p 33; Ronald Cant, *The parish church of the Holy Trinity St Andrews* (St Andrews, 1992).

19. W Hay (ed), *Charters, writs and public documents of the royal burgh of Dundee*, Scottish Burgh Records Society (1880), pp 19–23.

20. See the illustration in J Robertson, *The book of Bon Accord* (Aberdeen, 1839).

21. *Extracts from the council register of the burgh of Aberdeen*, Spalding Club (1844), pp 56–7 and 77–8.

22. See the illustration in J Cant, *Memorabilia of the city of Perth* (Perth, 1806).

23. Earlier uses of cylindrical piers may be found in the naves of the cathedrals at Aberdeen (started 1355x80) and Dunkeld (started 1406) and in the transept of St Andrews Cathedral (after 1409).

24. Similar piers were designed for Edinburgh Trinity College Church (founded 1460).

25. Similar piers were designed for Paisley Abbey nave

(circa 1445x59, but possibly started earlier) and for the north-west bay of Dunfermline Abbey nave (1446x82).

26. Related tracery is found in Melrose Abbey north transept (after 1385), Roslin Collegiate Church (started 1446) and Seton Collegiate Church (started before 1478).

27. Related tracery is found in Paisley Abbey nave (circa 1445x59) and Seton Collegiate Church (started before 1478).

28. Spiralling daggers within a circlet were a particularly common motif in late medieval Scotland.

29. Two types employed there, however, are rather less inventive. One, adjacent to the south transeptal chapel, is like a window in the chapter house at Elgin Cathedral (circa 1482x1501), and may be a later insertion.

30. For a slightly fuller discussion of the author's views on foreign influences see 'Late Gothic architecture in Scotland, considerations on the influence of the Low Countries', *Proceedings of the Society of Antiquaries of Scotland*, vol 112 (1982), pp 477–96; 'Scottish medieval window tracery' in D J Breeze (ed), *Studies in Scottish antiquity* (Edinburgh, 1984), pp 148–86; *Scottish architecture from the accession of the Stewarts to the Reformation 1371–1560* (Edinburgh, 1994); 'Architectural links between Scotland and the Low Countries in the later middle ages', The British Archaeological Association, *Transactions of the Utrecht conference* (Leeds, 1996), pp 172–82.

31. Jim Inglis, *The organ in Scotland before 1700* (Schagen, 1991), pp 9–10 and 49.

32. *Extracts from the records of the burgh of Edinburgh, 1528–1557*, Scottish Burgh Records Society (1871), pp 196–7.

3

IAN CAMPBELL

James IV and Edinburgh's First Triumphal Arches

THE Entry of Margaret Tudor to Edinburgh in 1503 included two temporary gates, which may have been the earliest Renaissance triumphal arches outside Italy.

Until the recent insight that the gateway of the James IV's Forework at Stirling Castle, built in the first decade of the sixteenth century, is a triumphal arch, the architecture of James III and James IV had been regarded almost exclusively in the fading light of the northern Middle Ages. Now we see their buildings were already touched by rays of the renascent Mediterranean sun, pushing Scotland into the vanguard of receiving (and disseminating) Italian Renaissance architecture north of the Alps.[1] The purpose of this essay is to see if two temporary gates erected for the Entry of Margaret Tudor, daughter of Henry VII, into Edinburgh on 7 August 1503, the day before her wedding to James IV, can be regarded as triumphal arches. Architectural historians have tended to neglect such festive conseits, but, as Howard Colvin observes:

> ... it was precisely the ephemeral character of festive displays ... that made them important vehicles for new architectural ideas. Being constructed only of insubstantial materials such as timber and canvas these temporary structures could represent accurately sophisticated architectural designs that could not easily be got through to an unlettered and untravelled mason ...[2]

The ceremonies of royalty entering cities became increasingly elaborate from the late fourteenth century, incorporating street pageants, temporary castles and fountains flowing with wine, in addition to older elements such as the presentation of the keys of the town, the homage of groups of citizens, both religious and lay.[3] From the mid-quattrocento, entries in Italy began to acquire the trappings of classical triumphs, although it took over a century for triumphal arches to supplant the *tableaux-vivants* throughout Europe.[4] In origin Roman triumphs were awarded to victorious military commanders, but later became reserved for the imperial family.[5] During the Renaissance, rulers came to be equated with heroes with or without military honours, and the immensely influential poem of Petrarch, *I Trionfi*, which describes a procession of chariots carrying the 'Triumphs' of Love, Chastity, Fame, etc, facilitated the widening of the definition of 'triumph' to embrace wedding celebrations. Thus, in Scotland, 'triumphs' is used in 1537 and 1538 to describe the entries prepared for the arrival of James V's first and second wives, Madeleine of Valois and Mary of Guise.[6]

A detailed description of Margaret Tudor's entry survives from the pen of John Yonge, an English herald, who accompanied her north. He relates that as James and Margaret entered the town they were first met by a procession of Franciscans and then Dominicans and then came to:

> ... a Yatt [gate] of Wood painted, with Two Towrells, and a window in the Midds. In the wich Towrells was, at the Windowes, Angells syngyng joyously for the Comynge of so noble a Lady; and at the sayd middle windowe was in lyk wys an Angell presenting the Kees to the said Qwene.
>
> Within the Town ny to the said Yatt came in Processyon the College of the Perysche of Seint

Gilles, rychly revested, with the Arme of that Seint, the wiche was presented to the Kynge for to kysse; wherof he did as before, and began to synge *Te Deum laudamus.*

In the Mydds of the Towne was a Crosse, new painted, and ny to that same a Fontayne, castynge forth of Wyn, and ychon drank that wold.

Ny to that Crosse was a Scarfawst [scaffold] maid, wher was represented Paris and the Thre Deessys, with Mercure, that gafe hym the Apyll of Gold, for to gyffe to the most fayre of the Thre, wiche he gave to Venus.

In the Scarfawst was represented also the Salutacion of Gabriell to the Virgyne, in sayinge *Ave gratia*, and sens after, the Sollempnizacioun of the varey Maryage betwix the said Vierge and Joseph.

More fourther was of new maid One other Yatt, apon the wiche was in Sieges [thrones] the iiij Vertuz. Theys is to weytt, *Justice*, holdynge in hyr right Haunde, a Swerde all naked, and in the t'other a Pair of Ballaunces, and she had under hyr Feet the Kyng Nero: *Force*, armed, holdyng in hyr Haund a Shafte, and under hyr Feete was Holofernes, all armed: *Temperance*, holdyng in hyr Haund a Bitt of an horse, and under hyr Feete was Epicurus: *Prudence*, holdynge in hyr Haunde a Syerge, and under hyr Sardenapalus. With thos war Tabretts that playd merrily, whill the noble Company past thorough. Under was a Licorne and a Greyhound, that held a Difference of one Chardon florysched, and a Red Rose entrelassed.

Then the noble Company passed out of the said Towne, to the Church of the Holy Crosse ... [7]

The entry can be seen to have all the standard elements of medieval entries. However, the 'Judgement of Paris' was the earliest appearance of classical mythology in the pageantry of Britain, heralding the arrival of the Renaissance and suggesting it is worth looking closely at the gates to see if they are triumphal in character.[8]

The first 1503 gate, which probably occupied the site of the later Bristo Port, Edinburgh, had two

towers flanking the gateway clearly imitating a castle.[9] Temporary castle-like architecture formed a constant feature of entries from the earliest recorded, being particularly popular for the staging of *tableaux-vivants*, as in the entry of Margaret of York into Bruges in 1468 (in which the Scottish merchants participated), where an observer describes 'a pageant made by subtille craffte, after the forme of a castle gatte ...'.[10] I illustrate a timber 'castle' erected by the Seventeen Trades in Bruges for the entry of Charles V in 1515, a lion occupying the central arch and two *tableaux-vivants* in front of towers which have inset turrets with conical caps, like those James IV built at Stirling (see Figure 1).[11]

What is unusual in medieval entries, however,

Figure 1. Temporary castle erected by the 'Seventeen Trades' for the entry to Bruges of the future Charles V in 1515 (woodcut from Remi Du Puys, Tryumphante entrée ...). The castle is a favourite device for staging pageants.

Figure 2. Temporary gate erected by the Spanish colony for the entry to Bruges of the future Charles V in 1515 (woodcut from Du Puys, Tryumphante entrée ...). The inclusion of all'antica motifs implies this is a triumphal arch.

is the use of temporary gates.[12] This is probably because most major European towns already had permanent defensive gateways, which could be decorated in the event of a ceremonial entry, but Edinburgh, having enjoyed over a century of peace, had spilled beyond its medieval defences.[13] The act of passing ceremonially under an arch inevitably evokes the idea of triumphal arches, and one authority does describe the Edinburgh entrance gate as such, arguing that the revived triumphal arches of the Renaissance 'borrowed much from the castle'.[14] Indeed, the earliest *all'antica* triumphal arch of the quattrocento stands between two drum towers of the Castelnuovo in Naples, commemorating Alfonso II's entry in 1443, and the genuine arches in Rome had been fortified in the Middle Ages, the Arch of Septimius Severus sporting battlements and a tower in Renaissance views.[15]

Figure 2 shows a temporary arch to be passed under, erected by the Spanish colony in Bruges in 1515. Its battlemented superstructure, arrow slits and gun loops refer to the castle, while the triple arches, portrait tondi (of the Stirling Head type), and probably the romanesque windows, allude to classical antiquity, and hence the arch is implicitly triumphal.[16] While nothing in the description of the Edinburgh gate suggests *all'antica* ornament, one would expect its architecture to resemble the contemporary Stirling Forework, with round-headed apertures, which may have been sufficient to evoke *romanitas*. In support of its triumphal character is the plausible (but unprovable) suggestion, that the angels on the gate were singing the poem 'Now fayre fayrest off the fayre', which refers to Margaret as 'Descendyd from imperyall blode', probably alluding to the Tudors' Welsh, ie British, and ultimately Trojan descent.[17] The Stewarts too had imperial imagery: both James III and James IV were portrayed wearing closed imperial crowns, echoed architecturally by the crown steeples of St Giles, Edinburgh, and King's College, Aberdeen.[18] Empire and triumph are intimately connected, *imperator* meaning both a military commander and emperor. Significantly, the Scottish Marchmont Herald, William Cumming, in 1494 commissioned 'The Deidis of Armorie', a manuscript on a variety of ceremonial and heraldic matters, including a tract on types of crown, wherein the 'crownn triumphal' is equated with the 'croun of an empriour'.[19] The marriage of members of the two imperial dynasties of Britain foreshadowed the union of the kingdoms under a single 'emperor', for which triumphal imagery would be entirely appropriate.[20] We can conclude, therefore, albeit tentatively, that the 1503 Edinburgh entrance gate was a triumphal arch.

The earliest date which has come to light for a temporary archway explicitly described as 'triumphal' is 1489, for the Milanese wedding of Giangaleazzo Sforza and Isabella of Aragon; followed by arches in Ferrara in 1491, Rome in 1492, and several for the entries of the French kings, Charles VIII and Louis XII, to Italian cities over the next two decades.[21]

Figure 3. Temporary arch at Porte Bourgneuf, Lyons, 1515 (miniature from Cod 86.4, Herzog August Bibliothek, Wolfenbüttel). One of the first two 'triumphal' arches in France, erected for entry of François Ier.

The earliest arches to be designated 'triumphal' north of the Alps are two in Lyons, erected in 1515 for the entry of François I, and two, erected by the Italian merchants, for the Bruges 1515 entry. Happily, illustrations and descriptions of both entries survive.[22] The arch decorating the Porte Bourgneuf in Lyons (see Figure 3) rested on 'deux grosses tours quarrées', (two large square piers), above which stood four allegorical figures in front of a painted backdrop showing François' family tree.[23] The illustrator, who depresses the arch to allow more space for the *tableau-vivant*, adds two

engaged Corinthian columns to the square imposts, which have rudimentary *all'antica* ornament. The arch at Bruges (see Figure 4), which stood at the exit of the Place de la Bourse, again stood on square piers, decorated with *all'antica* and heraldic motifs, and supported four classical heroes, offering gifts appropriate to a future emperor. From the woodcut the figures might be taken to be statues but the text describes them as 'personnages', implying that they were real people.[24]

What is striking about these arches is their general similarity to each other and to the second 1503 Edinburgh arch, which probably stood on the site of the later Netherbow, and which supported the four Cardinal Virtues resting their feet on mortals, exemplifying the opposite vices. Some have assumed that the Virtues were painted, as were probably the heraldic unicorn and greyhound holding the rose and the thistle, also on the arch, but on analogy with Lyons and Bruges, it seems more likely that they were real people, which explains why with them 'war Tabretts [drums] that playd merrily'.[25]

The Cardinal Virtues had appeared in medieval pageants, but here they are in explicitly triumphal mode, trampling on their vicious enemies (three from classical antiquity, one an archetypally bad Roman emperor and another a barbarian king).[26] Whether the arch included *all'antica* decoration cannot be ascertained, but is not impossible given the presence of craftsmen such as the French plasterer in Stirling in 1504, whose name 'Dorange', would suggest acquaintance with the great Arch of Tiberius at Orange. Later in 1510–11 we have Cressent, an Italian mason in royal service, and in 1512 the native glazier, Thomas Peblis, is paid for 'payntit roundis with chaiplatis' (wreathed tondi) at Holyrood.[27] Even without *all'antica* ornament, the presence of the triumphant Virtues over what was almost certainly a round-headed arch, and the closeness of the parallels at Bruges and Lyons allow us to conclude with more certainty than the first gate that it was a triumphal arch. The fact that Yonge does not explicitly describe it as such, unlike the Bruges and Lyons examples, may be explained by his being a foreign observer, who may not have

Figure 4. Temporary arch erected by the Italian merchants, Bruges 1515 (woodcut from Du Puys, Tryumphante entrée . . .). One of first two 'triumphal' arches in the Netherlands, erected by the Italians for the entry of the future Charles V.

understood the full significance of what he saw, whereas the texts of the two continental entries are official records, for which the writers would have had access to inside information to explain the underlying meaning. We do not know the intentions of the devisers of the Edinburgh entry which raises the question of who they were.

Poets, such as John Lydgate at the courts of Henry V and Henry VI could fulfil the rôle, but William Dunbar's involvement appears peripheral to James IV's wedding.[28] Certainly, Sir David Lindsay of the Mount, court poet to James V, organised the abortive triumphs for Madeleine of Valois in 1537 and the 'great treiumph' for Mary of Guise's Edinburgh entry in 1538. However, he was also Lord Lyon, and royal pageantry falls more within the province of heralds than poets.[29] In 1503, Henry Thomson was Lord Lyon and had

been in Rome in spring 1502, where, besides seeing real triumphal arches, he would have heard about the pageantry in December and January in honour of Lucrezia Borgia's wedding to Alfonso d'Este, which stretched from Rome to Ferrara, and included re-enactments of Roman triumphs and a representation of the Judgement of Paris.[30] Moreover, Thomson's deputy appears to have been Cumming, Marchmont Herald, whose interest in triumphal and imperial crowns has already been discussed Thus the decision to include triumphal arches, and possibly their design, in the 1503 entry is likely to have come from the heralds.[31]

In a wider context, the 1503 triumph can be seen as part of the transformation of Edinburgh from medieval burgh to Renaissance capital, initiated by James III.[32] That the judges of the College of Justice, founded in 1532, are styled 'Senators', and that the 'Octavians' were appointed to sort out royal finances in 1596 are pointers towards the self-image of Renaissance Scotland and its capital, which appears in the earliest printed view of the city.[33] The woodcut, from the 1550 Latin version of Muenster's *Cosmographia* (see Figure 5) with its domes and spires, cornices and pediments is obviously a romanticised view, but does have some basis in fact and deserves closer analysis than it has hitherto received, but here I only have space to refer to the accompanying text by Alexander Alesius, an Edinburgh-born Protestant divine, exiled in Germany. He describes his home town in terms which inevitably recall Rome, with its 'arx' (castle), 'capitolium' (tolbooth), 'basilica [Sanctae Crucis]' (Holyrood Abbey), 'monasteria et templa' (monasteries and churches), its 'Via Regia' (Royal Mile) paved with 'level square stones' and lined with buildings 'not constructed from bricks, but natural and square stones, so that even private houses can be compared with great palaces'. Even the Cowgate, in Latin 'Via Vaccarum', recalls the Roman Forum, known during the Renaissance as 'Campo Vaccino' (Cow Field). Alesius tells us that in it lived 'patricii et senatores urbis, et in qua sunt principum regni palatia' (nobles and councillors of the town and in which are the palaces of the most distinguished men of the kingdom).[34] It

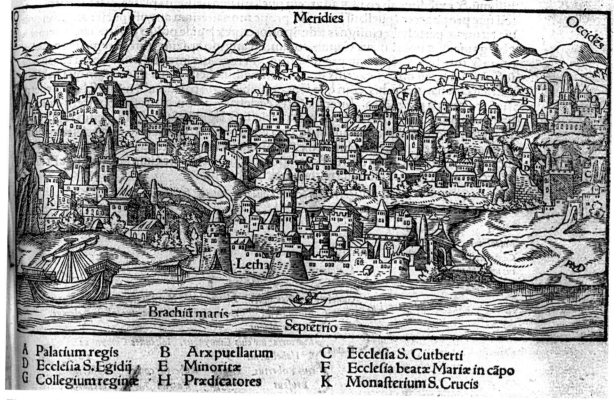

Alexander Alesius Scotus de Edinburgo.

A	Palatium regis	B	Arx puellarum	C	Ecclesia S. Cutberti
D	Ecclesia S. Egidij	E	Minoritæ	F	Ecclesia beatæ Mariæ in cãpo
G	Collegium reginæ	H	Prædicatores	K	Monasterium S. Crucis

Figure 5. Edinburgh in the time of James V (woodcut by Hans Rudolf Manuel ('Deutsch') in S Münster, Cosmographia, 1550). An idealised but recognisable view of Edinburgh as a Renaissance capital.

is fitting that the town which appears to have had the first two Renaissance temporary triumphal arches north of the Alps should inspire such comparisons.

The 1503 arches inaugurated more than a century of triumphs in Edinburgh, for some of which we know temporary arches were erected.[35] However, its most intriguing successor may be the 'New World' arch erected in Fleet Street for James VI's entry into London in 1604, symbolizing the union of the crowns of Scotland, England, France and Ireland. With its two towers and battlements, it is the only one of seven triumphal arches to have a castellated character, and, by also including the Cardinal Virtues, recalls both the 1503 Edinburgh arches. It is tempting to speculate that such a combination was deliberate since without Margaret Tudor's entry to Edinburgh, James VI would not have been entering London as James I.[36]

Acknowledgements

I gratefully acknowledge the help of Priscilla Bawcutt, Michael Bury, Margaret Campbell, Alistair Cherry, Howard Colvin, Douglas Gray, Norma Henderson, Aonghus MacKechnie, Norman Macdougall, Richard Schofield, Margaret Wilkes, and the Herzog August Bibliothek, Wolfenbüttel.

NOTES

1. A MacKechnie, 'Stirling's triumphal arch', *Welcome: News for Friends of Historic Scotland* (September 1991), p 5: see also I Campbell, 'A Romanesque revival and the early Renaissance in Scotland circa 1380–1513', *Journal of the Society of Architectural Historians*, liv (1995), pp 302–25; and 'Linlithgow's "princely palace" and its influence in Europe', *Architectural Heritage*, v (1995), pp 1–20.

2. H Colvin, 'Pompous entries and English Architecture', a forthcoming essay.

3. For an introduction to entries, see R Strong, *Art and power: Renaissance festivals 1450–1650* (Woodbridge, 1984), pp 3 ff.

4. Strong, *Art and Power*, pp 44–8; and R Baldwin, 'A bibliography of the literature on triumph' in *'All the world's a stage': Art and pageantry in the Renaissance and Baroque*, 2 vols, ed B Wisch and S S Munshower, *Part 1: Triumphal celebrations and the ritual of statecraft* (University Park, 1990), pp 359–76.

5. N G L Hammond and H H Scullard (eds), *The Oxford Classical Dictionary*, 2nd edn (Oxford, 1970), s v 'Triumph'.

6. On Petrarch, Strong, *Art and power*, p 44; on the influence of *I Trionfi* on Gavin Douglas' *Palice of Honour* (1501) see R D S Jack, *The Italian influence on Scottish literature* (Edinburgh, 1970), pp 23–7; on the 1537–38 entries, see R Lindsay of Pitscottie, *The Historie and Cronicle of Scotland*, ed J A G Mackay, 3 vols (Edinburgh and London, 1899–1901), ii, pp 368–81.

7. J Yonge, 'The fyancells of Margaret, eldest daughter of King Henry VII to James, king of Scotland …' in J Leland, *De rebus Britannicis collectanea*, 5 vols, ed T Hearne, 2nd edn (London, 1770), vol iv, pp 289–90; see also L O Fradenburg, *City, marriage, tournament* (Madison, 1991), pp 91–122.

8. R. Withington, *English pageantry: An historical outline*, 2 vols (Cambridge, Mass, 1918–20), i, p 81. The 'Judgement of Paris' had appeared in the entry of Joanna of Castile to Brussels in 1496, illustrated in M Herrmann, *Forschungen zur deutschen Theatergeschichte des Mittelalters und der Renaissance* (Berlin, 1914), p 391.

9. This is surmised from the royal couple's first encountering the Franciscans ('Greyfriars'): W Moir Bryce, 'The Flodden Wall of Edinburgh', *Book of the Old Edinburgh Club*, ii (1909), p 70.

10. T Phillips, 'Account of the ceremonial of the marriage of Princess Margaret … to Charles, duke of Burgundy in 1468', *Archaeologia*, xxxi (1846), p 331.

11. R du Puys, *La tryumphante entree de Charles Prince des Espagnes en Bruges 1515* [Paris], nd, reproduced with introduction by S Anglo, New York, nd, fols Ci^{r-v}, discussed pp 25–6.

12. I have only found reference to two: T Godefroy, *Le Ceremonial françois*, 2 vols (Paris, 1649), i, p 655, has Charles VII passing under 'une arcade' in his entry to Paris in 1437, but another account in B Guenée and F Lehoux, *Les entrées royales françaises de 1328 à 1515* (Paris, 1968), p 76 omits mention of the arcade. G R Kernodle, *From art to theatre: Form and convention in the Renaissance* (Chicago, 1944), p 92, refers to one in 1440 at the entrance to the market square in Bruges, for Philip the Good's entry.

13. See Withington, *English pageantry*, i, pp 162–4 for English and French examples.

14. Kernodle, *From art to theatre*, pp 90–2.

15. E Callmann, 'The triumphal entry into Naples of Alfonso I'; *Apollo*, cix (1979), pp 24–31.

16. Du Puys, *Tryumphante entrée*, fols Di^v–Dii^r, and p 14. On the use of romanesque motifs to represent Roman architecture, see Campbell, 'Romanesque revival', p 319.

17. On the poem, see J Kinsley (ed), *Poems of William Dunbar* (Oxford, 1979), No 24, l 6, pp 95–6: J Hughes and W S Ramson, *Poetry of the Stewart Court* (Canberra, 1982), pp 11–12. On the Tudors' imperial claims, see F Yates, *Astraea* (London, 1993), p 50 ff. The Stewarts too had originally claimed Trojan descent, but later found it politic to emphasise their Greek ancestry in common with the rest of the Scots, hence the popularity of Alexander as a royal name in the fifteenth century: R Nicholson, *Scotland: the later Middle Ages* (Edinburgh, 1974), p 185; and Campbell, 'Romanesque revival', pp 308–9. At the wedding banquet at Holyrood on 8 August, Yonge reports that there were tapestries of the 'Ystory of the old Troy' and the 'History of Hercules', referring to both origin myths (Leland, *De rebus*, iv, p 296).

18. See C Edington, *Court and culture in Renaissance Scotland: Sir David Lindsay of the Mount* (Edinburgh, 1995), pp 111–12; Campbell, 'Romanesque revival', pp 322–3, n 70.

19. Hammond, *Classical Dictionary*, s v 'Imperator'; L A J R Houwen (ed), *The Deidis of Armorie: a heraldic treatise and bestiary*, 2 vols (Aberdeen, 1994), Scottish Text Society; Houwen, 'The Seven Deeds of Honour and their crowns: Lydgate and a late fifteenth-century Scots chivalric treatise', *Studies in Scottish literature*, xxviii (1993), 159.

20. The naming of James and Margaret's first son, Arthur, alludes to this *renovatio imperii*: Norman

Macdougall has suggested that the triumphal arch at Stirling Castle, which has Arthurian associations, celebrates the birth of Arthur (personal communication to A MacKechnie).

21. R Schofield, ' A humanist description of the architecture for the wedding of Gian Galeazzo Sforza and Isabella d'Aragona (1489)', *Papers of the British School at Rome*, lvi (1988), p 215; T Tuohy, *Herculean Ferrara* (Cambridge, 1966), p 267; S Infessura, *Il diario della città di Roma*, ed O Tommasini (Rome, 1890) (Fonti per la storia d'Italia, v), p 282; J Chartrou, *Les entrées solennelles et triomphales à la Renaissance (1484–1551)* (Paris, 1928), pp 73–7.

22. Herzog August Bibliothek, Wolfenbüttel, Cod 86.4 'Extravagantium', discussed in A-M Lecoq, *François Ier imaginaire*, Paris [1987], pp 186–206; and Du Puys, *Tryumphante entrée*, fols Eiii^r-v and [E vi]^r-v and pp 16–17.

23. Lecoq, *François Ier*, pp 194–6: this arch was traditional in decorating an existing permanent gateway, and innovative only in its ornament.

24. Du Puys, *Tryumphante entrée*, fols E iii^r [E vi]^r-v and pp 16–17.

25. Leland, *De rebus*, iv, pp 289–90: P Bawcutt suggests that the Virtues were painted, in *Dunbar the makar* (Oxford, 1992), p 162.

26. On the Virtues triumphant, see A Katzenellenbogen, *Allegories of the Virtues and Vices in medieval art*, 2nd ed (New York, 1964), pp 14–21.

27. See *Compota thesariorum regum Scotorum: Accounts of the Lord High Treasurer of Scotland*, ed T Dickson and J Balfour Paul (Edinburgh, 1877), ii, p 377 on Dorange; iv, p 375 on Peblis; and on Cressent, iv, p 271; and Campbell, 'Romanesque revival', p 317.

28. Bawcutt questions the attribution to Dunbar of 'Now fayre fayrest ...' (*Dunbar*, p 32).

29. Pitscottie, *Cronicles*, ii, pp 368–77 and 381; and Edington, *Court and culture*, pp 107–10.

30. R L Mackie, *King James IV of Scotland* (Edinburgh, 1958), p 101: F Gregorovius, *Lucrezia Borgia* (London, 1948), pp 135 ff.

31. There seems to have been a close connection between architecture and heraldry at the Scottish court: Sir John Scrymgeour of Myres was a macer (between a herald and a pursuivant) and owned a copy of Cumming's 'Deidis', as well as being King's Master of Works from 1529–62; and William Schaw was both Master of Works (1583–1602) and Master of Ceremonies, and owned the Dunvegan Armorial: Houwen, *Deidis*, i, pp lxiii-lxx; and H M Paton (ed), *Accounts of the Masters of Works: Volume I 1529–1615* (Edinburgh, 1957), pp xxiii–iv, and xxviii–ix; D Stevenson, *The origins of Freemasonry: Scotland's century 1590–1710* (Cambridge, 1988), p 27: *Dunvegan Castle, Isle of Skye, Scotland*, np, nd, p 12.

32. Fradenburg, *City*, pp 20 ff.

33. M Lynch, *Scotland: a new history*, 2nd edn (London, 1992), p 107 and pp 234–5.

34. S Münster, *Cosmographia universalis*, libri VI (Basle, 1550), pp 51–2. The text is discussed and reproduced without the woodcut in 'Edinburghi regiae Scotorum urbis descriptio, per Alexandrum Alesium, S T D Tempore Jacobi V', *Bannatyne Club Miscellany*, i (Edinburgh, 1827), pp 180 ff. A translation appears in P Hume Brown, *Scotland before 1700 from contemporary documents* (Edinburgh, 1893), pp 106–8. For the woodcut, see R McClary, *The earliest views of Edinburgh 1544–1647* (Edinburgh, 1991), No III. On Alesius, T Fischer, *The Scots in Germany* (Edinburgh, 1902), pp 165 ff.

35. See Douglas Gray, 'The Royal entry in sixteenth-century Scotland', forthcoming in 1998 in a collection of essays, *The Rose and the Thistle*, edited by S Mapstone and J Wood, to be published by Tuckwell Press.

36. D M Bergeron, *English civic pageantry 1558–1642* (London, 1971), pp 84–5 and plate 7; Fradenburg, *City*, pp 121–2.

4

ANNE RICHES

The Teeth of an Ivory Comb: Travellers' Observations of Edinburgh and Glasgow, 1548–1830

TRAVELLERS to Scotland have been prodigious recorders of their visits, providing a rich legacy of impressions and observations, frequently mined for apt quotations by historians. Their personal diaries and journals can also be quarried more specifically to give a picture of the changing face of Scotland. Their glimpses, pinpointed in time, have an immediacy absent from formal historical documents. Before the middle of the sixteenth century accounts mainly dwelt on events, people or social habits with little description of places.[1] Later travellers' reports became increasingly visual, often written with publication in mind. They did, in effect, fill the place of guide books, influencing subsequent travellers' itineraries and ideas. With the growth of easier travel, especially travel for leisure, came the need for mass-produced guide books crammed with facts and figures. The personal travel journal, with all its idiosyncrasies, was relegated to the private archive.

Who were these travellers and why did they come? Before the Union with England the French were regular visitors. Jean de Beaugue, travelling with a French armed force, sent in 1548, to help the Scots against the continued English threat after the battle of Pinkie, came to advise on fortifications and recorded his findings.[2] With peace in Europe at the end of the sixteenth century, European travel became possible. The highly connected Duc de Rohan set out in 1600 and was received equally cordially in Scotland and England,[3] a foretaste of closer contacts between the two countries. This mood was detected two years previously by the

Englishman, Fynes Moryson,[4] who toured extensively throughout Europe. After the Act of Union the English began to explore Scotland; they made records and some published their discoveries, with the eighteenth century producing the best-known travellers, including Daniel Defoe, Richard Pococke, Thomas Pennant, Samuel Johnson and James Boswell. The genre was continued by less eminent diarists into the nineteenth century. Some observers were clerics, apparently unfettered by their livings or universities, some came on political or military assignments, some were natural scientists, some gentlemen, some simply avid travellers. The hazards of travel ensured that most travel was undertaken by men, but exceptions were found in Celia Fiennes, who on her travels in 1598, perhaps not surprisingly considering the date, barely penetrated the border and Dorothy Wordsworth (1803)[5] who, in the fashion of her day, sought out the picturesque qualities of Scotland.

By their nature the journals and diaries do not conform to any regular pattern. Some were clearly influenced by earlier publications and not all travellers kept daily records. Berian Botfield,[6] travelling in 1830 was scathing of those 'who trusted to memory what cannot be trusted safely to the eye and told by guess what a few hours before they had known with certainty'. Certain topics and places attracted most writers and they invariably focused on sights and customs which contrasted with their own environment. A consequence of this has been to highlight Scottishness. It is important to remember that different travellers

THE TEETH OF AN IVORY COMB / 35

had different aims and interests and the inclusions and omissions reflect their personal leanings. Jean de Beaugue (1548) focused on the fortification of vulnerable towns, recommending sites for citadels. In 1548 he described Perth as 'a very pretty place, pleasant and well-fitted to be the site of a good town, which might be rendered secure for its inhabitants by building a citadel where is now the church of the Holy Cross' (St John's). The advice was not heeded and the church was badly damaged in 1559. Perth was not the only town where the church was found to occupy the strongest site; in St Andrews too 'there is no commodious place for a citadel which would not risk much damage to the abbey ... a very large and beautiful structure'. Dundee, by contrast was 'one of the finest towns in Scotland ... and capable of being easily fortified'. Johnson and Boswell's purpose was to visit the Western Isles to 'contemplate a system of life almost totally different from what we had been accustomed to see'.[7] Most visitors were simply curious.

Edinburgh and Glasgow provide a focus for discussion because most travellers visited both cities. Through their comments will emerge a view of the townscapes of the two cities, with a closer focus on buildings, for the most part residential. The first graphic description of Edinburgh came from Fynes Moryson, who visited in 1598. Still conscious of the recent need for fortification, he was surprised by the neglect of Edinburgh's 1513 walls which were, he commented, 'built of little unpolished stones and seem ancient but are very narrow and exceedingly low, in other [parts] ruined', and the citizens had not used their powers of 1591 to collect money for strengthening them. John Taylor,[8] the 'King's Majesties Water Poet' (1618), on the other hand thought the walls to be strong, which, although true of parts, suggests that his knowledge of fortifications was superficial. Because he sets the pattern for subsequent travellers, Moryson's description of Edinburgh is worth quoting:
'The City is high seated, in a fruitfull soyle, and wholesome aire, and is adorned with many Noblemens Towers[9] lying about it, and aboundeth with many springs of sweet waters. At the end

towards the East is the Kings Pallace joyning to the Monastery of the Holy Crosse ... From the Kings Pallace at the East the City still riseth higher and higher towards the West, and consists especially of one broad and very faire street (which is the greatest part and sole ornament thereof), the rest of the side streetes and allies being of poore buildings and inhabited with very poore people, and this length from the East to the West is about a mile. At the furthest end towards the West is a very strong Castle which the Scots hold unexpugnable ... In the midst of the foresaid streete, the Cathedrall Church is built, which is large and lightsome, but little stately for building, and nothing at all for beauty and ornament'.

Edinburgh's dramatic natural site and the 'faire Streete' have never ceased to fascinate travellers. Taylor added embellishments to Moryson's description: the Royal Mile he described as the 'fairest and goodliest streete that ever mine eyes beheld, for I did never see or heare of a street of that length'. The contrast with English streets was marked: they may have opened into spacious market places, but did not compete for breadth and length. Taylor corrected Moryson's description of the closes off the Royal Mile 'wherein are gentlemens houses, much fairer than the buildings in the high-street', such houses as Baillie John McMorran's in Riddle's Court built circa 1590 and Tweeddale House built and added to by the Laing family 1576 and circa 1602, whose significance Moryson did not recognise.

Of particular interest is Moryson's account of domestic buildings

The houses are built of unpolished stone, and in the faire streete good part of them is freestone, which in the broade streete would make a good shew, but that the outsides of them are faced with wooden galleries, built upon the second story of the houses, yet these galleries give the owners a faire and pleasant prospect, into the said faire and broad streete, when they sit or stand in the same.

Some observers were misled by the timber galleries into assuming that many domestic buildings were timber-framed; Henri Duc de Rohan (1600) commented, erroneously, that 'almost all are constructed of wood', perhaps reflecting on the towns of Normandy. By the early seventeenth century the Royal Mile was lined with buildings five, six or seven stories high, with gable ends to the street and built of squared stone, for occupation by merchants and tradesmen. In the many closes were 'the gentlemens mansions and goodliest houses' as Taylor noted. The timber galleries did not always find admirers; Sir William Brereton,[10] familiar with the timber framing tradition of his native Cheshire, believed that the Cowgate would have been very stately 'were [the buildings] not lined to the outside and faced with boards, ... which is towards the street, doth much blemish it, and derogate from glory and beauty; as also the want of fair glass windows, whereof few or none are to be discerned towards the street ... This lining with boards (wherein are round holes shaped to the proportions of men's heads) and this encroachment into the street is a mighty disgrace unto it, for the walls (which were the outside) are stone; so as if this outside facing of boards were removed, and the houses built uniform all of the same height, it were the most complete street in Christendom'.

The scale of the Royal Mile continued to astonish visitors; Brereton proclaimed: 'it is the broadest street (except the Low Countries, where there is a navigable channel in the middle of the street) and the longest street I have seen, which begins at the palace, the gate whereof enters straight into the suburbs, and is placed at the lower end of the same. The suburbs [ie the Canongate] make a handsome street'. He admired the construction of the street: 'the best paved street with bowther [boulder] stones (which are very great ones) that I have seen: the channels are very conveniently contrived on both sides of the streets, so as there is none in the middle ... Here they usually walk in the middle of the street ... This street, which may indeed deserve to dominate the whole city, is always full thronged with people, it being the market place, and the only place where the gentlemen and merchants meet and walk ... there

were about sixty back lanes or streets, which were placed in the side of this street, and went out of it narrow and inconvenient straight lanes, some wider, some narrower, some built on both sides, others only on one side'.

Brereton provided one of the earliest accounts of Glasgow, distinguished by its spacious plan and unconstrained by city walls, a sharp contrast with Edinburgh's constricted site. Glasgow was 'famous for the church, which is fairest and stateliest in Scotland, for the Toll-boothe and Bridge'. It had 'two streets, which are built like a cross, in the middle of both which the cross is placed, which looks four ways into four streets, though indeed they be but two straight streets; the one reaching from the church to the bridge, a mile long, the other which crosseth it, that is much shorter'. The church is of course the Cathedral 'a brave and ancient piece'. After the Reformation, the nave was separated from the chancel, the latter and the lower church only being used in the seventeenth century. It was stone building which impressed Brereton, indeed he did not mention the timber houses on Glasgow's High Street, described in 1661 by Jorevin De Rocheford[11] as 'of wood ornamented with carvings', but turned his attention to public buildings. Near the Cross, the Tolbooth with its tall tower 'from the top of which, being leaded, you may take a full view and prospect of the whole city' was 'said to be the fairest in this kingdom'. Of particular interest in 1636 was the construction of the new university buildings, with one side of the quadrangle completed. An anonymous Royalist poet with an undisguised distrust for the new order wrote (1641):[12]

As we descend the street we take a view
Oth' Colledge, where the buildings were
   yet new,
And so must be the doctrine thats there
   taught
For now the old is quite worn out and
   naught.

The contrast between the buildings for the universities of Edinburgh and Glasgow was marked; John

Ray[13] circa 1662 found Edinburgh's university buildings to be 'mean and of no great capacity' while Glasgow had 'a pretty stone building, not inferior to Wadham and All Souls' at Oxford.

By the Restoration it was rare for a traveller to bypass either Edinburgh or Glasgow and for the most part they were attracted by the same things: the visual appearance of Edinburgh and in particular the height of the buildings, crammed within the city walls and the strength of the castle site; in Glasgow it was the drama of the cathedral, the spacious, symmetrical layout and the public buildings which dominated descriptions. John Ray failed to comment on Edinburgh's arresting town plan, maybe it was taken for granted but Glasgow he records as 'fair, large and well-built, cross-wise, somewhat like unto Oxford, the streets very broad and pleasant'. In 1661 de Rocheford noted that the city was situated upon a hill that extends gently to the brink of the river Clyd', with streets 'large and handsome, as if belonging to a new town'. He highlighted the contrast between Glasgow's favourable trading position and economic prosperity resulting in expansion, with the greater antiquity of Edinburgh, 'the capital town, and the handsomest in the kingdom'. He described the Royal Mile, extending from the castle gently to the bottom of the hill 'that seems on both sides enclosed by a valley, which serves for a ditch'; in the valley to the north were the gardens[14] (separated from the town by part of the city walls); to the south was the lower town. He had previously described the Cowgate, leading from the Grassmarket, as the most populous quarter of the town with 'little narrow streets mounting into the great one that forms the middle of the town ... This street is so wide that it seems a market-place throughout its whole extent'. He was among the first to comment on the St Giles' crown steeple which had recently been restored; the fact that earlier visitors had ignored this very striking and unusual feature – Moryson (1598) had dismissed St Giles as 'nothing at all for beauty and ornament' – perhaps suggests that before the 1648 restoration it was very decayed or even partially dismantled.

By the end of the seventeenth century Edinburgh had become overcrowded and cramped; it had ceased to impress travellers with its beauty and vitality. In 1689 Thomas Morer,[15] while still admiring the Royal Mile, found the 'little lanes of communication [between the Cowgate and the High Street] but very steepy and troublesome, and withal so nasty ... that Edinburgh is by some liken'd to an ivory comb, whose teeth on both sides are very foul, though the space between them is clean and sightly'. He indicated considerable development in urban housing. The old houses of the kind described by Brereton (1636) still existed in Edinburgh; their stairs projected into the street, which Morer found unsightly and inconvenient and they were sometimes 'so steepy, narrow and fenceless, that it requires care to go up and down for fear of falling' but 'their new houses are made of stone, with good windows modishly framed and glazed and so lofty that five or six stories is an ordinary height and one row of buildings there is near the Parliament Close with no less than fourteen [a feat which amazed most visitors]. The reason of it is their scantness of room, which, not allowing 'em large foundations, they are forced to make it up in the superstructure, to entertain comers, who are very desirous to be in or as near as they can to the city'. Stairs to the upper floors were removed to rear courts or were contained within the walls of the buildings and 'the ascent and descent is more decent and easie, and rids the street of an incumbrance which cannot be avoided in other houses'.

The traditional tenemental division of buildings was alien to most English travellers; Morer could only think of student accommodation in London's Inns-of-Court for comparison. He illustrated the increasing interest in proportion and scale when commenting on Parliament Yard, 'the pride of Edinburgh'. It was 'square and well-paved, beautiful with good buildings round about it; and the only fault is that it is no bigger, the height of the houses bearing no correspondence to the dimensions of the area'. On the other hand Glasgow, with no natural constraints to its development, was growing spaciously. 'A very pleasant city', recalled Ralph Thoresby[16] in 1681, 'far exceeding

Figure 1. Urbes Edinae latus septentrionale. The prospect of the North syde of Edinburgh. Nd – early eighteenth century. (Society of Antiquaries, Harley Collection, County Views, Vol 8)

Figure 2. View of Glasgow from the South West, 1764. (Foulis Academy Prints, Mitchell Library, Glasgow)

Figure 3. View of the new bridge, Edinburgh, with the adjacent buildings of the Old and New Town from the west. Nd, circa 1780. (RCAHMS)

Figure 4. Old and New Edinburgh with the North Bridge. Sir J Carr, 1809. (RCAHMS)

Figure 5. Glasgow from the east, drawn by W Wilson, engraved by C Bennet, 1818. (RCAHMS)

Edinburgh itself in the situation and cleanness'. For Morer (1689) it was 'a place of great extent and good situation; and has the reputation of the finest town in Scotland not excepting Edinburgh, tho' the royal city. The two main streets are made cross-wise, well paved and bounded with stately buildings, especially about the centre, where they are mostly new with piazzas under 'em'. In 1723 John Macky [17] called Glasgow 'the beautifullest little city I have seen in Britain' with its regular spacious streets. Like Morer he admired the Royal Mile in Edinburgh but lamented the state of the closes and concentrated his efforts on descriptions of individual, remarkable buildings and not the outmoded plan.

Perhaps the most interesting form of urban street building found in the second half of the seventeenth century was the arcaded or piazza form adopted for the best houses in the vicinity of Glasgow Cross, pointed out by Morer. The system was familiar to those who knew Covent Garden or the Place des Vosges, but the squat design was closer in spirit to the arcades of the French bastide towns. Defoe admired the Glasgow houses 'all of stone and generally equal and uniform in height, as well as in the front the lower story generally stands on vast dorick columns, not round pillars, and arches between give passage into the shops, adding to the strength as well as the beauty of the building'. [18] This form, although found in Edinburgh and seen in Gladstone's Land where the arches were discovered in the 1935 restoration, was never so regularly adopted there, except in an altogether more sophisticated way in the courtyard of Holyrood which was arcaded after the example of the Royal Exchange in London. Other towns too, for instance Elgin and Inverness, employed the arcade, disparaged by some for removing light from the often commercial ground-floor accommodation. The solidity of urban building caused Defoe to draw comparisons with the 'paper-built cities in England'. The Canongate boasted Edinburgh's grandest domestic building, Defoe noting 'several magnificent houses of the nobility'. Queensberry and Moray Houses were 'large and princely buildings, all of freestone with good gardens behind';

inside the walls the Earl of Tweeddale had 'a good city house with a plantation of lime trees behind it'. Handsome houses continued to be built within Edinburgh's narrow wynds and alleys which had they been 'set out in handsome streets, would have adorned a very noble city, but are here crowded together, as may be said, without much notice'.

Daniel Defoe set a new pattern for travel writing, taking the mantle of a modern critic. In Edinburgh he described the 'greate street' as 'perhaps, the largest, longest, and finest street for buildings and numbers of inhabitants, not in Britain but in the world' but, because of its site suffered 'infinite disadvantages, and lies under such scandalous inconveniences as are, by its enemies, made a subject of scorn and reproach ... yet I believe, this may be said with truth, that in no city in the world so many people live in so little room as Edinburgh'. Not content simply to assess the current situation, Defoe sought solutions and foresaw the advantages if the North Lough had been drained 'and fine beautiful streets would no doubt have been built there; nay I question much whether, in time, the high street would not have been forsaken, and the city, as we might say run all out of its gates to the north'. Defoe and his contemporaries lavished praise on Glasgow, 'a very fine city, the four principal streets are the fairest built that I have ever seen in one city together ... in a word it is the cleanest and beautifullest city in Britain, London excepted ... Could this city but have a communication with the Firth of Forth ... they would in a few years double their trade'. Over fifty years later the Forth and Clyde canal provided the link.

By Bishop Pococke's visit in 1756, [19] Glasgow had subtly divided into an old and new town, with the old around the Cathedral and the new, reflecting the trade boom, concentrated around the Cross and with several new streets crossing the earlier street pattern to make a grid. 'Several merchants have grand houses. They have a fine old town house and a beautiful new town house adjoining to it.' The plan of Edinburgh remained virtually unchanged, made up of '329 streets, wynds or lanes and squares or closes or courts and other openings'. But change was imminent: the city was about to expand first to the south with a series of small squares, but also, as Pococke reported, more radical plans were afoot – 'the first hill to the north is to be divided into three streets from east to west and the houses to be only three stories high, which will make it a most noble city'. A feeling for the romantic tinged Thomas Pennant's (1771) first impressions of Edinburgh, 'a city that possesses a boldness and grandeur of situation beyond any I had ever seen. It is built on the edges and side of a vast sloping rock of a great and precipitous height at the upper extremity and the sides declining very quick and steep into the plain'.[20] It was not however a situation he regarded as suitable for a modern city; more to his taste was the layout of George Square to the south, a small portion of which was built with 'small but commodious houses in the English fashion. Such is the spirit of improvement that within three years £60,000 have been expended in houses of the modern taste and £20,000 in the old'. The city's renaissance lay in the proposed New Town on the north side, 'planned with great judgement and will prove a magnificent addition to Edinburgh'. St Andrew's Square was already building, demonstrating the pattern for future living. But until Edinburgh's new town materialised, Glasgow remained the model by which standards were set. The elegant streets and market places underlined the growing prosperity of the city, a fact Dr Johnson did not miss, noting that 'the prosperity of commerce was shown in the greatness of many private houses and a general appearance of wealth'. But for a city so much frequented no description was required.

Towards the end of the eighteenth century the admiration pendulum was swinging towards Edinburgh. In 1786 the Frenchmen, François and Alexandre de la Rochefoucauld with their tutor Lazowski, travelled to Scotland.[21] The tutor's notebooks record his observation 'No room for carriages in Edinburgh, but plenty of sedan chairs' and he perhaps suffered from the 'perpetual climbing and descending almost vertically'. He was excited by the emerging New Town – 'In a few years Edinburgh will be a town quite as agreeable and a great deal more picturesque than any other

town in Europe'. Thomas Newte (1791) expressed the views of fellow observers when he declared that Edinburgh's buildings 'presented an assemblage scarcely to be exceeded by the imagination of painter or poet'.[22] Of the Old Town he wrote, 'choice would never have induced any man to build a house on this spot or live fourteen stories above the ground' but he had praise too: 'the Old [Town] excells the New in variety, boldness and grandeur of aspect', the New Town scored 'in beauty, elegance and commodeous as well as salubrious disposition and situation'.

The numbers of informed descriptions which existed by the end of the eighteenth century meant that later travellers rarely bothered to repeat the exercise except to add odd comments. An exception was Alexander Campbell who left little undescribed after his visit to Edinburgh in 1801.[23] He was particularly aware of the changing face of Edinburgh. The Grassmarket gave him a point of reference to the Old Town: 'the houses on either side of the street, will most probably exhibit to the eye of a stranger, an air of antiquity by no means ill-calculated to produce a characteristic impression of what in former times the Scottish capital displayed in point of amplitude and relative elegance of building'. In the High Street the scene was changing 'on either hand ... new buildings which exhibit a striking contrast to the old and weather-beaten houses, some of which have stood for centuries'. One improvement he praised was the demolition of houses around the Tron Church, but he noted that St Giles, 'a magnificent Gothic pile', was almost totally concealed by neighbouring houses and particularly the Luckenbooths. But the real contrast was the New Town: 'the uniformity of the straight lines is happily varied by the transverse sections of the streets that on either side branch off at right angles and join Queen Street on the north and Princes Streeet on the south'. The buildings too exhibited the same contrasts of uniformity and variety: the Physicians' Hall in George Street, 'built in so chaste, elegant and so simple a style as, on the slightest glance, to arrest the passengers' attention', contrasted with St Andrew's Church, 'so strangely constructed, that, although the workmanship is excellent, yet one is at a loss whether to bestow praise or blame on the architect of so peculiar a structure'.

In 1800 T Garnett described Glasgow as the most improving place in Britain although it must be noted that he did not visit Edinburgh where he would have encountered a similar vitality.[24] The romantic approach dominated Dorothy Wordsworth's (1803) diaries. Of Glasgow she wrote, 'we walked for considerable time in the streets, which are perhaps as handsome as streets can be ... The Trongate, an old street, is very picturesque ... The new town is built of fine stone in the best style of the very best London Streets at the west end of the town, but not being of brick they are greatly superior'. The shops she compared favourably with London shops and the coffee house on the Exchange also reminded her of London. But it was Edinburgh which thrilled her; she was 'exceedingly delighted with the old town with its irregular houses stage above stage, seen as we saw it, in the obscurity of a rainy day, it hardly resembles the work of man, it is more like a piling up of rocks, and I cannot attempt to describe what we saw so imperfectly, but must say that high as my expectations had been raised, the city of Edinburgh far surpassed all expectation'. No reference was made to the classical beauty of the New Town, indeed so far was she from appreciating symmetry, that the fact that Holyrood had sash windows and was a regular pile 'we could not but lament'. Sir John Carr (1807) shared the romance; he saw the Old and New Towns as 'Nature and art [which] seem to have happily exerted their energies in bringing within one view all the varieties of their powers';[25] he even went so far as to fantasise that if the North Loch and the Cowgate were filled with water, Edinburgh would in a considerable degree resemble Stockholm. He captured the New Town before the push north: 'The situation of Queen Street, which opens to the north, (the fashionable evening promenade), is grand and beautiful beyond description. The eye, enchanted, wanders over parks, plantations and villages, adorning a gradual slope of about two miles to the Frith (sic), which exhibits a noble expanse of water ... This fine prospect is beginning to be interrupted by the recent elevations of new streets, particularly by the houses on a piece of ground called Heriots Row'.

John Bowman (1826) did not share the Wordsworthian passion for the romantic.[26] For him Glasgow was a pleasant surprise:

so fine a city ... on account of its extent and the beauty and uniformity of its streets and buildings [it] is not inferior to the finest provincial cities in Britain. The principal streets are wide, and either at right angles or parallel to each other; the houses lofty, built of freestone and very handsome (particularly Argyle Street which is the principal thoroughfare) most of them being finished with fluted or plain pilasters, cornices etc. The whole environs are thickly sprinkled with manufactories, bleaching grounds, villas and gentlemen's houses, giving assurance of its wealth and commercial importance.

Of the public buildings picked out for comment, the Courts of Justice with the jail behind them, by the architect William Stark, made 'altogether a magnificent pile of building, with a facade of singular beauty and classic elegance facing the Clyde'. Stark's 'elegant and extensive' Lunatic Asylum, designed on the panopticon plan, was also applauded. Glasgow was the Liverpool of Scotland, Edinburgh the metropolis, 'the resort of nobility and gentry not connected with trade'. Drama dominated Bowman's description of Edinburgh; he marvelled at the subterranean street the Cowgate had become by the construction of the South Bridge and the impressive height of the North Bridge to the New Town. The New Town was a theatrical set-piece with 'streets generally terminated by some public building, as a church, a portico, a temple or a column'. The extent still 'increased our wonder at the splendour and opulence of this vast and superb city, by the high finish and uniformity of many a crescent, circus and square, in perfect Grecian architecture and Attic chastity'.

It was the expansion of Edinburgh which captivated the early nineteenth-century traveller; even if he were acquainted with London, Paris or Bath, 'the eyes of the stranger must be struck with amazement'. Bowman's description explains why: 'instead of considering the metropolis of one part of a great commercial nation, its classical elegance recalls to the fancy ideas of eastern magnificence. Athens, Babylon, Baghdad and Palmyra, seem to rise again from their ruins of countless centuries, and to reappear in all their splendour before his eyes. Porticoes of massive columns, fluted and plain and of every order, pilasters, domes, obelisks, pillars, and temples; streets of spacious width, intersecting each other at right angles and stretching in long and elegant perspective; houses of towering height, richly decorated with friezes and cornices, meet the eye on every side, all airy, chaste and classical. Every building is of freestone, beautifully clean and light, not a brick or even plaster or cement offends the eye ... As we went up one flight of steps after another, we observed that each storey was inhabited by a distinct family whose name appeared on the brass plate fixed to the principal door'.

In 1826 John Phillips, in his manuscript diary, provides the most poignant description.[27] For him Edinburgh manifestly represented the ancient and modern: 'it would be difficult to describe the mingled feelings of hope and anxiety and expectation which possess my mind at the entering, in the gloomy shroud of evening, a city which is thought to surpass in the beauty of its edifices as well as the romantic nature of its situation, the most boasted of the populous dwellings of man'. He specifically mentioned the 'romantic out line of the old Town, and the beautiful edifices of the new Town'. It is this view of Edinburgh which persisted in the wider sphere and eclipsed the eighteenth-century travellers' impressions of the beauty of Glasgow. Glasgow's great nineteenth-century period of expansion coincided with the advent of published guides and was not subjected to the personal portraiture of the individual traveller.

Acknowledgements

I am grateful to staff at the National Monuments Record of Scotland, the Mitchell Library Glasgow Room, Edinburgh Public Library Edinburgh Room and the Society of Antiquaries Library; also to Professor Roland Paxton and Norman Scarfe for their suggestions, and to Dr Deborah Mays and Juliet Clough for their help with the text.

NOTES

1. At the first mention of an author the full title of the publication is given but page references to Hume Brown or to the other publications would have made the notes intolerably lengthy.

   P Hume Brown, *Early Travellers in Scotland* (Edinburgh 1891). This selected collection of travel writing from the thirteenth century to 1700 has provided the main source for early accounts. It is not only valuable for the texts but for the editor's notes and wry comments.

2. J De Beaugue, *Histoire de la Guerre d'Ecosse* (Paris 1556).

3. Henri Duc de Rohan, *Voyage du Duc de Rohan, facit en l'an 1600*.

4. Fynes Moryson, *An Itinerary written by Fynes Moryson, gent. First in the Latin tongue and then translated by him into English: containing his ten yeeres' travell through the twelve Dominions of Germany, Bohemerland, Sweitzerland, Netherland, Denmarke, Poland, Italy, France, England, Scotland and Ireland* (London 1617).

5. E De Selincourt (ed), *The Journals of Dorothy Wordsworth* (London 1952).

6. Berian Botfield, *A Tour Through Scotland* (Norton Hall 1830).

7. R W Chapman (ed), *Johnson's Journey to the Western Islands of Scotland* and Boswell's *Journal of a Tour to the Hebrides with Samuel Johnson, LL. D.* (London 1924).

8. J Taylor, *The Pennyless Pilgrimage, or the Moneyless Perambulation of John Taylor, alias, The King's Majesties Water-Poet: How he travailed on foot from London to or fro, neither begging, borrowing, or asking meate, drinke, or lodgings* (1618). His expedition was a ploy intended to outdo Ben Jonson, who was also set on walking to Scotland despite his age and girth. Unfortunately there is no record of Jonson's 1618 visit, but Taylor's, if lacking Jonson's style, displays a keen visual awareness and light-hearted wit.

9. The numerous residences in the vicinity of Edinburgh are recorded by most travellers. See Brereton:

'gentlemen's (here called lairds) houses built all castle-wise', Hume Brown, p 148.

10. Sir William Brereton, *Travels of Sir William Brereton* (Chetham Society, 1844). William Brereton, travelling in 1636, prepared his journal from jottings taken on his travels but with no intention of publication. He was particularly interested in the appearance and the administration (ecclesiastical and secular) of the towns he visited.

11. *A Scottish Journie* (1641). Miscellany of Scottish History Society, vol 2 (1904), No 44, pp 224–28.

12. John Ray, *Itinerary*. John Ray known as Ray the naturalist (ed), *Select remains of the learned John Ray* (London 1760).

13. J De Rocheford, *Travels*, included in book of travels published Paris 1672. *Antiquarian Repertory* vol 4 (1809).

14. These were the Botanical Gardens roughly on the site of Waverley Station.

15. T Morer, *A Short Account of Scotland* (London 1715).

16. P Hume Brown (ed), *Early Tours in Scotland by Thomas Kirk and Ralph Thoresby 1677 & 1681* (Edinburgh 1892).

17. J Macky, *A Journey through Scotland in familiar letters from a gentleman here to his friends abroad* (1723).

18. D Defoe, *A tour through the whole island of Great Britain 1722–26* (Folio Society, London 1983).

19. R Pococke, *Tours in Scotland 1747, 1750, 1760* D W Kemp (ed) (Edinburgh 1887).

20. T Pennant, *A Tour in Scotland* (1769, 5th edn, 1790). It appears that Thomas Pennant had seen and used Richard Pococke's letters, which were subsequently lost and not published until 1887, to formulate his own travels; indeed they appear to have influenced his much better known comments on the state of Scotland made after his visit in 1771. So influential were Pennant's observations that T Garnett, writing his journal in 1798, specifically omitted places discussed in detail by Pennant, except for obvious new developments, and turned his attention to the picturesque landscape.

21. I am grateful to Norman Scarfe for information from his preliminary work on the notebooks of the Frenchmen, Alexandre and François de la Rochefoucauld and their tutor, Maximilian de Lazowski who travelled through Scotland in 1786. Their views on Glasgow are awaited with interest, particularly as on their tour of England in 1785 they gave detailed descriptions of industrial and commercial growth.

22. T Newte, *Prospects and observations on a tour in England and Scotland* (London 1791).

23. T Garnett, *Observations on a tour through the Highlands and part of the Western Islands of Scotland* (London 1800).

24. A Campbell, *A journey from Edinburgh through parts of North Britain 1801* (London 1802).

25. Sir John Carr, *Caledonian sketches or tour through Scotland in 1807* (London 1809).

26. J Bowman, *The Highlands and Islands: a nineteenth century tour*, E Barry (ed) (Gloucester 1986).

27. J Phillips, MS Mitchell Library, Glasgow, 'A Tour of Scotland' (1826). Phillips was a geologist and his accounts show a particular interest in building materials.

5

DUNCAN MACMILLAN

'The Busie Humm Of Men':
Visions of the City in Scottish Art

JOHN SLEZER's *Theatrum Scotiae* was the first extended account of the appearance of Scotland and it is clear that for Slezer the country was the sum of its great houses and its towns. These are its social units. His was a social vision and as such, surely it is sound? His Scotland is still the kingdom of the Scots, of its people, and what country would choose to be known, as Scotland now is, largely by images of wild and barren mountains, romantic and beautiful though they may be? But in portraying the towns, Slezer always observes them from outside. They are distinct units, each with its own distinctive profile.[1] They seem immutable and as they sit in the landscape they are as much permanent features of it as if, indeed, they were mountains.

Such images clearly reflect the small size of Scottish towns at the end of the seventeenth century and also their homogeneity, but it also suggests that the artist saw the town as naturally dominant and the country as no more than its setting. Slezer's younger contemporaries, James Thomson, Allan Ramsay and John Clerk of Penicuik, saw things very differently, however. Thomson laid the foundation for the Virgilian view that landscape is nature, untouched by such things as towns; the view that has remained dominant ever since. At the same time, Clerk in his *Country Seat* and Ramsay in the creation of his own villa where it still stands on Castle Hill – at the time it was a suburban villa – adopted a Horatian attitude to the country. It involved a stated and self-conscious awareness of the difference between town and country and the belief that the poet's place was firmly in the latter, though from that vantage point, he could observe the foibles of the city.

This opposition of town and country had already been introduced into Scots literature by Henryson in his adaptation of Aesop, *The Tale of the Uponlandis Mous and the Burges Mous*. The moral was simple, and it is a theme that runs through much later Scottish poetry:

Blissit be simple life withouten dreid;
Blissit be sober feist in quietie
Wha has aneuch, of na mair has he need
Though it be little into quantitie.

Nature in Thomson's sense of the word becomes the subject of painters like Charles Steuart and Jacob More in their pioneering views of waterfalls. In fact More's paintings of the Falls of Clyde are specifically Thomsonian. Alexander Runciman in Ossian's Hall went even further in seeing Ossian's poetry as part of the landscape and in this he was encouraged by James MacPherson and Hugh Blair in their interpretation of the essential symbiosis between such poetry and the landscape from which it grew and in which it survived as oral tradition.

Allan Ramsay junior, no doubt out of piety to his father's memory, also devoted a good deal of his later life to trying to establish the site of Horace's villa and thus prove just such a symbiotic relationship between Horace's poetry and the rural landscape that he inhabited. Horace of course differed from Thomson or MacPherson in that the savour of his poetry depended a good deal on his awareness of the town viewed from a distance as it were and it was this opposition of town and country that was the subject of Alexander Runciman's painting of the *Allegro* painted in 1773. The painting takes its title from Milton's eponymous poem. In a memorable image in the poem, Milton suggests a beehive as he invokes the town as the 'busie humm of men'. Robert Fergusson in his poem *Hame Content* also pays homage to this when he opens his own poem with a description of the city as a beehive:

> Some fock, like bees, fu' glegly rin
> To bykes bang'd fu' o' strife and din
> And thieve and huddle crumb by crumb.

Milton does not pass judgement on the town, but Fergusson adapts the image to a vivid evocation of Henryson's moral opposition of town and country. He then continues to propose his own preference for the health and relaxation of the countryside:

> May I lie streekit at my ease
> Beneath the caller shady trees
> (far frae the din o'Borrowstown).
> 'Mang herds and honest cottar fowk ...

As the poem continues, he develops Henryson's sentiment, 'Wha has aneuch, of na mair has he need'.

Runciman's painting and Fergusson's poem were contemporary and at the time the two were close friends. The painting echoes Fergusson's contrast by showing in the foreground a scene that Milton describes of the tranquil simplicity of a rural meal while in the far distance 'the busie humm of men', or 'the din of Borrowstown', is represented by the city of Perth. (In the middle distance Milton's 'towers embosomed in the trees' become the towers of Scone Palace). Perth is described very much as Slezer had seen it, but now it is visibly distanced to draw the contrast between the city and the simple healthy scene in the foreground.

This opposition is still a conventional one, however, for Fergusson, even though he wrote such fine bucolic poetry as this or the 'Farmer's Ingle',

was a great poet of the city. His 'Auld Reekie' is a wonderfully vivid evocation of the animation in the sounds and smells of Edinburgh:

> Now morn, with bony purpie-smiles
> Kisses the air-cock o' St Giles;
> Rakin their ein, the servant lasses
> Early begin their lies and clashes ...
> On stair wi' tub or pat in hand,
> The barefoot housemaids looe to stand
> That antrin fock may ken how snell
> Auld Reekie will at morning smell ...

Alexander Runciman literally matched the ambition of Fergusson's 'panoramic' poem with a view of Edinburgh that sadly does not survive, but which was taken from a chimney top. It may have related to the view of the city and the Firth of Forth that he painted in the scene of the *Ascension of St Margaret* at Penicuik, but this does not survive either. There is a group of anonymous drawings in the National Gallery of Scotland from this period which suggest some kind of panorama, but the closest that any contemporary came to Fergusson's vision of the city in a surviving image is John Runciman in his brilliant etching of the *Taking Down of the Netherbow Port* in 1764 (see Figure 1).

Prefiguring later battles, it was not without protest that the sixteenth-century port was taken down 'to improve the circulation of traffic' for it seems John Runciman's etching was connected with a campaign against demolition of it as a historical monument, as at the same date James Wilson published a broadside *The Last Speech and Confession and Dying Words of the Netherbow Porch of Edinburgh which was exposed to roup and sale on Thursday 9 August 1764*. John's etching also has a parallel in a drawing that his brother made of the demolished gate to Holyrood which was the subject of a similar broadside by James Wilson. Given the antiquarian interests of such members of the Runcimans' circle as James Cumming and George Paton, founder members of the Society of Antiquaries, there can be little doubt that both works reflected these early conservationist interests and were intended to record these objects for posterity.

In making his etching, however, John Runciman

Figure 1. John Runciman, The Taking Down of the Netherbow Port. (National Galleries of Scotland)

did more than record a historical building. He set it in the daily life of the city in which the actual act of demolition becomes part of the city's own continuing process of change through decay and renewal. John Runciman prefigures Geddes in his vision of the city, not as something static and permanent in the way that Slezer saw it, but as an organism subject to growth and decay. As a street scene, the etching has precedent, but no rival in Paul Sandby's drawings of Edinburgh done some fifteen years earlier, but John Runciman's image is closer to Hogarth's series *Morning, Noon* and *Night* in the way it captures the mood of the city. In the rough, improvised way that he uses the medium of etching, Runciman also captures the improvisation of city life, the clarty untidiness that reflects its particular vitality which Fergusson captured so well in *Auld Reekie*. Indeed in that poem, Fergusson too comments directly on the processes that shaped and are still shaping the city for better or for worse.

Among the Runcimans' contemporaries, though like Slezer he took a distant viewpoint, John Clerk of Eldin produced some dramatic views of Edinburgh which have something of the same vitality as John Runciman's etching (see Figure 2). Another contemporary, David Allan, took up the theme of life within the city in his drawings of particular city types and in broader views of the streets like his two views of the High Street, Edinburgh, or his memorable print of the laying of the foundation stone of the new College building, now Old College. Here too there were important precedents, not only in Sandby, but behind Sandby in the whole tradition of vedute painting that had been naturalised in England by Canaletto and Samuel Scott. In Allan's case though it was the Neapolitan variation on the tradition in the hands of painters like Antonio Joli or Pietro Fabris that was his primary inspiration. Perhaps because of the Dutch influence through Gaspar van Wittel, in Naples town vedute painting was as much concerned with the citizens as the city. Allan's own first essay in this genre was his set of drawings of the Roman Carnival later etched by Sandby. They are studies in 'manners' in which the urban setting is incidental.

Allan's Edinburgh drawings are also contemporary with the first Panorama. The form began in Edinburgh with Robert Barker's first 180 degree view from the Calton Hill in 1788 which he followed with a full 360 degree view the following year. The latter is recorded in a set of prints for which the drawings survive in Edinburgh University Library. Barker christened the Panorama with a word of his own coining that has passed into the language. It was a direct development of the vedute, but also of that impulse in seventeenth-century Dutch painting that Svetlana Alpers has christened 'the art of describing'. The objective was information, though information presented as entertainment, dramatically, with the conviction of

Figure 2. John Clerk of Eldin, a view illustrated in Views of Edinburgh. *(Joe Rock)*

Figure 3. Alexander Nasmyth, Edinburgh from Calton Hill. (Clydesdale Bank plc) (Joe Rock, photographer)

direct experience. You went inside the Panorama and as you looked around, the cylindrical image surrounded you exactly as your field of vision would have done if you were at the centre of an actual view.

The Panorama became the supreme form of city painting and one of the most popular entertainments of the nineteenth century. At the latter end of the century, it shaded imperceptibly into cinema and the modern world. Indeed the Poole family who ran several Edinburgh cinemas including the eponymous Poole's Synod Hall began as impresarios in the business of the panorama and its offshoot the diorama. The Panorama was therefore 'urban' under two counts. The early Panoramas tended to be views of cities, first Edinburgh and then London, but as popular entertainment the Panorama itself became part of the fabric of city life. It has been argued, for instance, that the location of Thomas Barker's Panorama in Leicester Square when he moved south was responsible for the later development of that square as the centre for London cinema.[2]

The greatest Scottish city paintings however are Alexander Nasmyth's views of Edinburgh. There are several of these, but the two principal ones are *Edinburgh from Princes Street* and *Edinburgh from the Calton Hill* (see Figure 3). These were certainly indebted to the Panorama. The latter for example takes a viewpoint close to Barker's on the Calton Hill, but they extend the Panorama's matter-of-fact imagery into the realm of social philosophy. They present not just the image of the city as so much building and so many streets, but the idea of it as the animate fabric of society. As Nasmyth sees it, the city is as natural to man as the coral reef is to the polyp, or the ant-hill to the ant. This is society as Hume and Adam Smith saw it. Thus Nasmyth's pictures offer comment on the underlying motives of the largest architectural project in Scottish history since Hadrian's wall, the building of the Edinburgh New Town. For it is this Enlightenment idea of society that was monumentally expressed there in its judicious balance of architectural order with the freedom of nature in the gardens and distant views. The architecture is not a utilitarian, mechanistic, or accidental environment, but the formal expression of what is ultimately a metaphysical idea of society as the embodiment of humane values.

In Nasmyth's *Edinburgh from Princes Street* we do indeed have 'the busie humm of men'. The people go about their business in the middle of the day and the most conspicuous activity is the building work on the Royal Institution, now known as the Royal Scottish Academy. (This construction is in contrast to the demolition work that animated John Runciman's etching). It is fitting that art should take a central place in the city's active life. In the second picture, the citizens are enjoying their well-earned leisure in the evening sun. Thus the two pictures represent the vital balance in a healthy society between work and recreation. We are reminded too of the practical power of recreation in its proper sense by the Calton Jail in the foreground, at the time a potent symbol of social reform, while the ruling genius of philosophy, the product of creative leisure, is invoked by Hume's tomb, discreetly emphasised by its placing on the exact central line of the composition. There is balance, too, between the Old Town and the New Town, thus between past and present, and between man and nature in the way that the city is clearly seen, though from within, as part of the natural world beyond.

The picture which anticipates these two great paintings in Nasmyth's oeuvre, *Inverary from the Sea*, also reflects this kind of balance. It is a view of the town and its castle seen from a distance, just as Runciman saw Perth, or as Slezer might have seen it even. The difference lies in the fact that Inverary was a new town and Nasmyth's painting seems to have been connected in some way with its development. It is not time that has made it harmonious with its surroundings, therefore, is design. Nasmyth makes the same point here as in his two Edinburgh paintings as he shows us that it is possible to create a city which is at one with the natural world. To do so depends on the belief that man's gifts do not put him at odds with his environment, but properly disposed they are the expression of his community with it.

Nasmyth's representation of the city is optimistic and progressive. There can be little doubt, however, that one of the things that stimulated him was the pageantry surrounding the visit of George IV, or at least the artistic response to it. The spectacle of the city as theatre presented by the royal visit gave an immense boost to the trade in pictures of it. Turner and Wilkie both came to Edinburgh and planned suitably theatrical responses to the spectacle. Ewbank and Carse painted more prosaically topographical pictures in which the royal subject was central and Lizars and others produced a wide variety of prints recording the event (see Figure 4). Like his contemporaries, Nasmyth's attitude is one of celebration, but it is the city and its citizens that he celebrates. He studiously avoids any reference to the pageantry of the royal visit. Pointedly, his hero is the common citizen, not a puffed-up prince. In his paintings, too, history is present, but it is balanced by a sense of the future as in these pictures we encounter once again the vision of the city as dynamic, indeed organic and capable of growth, represented by the building work.

Nasmyth himself was not immune to the drama of history, of course. He witnessed the demolition of the Tolbooth in company with Scott whose own response to this ambiguous event was to write *The Heart of Midlothian*, his novel of the city in which he takes the moral opposition of town and country as his theme. The drawings for Nasmyth's sets for the stage version of the novel show that he understood the importance of the city in its imagery. In his paintings, too, his subjects are frequently historical and picturesque. Indeed he provided forty-three vignettes to the Waverley Novels in

Figure 4. Alexander Carse, George IV Landing at Leith, 1822. (Duncan Macmillan)

Constable's edition of 1821–23, but Scott himself seems to have found his pictures too old-fashioned, or perhaps lacking in drama. Certainly we can see that Nasmyth's radical, Utopian vision of Edinburgh was very much at odds with, for instance, Scott's account of it as the setting of the primitive drama of the Porteous riots. If this was so, it reflected a real change in attitudes to the representation of the past and especially the city that took place under Scott's influence.

Throughout the last years of the eighteenth century and the first two decades of the nineteenth there had been a steady stream of topographical engravings of Scotland, John Knox's paintings of Glasgow following directly from the inspiration of Nasmyth's great paintings. But the growth market was in prints of Edinburgh after artists like Carse and Geikie, and by printmakers like Scott, Clark and Lizars. Initially these were as much of modern buildings as of buildings of antiquarian interest. The royal visit was the catalyst in a change of attitude which was in part due to the way that Scott animated the ancient remains of the city, but there was also a powerful move towards preservation and record. There are for example over two hundred drawings by James Skene of old Edinburgh and there are similar numbers by Walter Geikie, Daniel Wilson, James Drummond and

others as well as such prints as those published by Lizars in *Edinburgh Delineated* and *Picturesque Views of Edinburgh* or lithographs after the drawings of T H Shepherd or George Cattermole.

The immense energy which went into this is itself remarkable as the city became an object of study and of record on a quite new scale. The stimulus no doubt came from Scott who gave an imaginative dimension to simple antiquarianism, but Scott alone cannot have been responsible for all this activity. Other motives included the evolution of the antiquarian interests that had inspired Scott himself, but also a more modern though less focused feeling that the past enshrined values which were threatened by the unfamiliar developments which seemed to undermine the Enlightenment vision of society, even though they were themselves the product of economic forces unleashed by the Enlightenment itself. There is something retrospective about this too. Cattermole's prints in the 1850s, for instance, seem to be inhabited by people in the costume of thirty years earlier. The paintings of James Drummond are explicitly set in the past. The city is a stage for history, but in anticipation of the modern attitude, history itself, or at least the past, is a refuge from the grimmer realities of the present.

This is very much in contrast to Nasmyth's

Street Auctioneer.

Figure 5. Walter Geikie, Etching, Street Auctioneer.

positive view of society and of the properly functioning city as its natural expression, but there are not many pictures of the city in the nineteenth century anywhere that preserve or extend this view. Indeed the real life of cities tends to drop out of view. There are exceptions though and one of the most remarkable city artists of the period was Walter Geikie. His etchings at times undoubtedly reflect his antiquarian interests, but in them we nevertheless see the human life of the city warts and all; we see it integrated with the architecture which is its environment in a completely organic way (see Figure 5).

Walter Geikie was himself part of this street life. His great niece once told me how her grandmother, wife of the artist's nephew the geologist Sir Archibald Geikie, was not keen to acknowledge kinship with the artist as he had the habit of mixing with the unwashed children in the street. His is the smelly organic city of real life. It is also never identifiable as the New Town, suggesting that, in spite of Nasmyth's advocacy, Geikie shared Cockburn's aversion for that project which, although it was inspired by such high ideals, as the consequences of the Enlightenment became apparent, could also be seen to enshrine different and more sinister values. In this kind of engagement with the reality of city life, too, Geikie's etchings are in many ways closest to Robert Fergusson's vision of the city. Indeed one set of etchings includes captions in the vernacular which are amongst some of the most vivid evocations of actual speech from the period that we have, though as Geikie himself was deaf and dumb, it is not clear who was responsible for them.

In most of these etchings the city is implied only by its people, but Geikie was a topographer as well as a social observer. He was a fine draughtsman and he is most interesting when he is least conventional as when he chose to record the ruinous closes of the High Street and broken down rural houses in the environs of Edinburgh in a topographical record which is unique. Geikie's concern with humanity informs all his works and no doubt, in recording these decaying relics of another time, he was motivated by historical interest, but it is a historical interest more than just tempered by this humanity. As his remarkable kitchen drawings show, he is concerned with the places where people live. If the buildings are old, it expresses the continuity in their lives, however much they are constrained in other ways.

Thomas Annan's photographs of Glasgow follow in this tradition and this is a side of the motivation of the pioneer conservationists that we too easily lose from sight. Their antiquarianism was informed by a vivid sense of history as the story of people's lives and their eccentricities. This is what marks Cockburn, and if we read Daniel Wilson or James Grant it is humanity in all its variety running through their texts that brings them to life. Daniel Wilson's drawings are not unlike Geikie's in some ways and in them we can see how his love of the buildings that he recorded was a reflection of the values that he saw enshrined in them.

This need to record things, not only for their own sakes as aesthetic objects, but because of what they stood for, assumed a new urgency in the face of accelerating change and as the modern perspective of past and present was established. In 1812, Alexander Carse painted one of the most memorable city interiors in Scottish art, *The Visit of the Country Relations*. Seen simply as documentary, it is a fascinating picture. It shows the interior of an Old Town or Southside flat in Edinburgh with all the latest furnishings, but its real point is social. It contrasts this awareness of style and fashion in the town family with the simplicity of their country cousins. Among them, it is the girls who are most conscious of the contrast. The poor country girl is mortified by the supercilious stare of her town cousins. Out of place in her country costume, she is the 'Uponlandis mous'.

The country mouse returned to live happily in simplicity, but this poor lass bears some resemblance to the doomed girl in the first scene of the *Harlot's Progress*, innocently arriving in London in her country costume. The Harlot has a goose labelled as a present for her town cousins and, whether she is a goose or a sacrificial lamb, she is met by Mother Needham, a very sophisticated lady on the look-out for new talent. In Carse's picture, too, the country cousin's life will not be the same after this encounter and so there is a frisson of moral peril. It anticipates the theme of *The Heart of Midlothian* which was perhaps also indebted to Hogarth's example and more immediately to Wilkie's too.

In the *Letter of Introduction*, Wilkie took up this theme and in it we sense the moral tension of this whole evolving situation. It is only hinted at by the old man's manifest lack of sympathy for his young country visitor, but sympathy, as Adam Smith described it, was the vital cement of the whole social fabric. On the surface, even less than Carse's picture is this a painting of the city, however. There is nothing to say that it is urban except the fact of the letter itself, but Wilkie's own experience of arriving in London, a rustic stranger, informs it. The tension between natural and artificial in the *Letter of Introduction* is voiced more explicitly in Wilkie's *Penny Wedding* and *Distraining for Rent*. Though neither of these is an urban picture, they are very much pictures about the nature of society; about how a natural and harmonious society was being replaced by one that was inhuman and lacking in natural sympathy. In the pictures, this is expressed in the opposition of old and new, of past and present. In a way it is the old opposition of town and country given a new form born in the consciousness of change, and it gives a different perspective to the antiquarian interest in the city environment, for it was in the city that the changes were most visible. When Thomas Chalmers decided that, as a minister, he must be practically engaged with the world, it was to the deprived people of the city of Glasgow that he took his mission.

In architectural terms, this was a response to the development of unhygienic and inhuman slums and the sense of the loss of a more human architecture in which value and identity was invested. It was in the city, too, that the drama of the Disruption was acted out in a piece of history that, unlike the royal visit, was real not fictional. In it, the underlying issue was the preservation of the idea of society as enshrining a metaphysical ideal and therefore as susceptible to a spiritual cure at least for some of its ills.

Indirectly, the Disruption produced some memorable images of the city in Hill and Adamson's photographs of St Andrews and Edinburgh, but at a deeper level it reflects the resurgence of the practical and active concern with the nature of society that had been expressed twenty years earlier by Nasmyth. It was Patrick Geddes who formulated this as a coherent, theoretical critique of society. Chalmers, Cockburn, Geikie, Daniel Wilson and Geddes, to name only a few, belong together in a single tradition in which architecture in the broadest sense was not merely a material manifestation of the past, of greater or lesser aesthetic and historical interest, but a vehicle for enshrining and transmitting ideals of social value.

This of course is Ruskin's position and Ruskin had a profound influence on Geddes, but Ruskin's own Scottish roots have yet to be examined and Geddes's view does not simply grow out of Ruskin. It comes out of a complex variety of sources which certainly included a sense of the imaginative importance of history as one of the basic elements of the identity which is one of the *a priori* of a society, as opposed to *society* itself which is the sum of such units. In this, Geddes looked back to Scott as did so many throughout Europe in the nineteenth century, but in this broader sense of society as much more than a mere arithmetical calculation, Geddes was descended from the wider Scottish tradition, not just since the Enlightenment, but leading from there back to the Reformation itself.

It was in this perspective that Geddes

Figure 6. Muirhead Bone, Demolition of the Old Sugar Exchange, Glasgow.

approached the townscape, and though he went on to have a world-wide influence, at first, like Nasmyth, Cockburn, or Daniel Wilson and perhaps Scott himself, Edinburgh was his subject. In his vision of society, he saw the rôle of art, much as Nasmyth did in *Edinburgh from Princes Street*, as the highest expression of the idea of labour. It was the means by which society declared its identity, both to others and to itself. Geddes therefore did not approach the description of townscape as a

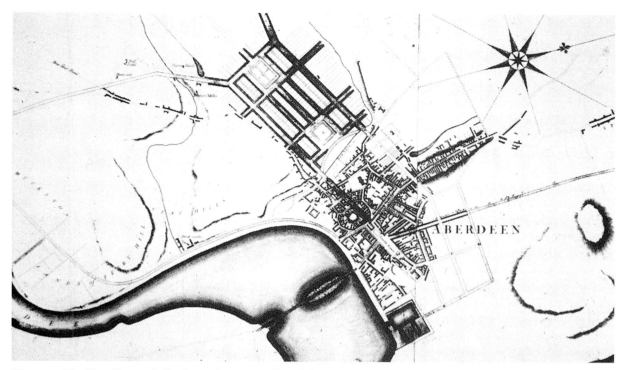

Figure 4. The New Town of Aberdeen, circa 1800. (Permission to reproduce courtesy of I Adams)

The position is entirely different in Aberdeen where a later but much bolder policy of expansion, which reduced the city fathers to temporary bankruptcy, has endowed the town with the urban form and much of the architecture that still give it its characteristic austere elegance almost 200 years later. When Dr Johnson visited the city in 1773 he noted that 'the houses are large and lofty, and the streets spacious and clean',[25] but although improvements at the harbour and between the harbour and the Castlegate were then in train, and various new streets relieving congestion in the medieval town were about to be laid down, it was not until just before the end of the century that the brief for a co-ordinated plan emerged in a scheme for *Further Improvements* prepared by surveyor Charles Abercrombie. In 1800, the Aberdeen New Streets Act was passed and a competition held; from seven entrants the layout designed by the Glasgow architect David Hamilton was chosen in 1801.

The improvement proposals had much in common with Craig's Edinburgh. As in the capital the new town development had to be linked to the old by bridging a deep valley, while the pattern of the new streets was also an elongated rectangular grid with square squares. Moreover, this new network of parallel streets followed the same dominant east-west alignment, although the connection back to the old had to be a continuation of the southernmost of these streets – the present grand avenue of Aberdeen, Union Street – and not a north-south link as in Edinburgh. Nonetheless, the similarities in conception were striking even if what was achieved on the ground, however remarkable, proved far less comprehensive (see Figure 4).

Several aspects of Aberdeen's early nineteenth-century development merit comment. First, the long line of Union Street rapidly became the principal axis of the town's growth and, although progress in building was slow, its architectural qualities were never in doubt thanks largely to the splendid contributions made all along its length by architects Archibald Simpson and John Smith.

Secondly, although the New Town across the Den Burn was never realised, one open square in its grid was. Golden Square (1810–21), though of course spatially focused, does not, however, form 'an architecturally unified composition'.[26] Instead, maintaining a design commitment to the part rather than the whole, it establishes the standard two-storey classical terrace-house unit for much of the city's later development. Thirdly, an effort was made to bring the streets north of School Hill into a better geometrical relationship with the Union Street spine. St Nicholas Street was cut north to meet the recently formed Tannery Street and then continued as a long straight northern route – another George Street – around which a fairly primitive square gridiron began to evolve. Finally, just as the Campbell family in Glasgow had responded to the opportunities created by municipal expansion, so, at the west end of Aberdeen's Union Street, James Skene of Rubislaw saw the chance to profit from the development of his estate. Living

in Edinburgh, he engaged Archibald Elliot to prepare a layout scheme and although his *Design for Feuing the Dam Lands of Rubislaw* (1819) was never carried out, except in small part at Albyn Place (1835), its forms show very clearly, both in respect of Craig's original schemata and also in the application of pavilioned terraces and crescents, just how much the attraction and influence of the capital's developing New Town had penetrated north.

In Dundee, however, despite its industrial boom and rapidly rising population, no New Town developed. Instead, new buildings and some new streets were inserted into the city's medieval plan – a plan anatomically elongated in street limbs stretched out like 'a man on his back'[27] lying between the Law Hill and the River Tay (see Figure 5). South Tay Street (1792) was laid out to connect the 'legs' of Nethergate and Hawkhill, though its three-storey classical terraces by David Neave were not completed until a generation later (1819–29), while over the same period King Street, extended

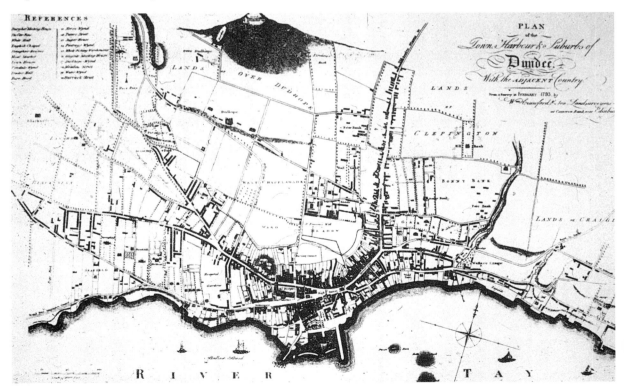

Figure 5. Plan of the Town, Harbour and Suburbs of Dundee, 1793 (Crawford). (Taken ultimately from Mitchell Library, Glasgow)

the town's north-east 'leg' of Murraygate towards Forfar, 'with substantial, regular and handsome buildings erected on each side'.[28] In the early 1820s the Edinburgh architect William Burn advised the Town Council of possible improvements to alleviate congestion, as a result of which Union Street, Lindsay Street, Panmure Street and Reform Street – all isolated schemes – were later opened up. Reform Street, running north from the centre, was outstanding, 'visualised from the first as a simple single architectural composition'.[29] At its northern end stood the hexastyle Doric portico of the High School, so effective as a *point de vue* that the symmetrical balance of the street needed only to be treated with a scrupulous architectural restraint. And this it received from George Angus whose terraces of shops and flats (1832), curving elegantly into Nethergate, are Dundee's finest example of Neo-classical townscape, though not realised *in toto* and much abused at street level.

Quite why Dundee never acquired a New Town is something of a mystery. Suggestions have been made that the incidence of cholera outbreaks in the town inclined middle-class preference towards detached villa development rather than urban terraces or tenements. It might also be argued that a relatively confined riparian location inhibited large-scale planned renewal. But neither explanation is convincing, a simpler and more likely reason being 'the absence of enlightened and strong-minded landowners'[30] prepared to speculate. In the event, several civic buildings of considerable architectural merit were erected and a measure of unco-ordinated street regularisation achieved. Ironically, while more salubrious development stretched west along the Tay and to the east the village of Broughty Ferry, expanding on a grid-iron plan which 'appears to be inspired by'[31] Edinburgh New Town, lured Dundee's richer citizens away from the docklands, factories and jute mills, the country's most intensive build-up of working-class tenements, distinguished by their cheap construction, open 'plattie' access galleries and general squalor, continued to spread uncontrolled in and around the town's medieval core.

Just how specious is the argument that limited location alone prevented the growth of a New Town quarter in Dundee is shown by the case of Greenock. Lying on the south bank of the Clyde on a narrow coastal strip below the Renfrewshire hills, Greenock perfectly mirrors the topographical conditions on Tayside. Yet, unlike Dundee, Greenock was to become a town of grids.[32]

In the last years of the eighteenth century at least two plans had been prepared to give some spatial order to the rapidly growing port. Incorporated into these proposals were two planned squares each at opposite ends of the town: in the older east end, St Andrew's Square, strongly formal in layout with four streets entering symmetrically at right angles; in the west, George Square, somewhat less defined, in an oblique relationship with the edge of the Old Town and clearly intended to be a gateway to some new suburb yet to be determined. But it was not until 1818 that David Reid's definitive *Plan of the Town of Greenock and Its Environs, with Intended Improvements ...* appeared. This comprehensive document, both record and proposal, delineated no less than four gridded networks disposed around the Old Town.

The earliest of the four, almost certainly conceived in the late eighteenth century, lay closest to the harbours and the town centre east of the West Burn. Not surprisingly, this north-west grid, which followed, albeit somewhat crudely, the familiar pattern of three elongated streets, was developed first – tenements at the busy east end, Venetian-windowed mansions in the more suburban west. South of the Old Town above Well Park two more open grids spread uphill, each a right-angled network of streets far from precise in geometry and entirely without focus or hierarchy (see Figure 6).

But the most remarkable of Greenock's grids was that proposed for the West End. A proposal for this wonderful location with its prospects across the Clyde to the Cowal Hills and Argyll had been prepared circa 1810 by the Edinburgh architect William Sibbald. In 1802 Sibbald, with another Reid, Robert Reid, had designed the first expansion of Edinburgh's New Town. The provenance of his Greenock plan is clear enough, though the built-up grid of terraced streets and mews lanes has the added delight of a riverside crescent and harbour

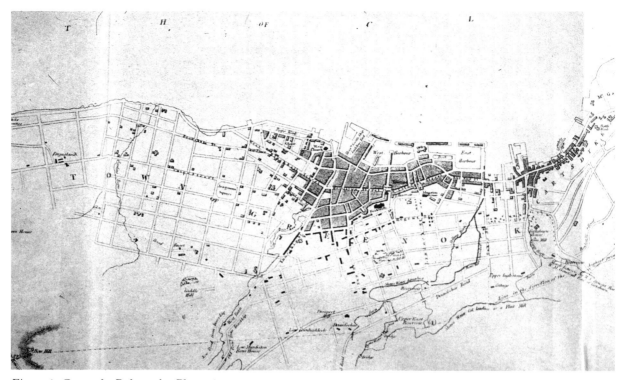

Figure 6. Greenock, Reform Act Plan, 1832.

basin. What was realised, however, was much less ambitious. Again, the network was Hippodamian, though without the relentless regularity of Glasgow's contemporary Second New Town. Some articulation of the urban form was attempted – along the sea-front Esplanade, in the creation of Ardgowan Square (comparable in its rather casual siting as in its estate-orientated appellation to Blythswood Square in Glasgow) and in the alignment of Union Street out from the urban hinge of George Square – but all this received at first no architectural reinforcement. On the contrary, the West End became the setting for the Georgian mansions aspired to by Greenock's merchants and shipbuilders; each house proudly independent in its own plot, sometimes pedimented, frequently porched, always symmetrical. Not until David Cousin's steepled Old Kirk (1839–55) was placed as a *point de vue* on the axis of Brisbane Street was any calculated relationship between urban and architectural form attained.

The coincidental eponymous confusion of English national saint and British king hints with more sinister coincidence at imperialist pretension; certainly there was no suggestion of a federal relationship or marriage of equal partners in the economic and parliamentary conjunction of the two countries which followed the 1707 Act of Union. Union Streets were laid down in Glasgow and Dundee and played a central rôle in the new townscape of Aberdeen and Greenock, but a preferential deference to the London-based monarchy was more marked. Edinburgh, Glasgow, Aberdeen and Paisley all had their George Streets, each a long, straight thoroughfare which, by virtue of its location in the spatial order of late eighteenth-century expansion, evidently merited its royal name. And even if, despite Craig's original intention, there proved to be no St George's Squares, there were, in fact, George Squares (or George's Squares) in Edinburgh, Glasgow and Greenock which further flattered the king who ruled from England. True, there *were* also St Andrew's Squares in these same three towns, as well as a St Andrew's Street in new Aberdeen, but the longer-

Figure 1. Calton Hill Viaduct. Adam's ideal sketch of Edinburgh as a city of monuments – including an early panopticon Bridewell – the centrepiece of which is his 'megastructure' proposed to link Calton Hill with Princes Street. (Sir John Soane's Museum, Vol 2, No 50)

simply cutting swathes through the urban fabric, or establishing broad lines of suburban development. This is true in Glasgow where Adam carried out most of his late work, and in Edinburgh where development, although briefly to the south, required massive bridging schemes to link the first New Town with the Old Town and with the second phase of development on Calton Hill and south to Leith (see Figure 1).

Although the 'idea' of a bridge is essentially that of some public work designed to improve communications and to stimulate economic growth, in its capacity as public work it might also stimulate 'private emulation'. This theory was propounded originally by Shaftesbury and, later, by Lord Kames.[4] It was put into propagandist style by John Gwynn[5] and to some extent by the Adam brothers. With bridges more than other structures this desired emulation was essential. It was during this period, chiefly the later eighteenth century and early nineteenth century, that the bridge as a recognisable type with an aesthetic all of its own was developed, mainly by Smeaton, Mylne, Rennie, Alexander Stevens, and Telford himself. Robert Adam is unique among eighteenth-century architects in having made the majority of his bridge designs for private clients. However, as in his private buildings, especially in his later career, Adam often aspires to public grandeur within a private framework. Kirk-

dale, for example, or the monumental single-span Montagu Bridge at Dalkeith which is semi-private rather than completely so, are both on a public scale of grandeur (see Figure 2). A distinction has to be drawn between those bridges which are public but have been put up mostly at the expense of the local landowner, and the private or estate bridges. A few in this latter category can verge on the whimsical. Of the wholly private schemes, perhaps the most interesting because it illustrates the almost bizarre, intellectually inaccessible aspect of the picturesque mentality is the 'ruined' bridge. Typical of this type would be Adam's designs for Bowood,[6] Syon (unbuilt, see Figure 3)[7] and for the viaduct spanning the gorge at Culzean. The Culzean bridge was designed in such a way that every ounce of climactic effect is squeezed from the curving approach to the house. This was a dramatically simple device used time and again throughout the nineteenth and twentieth centuries. It was recommended by the normally prosaic Telford so that a bridge's profile might be fully appreciated by the carriage-borne traveller. The picturesque is therefore not absent from public bridges any more than it is from town plans where its principles of scale, incident, rhythm, and vista are applied. In the case of bridging schemes where a dramatic geography already exists, these principles are carried through that much more effectively.

Figure 2. Montagu Bridge, Dalkeith, designed by Robert Adam 1792.

By the time that Adam came to be designing bridges the practice had become a well-established part of the architect's brief. James Paine had built many public bridges. There were other architects who came to specialise in bridge building in this era before the great civil engineers. John Gwynn, whose conventional architectural output was slight, was one of these. In his book, *London and Westminster Improved* (1766), Gwynn was to provide the arguments for public spending in architectural and civil engineering works in order to promote economic growth. It was undoubtedly this species of polemic that Adam Smith was rebutting when he argued in *The Wealth of Nations* that fine bridges were a *result* of economic growth rather than a necessary pre-cursor. The canonical Blackfriars

Bridge, the most important English bridge commission since Westminster Bridge of the 1740s, was begun in 1759. The designer was a young Robert Mylne, a friend of Adam's who was, as Adam put it, going to 'throw a bridge over the Thames'[8] while Adam himself was still learning his trade in Italy.

Mylne had won the Concorso Clementino during his studies in Italy but had gone on to specialise in bridge design. The winning of the Blackfriars competition was a remarkable achievement and because bridge-building was a relatively new 'science' informed by the arcane study of 'hydraulic architecture', there followed a great deal of public debate, most of it centring on the issue of elliptical (Mylne's design) versus round arches

Figure 3. The 'ruined' bridge at Syon, engraved for the brothers' Works in Architecture, *Vol 11, No IV, Pl VII. (Reproduced from Robert Oresko, ed,* The Works in Architecture of Robert and James Adam *(London, 1975, p 72)*

which form went rapidly out of date from the 1770s. However the debate also concerned itself with the architecture of the bridge, that is the applied decoration of the structure. Mylne's winning design was solidly Roman and included simple coupled columns on each cutwater. It did not approach the Piranesian vision of Chambers' or Gwynn's competition entries which were clearly based on triumphal arches, covered in applied sculpture and bold relief decoration. What appears to have been developing in Mylne's design, and to judge from its countless imitators successfully so, was an aesthetic based on frankness of engineering structure rather than architectural ornament. In Chambers and Gwynn the bridge appears as little more than an armature for applied decoration whereas in Mylne, and to some extent Adam, the gracefulness of the structure itself is given some expression.

Adam Bridges

Clearly for Adam, bridges had diverse picturesque architectural and town planning as well as commercial potential. The terrific increase in the number of public bridge building schemes, and the necessary attendant improvements in roads, may be explained either as cause or effect of the early stirrings of the first Industrial Revolution. By contrast, the great number of estate bridges erected during the period – practical, ornamental or both – may require a less materialist analysis. Carriage 'drives' necessitate demesne bridges. Adam's published, but unbuilt, design for a bridge at Syon House [9] is unmistakably private (see Figure 4), whimsical to the extent of folly. Instead of columns, which he rarely used in bridge design, four caryatids linked by heavy swags carry the parapet. It is only in the swept parapet – a characteristic

Figure 4. Estate bridge at Syon House, from the Works in Architecture of Robert and James Adam *(London, 1975, p 70)*

feature of Adam landscape bridges – that we are reminded of his father's bridge at Aberfeldy. Syon is an intentional travesty, light-hearted and ironically guarded by sphinxes at the wing-wall ends. However it is only within the sober, grandiose, and often pompous tradition of bridge design that the 'joke' has any meaning. Within the severe intellectual context of the Blackfriars debate, and the theory and counter-theory that it produced, perhaps Syon represents a flight from the solemnity and moral grandeur of scientific righteousness, the folly for its own sake in the age of reason. Certainly, we know that Adam was capable of Rowlandsonesque deflating visual wit.[10]

Adam made more than a hundred named designs for private bridges and very many more that can be positively identified or tentatively linked to actual projects. However it is in the area of public bridges that we find Adam at his most original.

Here it is that he has the opportunity to put up monuments to his genius. The central feature of a very sketchy design for the Calton Hill viaduct is a prominent inscribed tablet with the words, 'Robert Adam, Architect' (see Figure 1). In the ideal surroundings, the buildings are all Adam, including the vast, polygonal Bridewell on Calton Hill. It would be with bridges and monumental bridging schemes that Adam would strive finally to make his mark, rather than with his later small country house commissions.

In the eighteenth century bridges came to be regarded as the very symbols of economic progress and political power. In later eighteenth-century Dublin, for example, the development of bridges in conjunction with road-widening schemes, all carried out in an official, sub-Chambers style, came physically to express the colonial presence.[11] In France too public improvements came to symbolise the power of a centralising state authority. In 1755 the inhabitants of Nantes felt that they were late in aggrandising their town with the type of improvements that had been carried out by Gabriel at Bordeaux. In England, John Gwynn campaigned for improvements of this kind, as had Chambers in the *Treatise*,[12] where he associated the issue with national and international trade. Laugier's *Essai*[13] had a section devoted to utilitarian and commercial buildings.

Adam 'Megastructures'

In 1771 Adam made a design for Sir William Pulteney for laying out a new town, Bathwick, and for connecting it with Bath on the opposite side of the river Avon (see Figure 5). This was to be achieved by means of the now famous covered shopping bridge.[14] The bridge is in itself remarkable, since it re-establishes the medieval and Renaissance European type with houses upon it, so many of which were pulled down during the 'improving' eighteenth century. However Adam's bridge is not backward-looking. Rather it creates the proper environment for the sophisticated urban pursuit of shopping – in purpose-built shops within a 'promenade' rather than in houses converted for the purpose. In this it is typical of Adam's emphasis on urban structures which are both architecturally

monumental and commercially profitable. However, the main part of the scheme for which the bridge was to be the hub, was the houses of the potential customers. This was a massive four-storey 'tenemental' block of houses on either side of a central building closing the vista from the other side of the river. The scheme includes an embanked wall, like Gabriel's at Bordeaux,[15] with architectural stairways leading down to the riverside. Adam's huge colour drawing for the scheme[16] illustrates precisely the tendency towards what we might call 'graduated zoning', an idea realised at the Adelphi, further explored at Bathwick, and proposed again at the South Bridge in Edinburgh. The curving embankment in the Bathwick scheme effectively separates commercial life from polite society. This drawing even depicts a disturbance at riverside level, possibly as a Piranesian 'incident', but also, perhaps, as a demonstration of how effectively the design will mitigate the unfortunate nuisances of town life, even, afford some amusement to the town-dwellers. It is therefore within the context of contemporary, probably unpleasant, town life that the Bathwick design can be understood. The ideal representation of Bathwick is to some extent as Utopian as the later eighteenth- and early nineteenth-century model townships. It offers an idealised relationship of

Figure 5. Adam's proposed new town at Bathwick, Bath. The original drawing is a massive colour-washed elevation, one of a number held in Sir John Soane's Museum, Vol 38, Nos 1, 6 and 9, and Vol 10, Nos 79–82.

polite and commercial life which it proposes to establish through architecture.

The proposal to build at Bathwick originated in 1726 with William Pulteney, earl of Bath. His scheme had failed because no agreement could be reached on the crucial bridge to the town of Bath itself. The idea of building on the site was re-introduced by William Johnstone of Westerhall when he took lifetime control of the entailed estate through his marriage to the earl's grand-daughter. Pulteney had hardly succeeded when he wrote in 1768: 'If a bridge is built over the Avon somewhere near the city it is expected that a good deal of the Ground near the Bridge will be taken by builders for erecting Houses and that they will agree to pay considerable rents.' [17] A drawing in the Soane collection shows buildings on the opposite side of the Avon from Grand Parade, to either side of the projected bridge, which are little more than front-ages on an architecturally treated embankment. The arrangement is symmetrical and has two massive triumphal arches with coupled columns of the type noticed in the later public style. The bridge was to be the most important of the new buildings, since its function was to draw fashion-able Bath society seamlessly over the river to Pulteney's new town. The original bridge design had been plain and simple, providing effective communication for the proposed new suburb. The approach changed radically with Adam's involve-ment.

Pulteney had engaged William Paty to make the design but for some reason, not documented, Pult-eney suddenly dismissed Paty and brought in the Adam brothers. Pulteney may have been pre-disposed to his own countrymen – he was Thomas Telford's first and greatest private client – but it may also have been that the Adams had a keener eye for the commercial potential of the scheme. The bridge itself was now changed from a single to a triple arch scheme in order to flatten the profile. This is borne out by other projects such as the South Bridge and the Leith Road scheme at Edinburgh which were partially to finance them-selves with shop rentals or, at the Adelphi, where docking privileges and storage for the Board of Ordnance were to be leased. James Adam wrote to Pulteney persuading him to abandon the ac-cepted design and to introduce shops. Remarkably – for the work was well underway – Pulteney was persuaded.

The new design was accepted, if not by Bath Corporation, who were bemused by the idea and advised Pulteney that the shops should be omitted. The combination of shops and bridge was seen by many contemporary observers as ludicrously old-fashioned. As we have seen this was the epoch of the streamlined, modern bridge, but for the Adams this was an opportunity to create a bridge which would pay dividends. The profits would arise not through tolls, themselves an encumbrance, but through rental of shops and warehouses. Stylisti-cally, there are of course references to covered bridges both in Palladio's *Quattro Libri* [18] and their eighteenth-century derivative examples such as the covered bridge at Stow.

Nothing came of the Adam design for the new town of Bathwick, but the concept is clear enough. It involved private speculation on a massive scale, the bridge itself costing four times that of the North Bridge at Edinburgh. Pulteney exorbitantly fin-anced the scheme on the advice of the Adams, who had come so close to ruining themselves in a very similar adventure at the Adelphi. In Scotland, the design at Ayr carried out for the Town Council, proposed a bridge with flanking housing forming a 'gateway' to the Sandgate at a higher level and wharves at the riverside (see Figure 6). This was a smaller scale version of the Bathwick idea.

In Edinburgh, three major bridging schemes were proposed in the 1780s by a Town Council who had become accustomed to self-improvement. They had themselves paid for Parliament House in the 1630s and every major building since (except for the Custom House and Register House). Be-cause of the nature of their function and design, none of these might simply be called a 'bridge'. Their purpose was more to level out the upper social plane of Edinburgh life rather than to link any two pre-existing places. Each scheme is con-cerned to bring disparate and inaccessible parts of the town together, as a pre-condition rather than

Figure 6. A version of Adam's scheme for a 'bridge street' at Ayr, drawn by an unknown hand. (Carnegie Library, Ayr)

an aid to their existence. In 1785 Adam designed a line of houses and shops for the Leith Road which, as well as forming a curving 'bridge' between Princes Street and York Place, was a speculative development in itself. Although York Place appears to have been feued until 1793, it is marked down as a continuation of Queen Street in Craig's first New Town plan. By executing Adam's Leith Road scheme there would therefore be created an incentive to develop the eastern end of the New Town. Where the ground falls away sharply to Calton Hill, the terrace was banked up with shops and service entrances below. There was a layer of shop and house entrances above, reminiscent of the Adelphi double basement arrangement. Seen in a European context, the Leith Road scheme is a remarkable concept which packs the various elements of town life into one building of truly urban character.

Another bridging, or viaduct, scheme of the 1780s, involved making easier access to the proposed Bridewell on Calton Hill. This was to be done by forming an arch over St Ninian's Wynd or the 'Low Calton'; a project eventually realised with Archibald Elliot's Regent Bridge or Waterloo Place (1815). With the change in style of Adam's 'Bridge of Communication',[19] we can associate the early change in the development of the Bridewell scheme – on which the whole project hinged – from classical to castle style. In the visual sweep from west to east beyond Register House, the style of the Bridewell is picked up and used at the new 'entry' to this group of buildings at the eastern end of Princes Street, beyond the strictly classical New Town.

The essence of English urban planning had been the creation of spatial exclusiveness by the use of, often gated, squares and circuses. In Scotland,

Adam's South Bridge addresses the same problem, but finds the solution through the use of a vertical hierarchy. However, as Professor Rowan showed in the preceding chapter, the scheme as built did not approach the complex grandeur of the Adam proposal, whose most novel aspect is the treatment of bridges and viaducts as buildings in themselves, related thematically to others within the townscape.

NOTES

1. See Ted Ruddock, *Arch Builders and their Builders 1735–1835* (Cambridge, 1979).

2. R MacInnes, 'Robert Adam's Public Building' in John Lowrey ed. *Architectural Heritage IV 'Robert Adam,* p 20 n1 (Edinburgh, 1993).

3. In those countries, such as The Netherlands or England, where urban development took the form of thin, vertical 'slices', stacked in horizontal lines, it is less relevant.

4. Henry Homes, Lord Kames *Elements of Criticism* (Edinburgh, 1785).

5. John Gwynn *London and Westminster Improved* (London, 1766).

6. Illustrated Robert Oresko (ed) *The Works in Architecture of Robert and James Adam* (London, 1975), p 163.

7. Illustrated in Oresko, *Works in Architecture*, p 72.

8. Quoted in John Fleming *Robert Adam and His Circle* (London, 1962), p 272.

9. Illustrated in Oresko, *Works in Architecture*, p 70.

10. See for example Robert Adam's attributed drawing of a 'Public Lavatory' illustrated in Alistair Rowan's *Catalogues of Drawings in the Victoria and Albert Museum: Robert Adam* (London, 1988).

11. Murray Fraser, 'Public Buildings and Colonial Policy in Dublin, 1760–1800', *Architectural History*, Vol 28 (1985), pp 102–24.

12. Sir William Chambers *A Treatise on the Decorative Part of Civil Architecture* (London, 1758).

13. Marc-Antoine Laugier *Essai sur l'Architecture* (London, 1755. English translation S Wale).

14. See R S Neale, *Bath 1680–1850 A Social History* (London, 1981), pp 226–45.

15. For a discussion of this and other related projects by Gabriel, see Jean-Paul Avisseau, 'La Place royale de Bordeaux' in *Monuments Historiques,* No 120 (March/April, 1982) 'Gabriel et l'Urbanisme' pp 16–30.

16. Sir John Soane's Museum, Vol 38, Nos 1, 6–9 and Vol 10, Nos 79–82.

17. Quoted in Neale, *Bath 1680–1850,* p 228.

18. See Jean Manco, 'Pulteney Bridge' in *Architectural History*, Vol 38 (1995), pp 129–45.

19. Robert Adam, 'Sketch of A Bridge of Communication', 1791, Sir John Soane's Museum, illustrated in R MacInnes in *Architectural Heritage IV*, p 16, fig 2.5.

IAN GOW

Charlotte Square Buteified

CHARLOTTE SQUARE is recognised throughout the world as a jewel of Georgian Town Planning by Robert Adam, an undisputed master (see Figure 1). This perfection has not been inherited directly but rather actively recreated as a result of the strenuous efforts of the Fourth Marquess of Bute (1881–1947) to an extent where the Square can also be viewed as a victory in the history of the Conservation Movement in Scotland. This article sets out the steps by which the Marquess established control and influence over a substantial part of the design. It also pays tribute to the genius of the late Marquess of Bute who gave the Square a visionary new purpose in the national life of Scotland.

The history of the City's commission to Robert Adam in March 1791 is too well known to need repetition here. A discarded design, by an unidentified architect in the Heriot's Trust Collection, is a reminder of the brilliance of Adam's solution which set a new pattern for articulating Palace fronts in all subsequent developments (see Figure 2).[1]

The destruction of this eloquent exposition of the merits of ordering urban space by subordinating the individual to the greater good is less well charted and arose through a combination of changing fashions and taste. Earlier New Town houses were brought in line with the later Palaces of Moray Place through the dropping of the Drawing Room cills and the introduction of double doors to connect circuits of reception rooms. Because Charlotte Square became the Harley Street of Victorian Scotland, its houses were constantly adapted. The low point in architectural enthusiasm for the taste of the New Town came in Ruskin's 1853 Edinburgh lecture: 'Nothing but Square-cut stone – square-cut stone – a wilderness of square-cut stone for ever and ever';[2] and the Victorianisation of the Square was completed in 1876 when the Albert Memorial was unveiled by Queen Victoria.

The tide began to turn, however, in 1903 when the Fourth Marquess of Bute purchased 5 Charlotte Square and commissioned the Edinburgh architect, Balfour Paul (1875–1938), to restore it to a classical harmony (see Figure 3). His purchase reflected a renewed appreciation of the New Town

Figure 1. Robert Adam's design for the North Side of Charlotte Square. (RCAHMS)

which may have been kicked off by a taste for Adam Revival Drawing Rooms, like that at 37 Drumsheugh Gardens in the fashionable West End of the City and which may, through the Edinburgh decorator, Thomas Bonnar, be linked directly to the first stirrings of the Adam Revival that Lord Tweedmouth initiated in Scotland at, first, Guisachan, and then at Haddo, his daughter's home.

Lord Bute's central role in the Scottish Conservation Movement has been charted by David

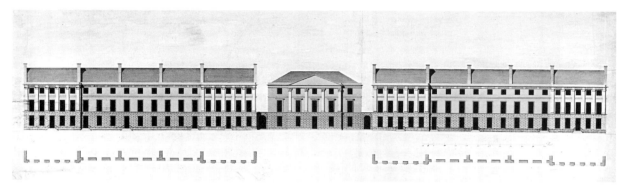

Figure 2. Unexecuted design for Charlotte Square. (RCAHMS, George Heriot's Trust)

Figure 3. Charlotte Square from John Swarbrick, Robert Adam and his Brothers *(1915). (RCAHMS)*

Walker,[3] and Charlotte Square reflected his particular enthusiasm for townscape and the 'group-value' that could arise from an association of often individually undistinguished houses on the grandest possible scale. His feeling for Adam's work must have been shaped by his possession of one of the brothers' earliest works, Dumfries House of 1754, which had been extended by Weir Schultz in Adam-Revival style for his father, the Third Marquess. The family was also surrounded by many fragments of Robert Adam's most original, but still underrated, country house at Luton, designed for the Prime Minister Earl of Bute in 1766.[4] Because the Fourth Marquess was secretive and cautious by nature, much about his precise intentions at Charlotte Square remains unclear.

To an architectural enthusiast, familiar with Adam's finest work, the interior of No 5 could not but disappoint and, like the exterior, it was capable of improvement. Little Georgian grace had survived in the birthplace of Elizabeth Grant of Rothiemurchus. In January 1871, Watherston and Sons had not only dropped the Drawing Room windows through Adam's stone belt, but also suppressed the eastern Venetian window of the northern centrepiece, removing its pilasters and filling the space with plain ashlars. Their drawing in the Edinburgh Dean of Guild Collection shows plate glass in all of the windows as well as in the lunette above an entrance door with fancy panels (see Figure 3). This alteration was repeated, with a sense of symmetry, in the same year, by Watherston at Lord Neave's No 7, across the central axis of the north side. In his petition to the Dean of Guild, Lord Neave stated that 'The proposed alterations will be beneficial to the Petitioner's property' but the all-important rhythm of Adam's design thus vanished for ever.

Watherston's internal alterations for George Ramsay were perhaps less controversial. The Dean of Guild plans show that the existing plan of the Dining Room flat had been extraordinary with the front room partitioned into two narrow awkward rooms as well as a lobby leading to a backstair in the sideboard recess of the Dining Room at the back of the house. This very unusual arrangement may reflect the requirements of the previous occupant, R Nasmyth, a Surgeon-dentist, who had succeeded the forty-year residency by the Fergussons of Kilkerran.

George Ramsay had the front room restored to a single unit, but created a narrow slip of two cupboard-like spaces between this restored front room and the lobby, which, through the introduction of some steelwork, was opened up to the stairwell. The lowest flight of the stairs was turned through forty-five degrees to face visitors on arrival. The proportions of the long narrow Dining Room at the rear were improved with a sideboard recess facing the windows. Similarly in the Drawing Rooms, the sliding doors dividing them were replaced with a deepened opening, reducing the length of the long thin Back Drawing Room, again with assistance of a certain amount of steelwork.

In February 1890, Mrs Beatrice Dick Lauder, or Ramsay, asked Watherston and Sons to further diminish Adam's intended effect through the addition of a set of obtrusive box dormers; but with a certain respect for symmetry, they closely followed the box dormers they had previously added to No 7 in April 1889.

Externally, Lord Bute replaced the plate glasses with astragals and put back a fanlight, but it is a measure of the general lack of any standard of classical proportions in the Square that he not only felt no compunction to raise the dropped Drawing Room windows but that his new sashes were over-astragalled, creating fussy too-small panes. Internally, the major alteration was in the entrance Lobby. The curious slip of cupboards, probably a legacy from the dental surgery, was partially suppressed and the space added to an inner lobby to broaden the proportions of an uncomfortably narrow Lobby. With the help of yet more steelwork, the new partition between the widened Lobby and Library at the front of the house gave provision for a run of deeper shelves in the bookcases. The smaller cupboard, nearest the outside wall, was adapted to create a safe, opening off the new Library. The narrow neck that resulted at the front door became a glazed internal 'porch'.

The obviously Victorian sideboard recess and

connection between the two Drawing Rooms were suppressed recreating the original long and narrow proportions of the rear rooms. The most dramatic changes were made in the spacious basement which was approached down a new service stair behind the principal stair. Accommodation in the basement was provided for a Butler, two footmen and a Housekeeper, with a brushing room in the sub-basement, to minister to the requirements of an Edwardian Marquess. Such extensive staff accommodation was unusual in predominantly middle-class Edinburgh where domestic staff had often lived out.

These architectural adjustments provided the matrix for a dazzling display of what can only be dubbed Fabergé Adam as the Marquess's designers endeavoured to supply the interior that he felt a house designed by Adam in Charlotte Square ought to have had. Because almost no element of decoration now visible in No 5 dates from before 1903, it can perhaps be inferred that the internal Victorianisation of the house had been thorough.

In 1992, when a modern flock wallpaper was removed from the Front Drawing Room, a painted scheme, characteristic of the work of the leading Edinburgh decorator, D R Hay (1797–1866), came to light with a pattern of small motifs in gold stencilling on a white painted ground complete with the dust-shadow of a curvaceous waisted glass over the chimney.

Although the plans handed in to the Dean of Guild were submitted by Balfour Paul, the internal fitting up was the responsibility of Scott Morton and Co. After a spell in London, William Scott Morton (1840–1903) had established his workshops in the Tynecastle district of Edinburgh in 1870, in order to capitalise on what he considered were the exceptional talents of his fellow Scots.[5] An inventive genius, his firm soon bifurcated into architectural woodworkers and a wallcovering establishment. But wallpaper is an inadequate description of his Tynecastle Canvas, a form of papier-mâché strengthened with canvas, which could be moulded into relief patterns and imitations of panelling and plasterwork, to say nothing of picture frames – one of the firm's zanier lines.

Indeed, as their 'Adams' catalogue demonstrates, the Tynecastle Canvas was an ideal medium for Adamesque ceiling ornaments.

Lord Bute's requirements were more substantial and the great strength of Scott Morton and Co lay in its Drawing Office. Many Scottish architects, including Sir Robert Lorimer, relied on the outstanding abilities of their draughtsmen, led by David Ramsay, to realise working drawings for their projects. Although this commission is not documented in the Scott Morton Letterbooks, now in the National Monuments Record of Scotland,[6] a design by the firm for the Dining Room curtain boxes, dated 1904, survives at Whytock and Reid, who acquired the goodwill when the firm closed in 1966.[7]

The combined talents of Scott Morton and Co, Balfour Paul and the Bute family's own team of craftsmen were to transform No 5 into one of the most ambitious and important set of Edwardian interiors in the City, whose only rival is Manderston and whose cost would surely have startled Robert Adam himself. As was the convention, the Drawing Rooms attracted the largest proportion of the total outlay.

Scott Morton's solution could not have been more appropriate in that they adapted, as John Gifford has shown in *Edinburgh*, the engraved design for Lady Bute's Dressing Room at Luton, which had been published by Adam in his *Works in Architecture*, to fit both rooms (see Figures 4, 5). Although this had been designed for a room with apsidal ends, by judicious re-arrangement of Adam's own ribbons and lines of bellflowers, the engraving was adapted ingeniously to fit the rectangular spaces. The decorative painting of the original by Zucchi, however, was never to be replicated.

A run of splendid chimneypieces was installed, with the finest of white statuary marble inlaid with coloured marble fluting and slips in the Front Drawing Room and holding a basket grate with vases which were repeated on the pierced *en suite* fender and fire-irons. This splendour was partnered by no less luxurious carved Adamesque woodwork of cedar creating an opulence to which

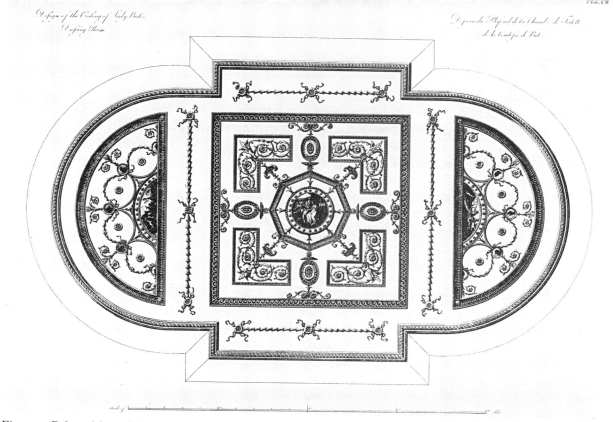

Figure 4. Robert Adam, Ceiling of Lady Bute's dressing room at Luton from Robert and James Adam, Works in Architecture. (RCAHMS)

Figure 5. Ceiling of No 5 Charlotte Square. (RCAHMS, ED/8599)

few of Adam's own patrons would have been willing to rise. As in his finest drawing rooms, however, the colour scheme followed the choice of the silk wallhangings. Again while Adam might have been satisfied with mere damask, No 5 had a lampas woven from several colours of silk depicting baskets of flowers interlinked by floral garlands. Although sadly this no longer survives, in 1991, when the room was being decorated and the modern picture rail was removed, a strip of this silk about one inch deep and a hundred feet long with a brilliant unfaded apple-green ground was discovered. A similar sky-blue lampas survives in another Bute Drawing Room at House of Falkland. The colours in the lampas, as in Adam's own Drawing Rooms, were the starting point for the tinting of the ceiling colours.

Perhaps the most remarkable feature of the front Drawing Room ceiling at No 5 were the parti-colours on the rinceau grotesques framing the central ornament (they were partly painted over in 1991) which seem to betray a knowledge of eighteenth-century practice. The plasterwork must have been painted by the same craftsmen who decorated the contemporary Adamesque corridor at Dumfries House with similar elaborate parti-coloured picking-out.

If this decoration was sober thus far, it was brought to glittering life by two gilt rococo glasses, comprising an overmantle glass, topped by ho-ho birds and with brackets for ceramics, which reflected a large pier glass, crowned with a Chinese Temple to hold a porcelain figure, on the opposite wall. The chimney-glass fitted its supporting chimney-piece so well that the two were surely conceived as a unit, but the glass, at least, was antique and is identical with one photographed circa 1879 in the Countess of Fife's Boudoir at Duff House in Banffshire.[8] The glasses were almost certainly supplied from London by the cabinet-maker James Mackie, whose patrons included several members of the Clan Duff. After the sale of the contents of Duff House in 1906, the glasses were acquired by Partridges, the London art dealers, and are described, but not illustrated, in their *Specimens of Ancient Furniture in the Possession of Partridge, Lewis and Simmons* (no date). This luxurious interior was completed by a large carpet, especially made for the room, with a matching hearth-rug, which is now in the Dining Room at Mount Stuart (see Figure 11).

A photograph of 1926 taken by the Royal Commission shows this attractive sunny room in use by Lord Bute with a comfortable and distinctly un-Adamesque chaise longue pulled up to the desk in the sunny window and the distinctive Byzantine electrical lighting of suspended glass lamps, favoured by the Bute family, augmented by a standard lamp.

The Back Drawing Room had a matching ceiling, a handsome white statuary marble chimney-piece and the room was hung with a similar floral lampas creating a harmony between the two rooms when the big cedar dividing doors slid back into the walls.

The most elaborate of the other rooms was the Library occupying the front room of the Dining Room flat which was entirely lined with glazed cases in a Chippendale style. The cornice in the Library may be the only surviving run of late-Georgian plasterwork in the entire house. The long proportions of the Dining Room were improved by a deep sideboard arch at the south end. Scott Morton and Co's design for the curtain boxes in this room were a recreation of those designed by Adam for Luton and published in the *Works in Architecture* (see Figure 6).

The Vestibule and Hall were panelled in oak and the ribbon frieze, in an otherwise historicist house, has just a kick of Art Nouveau. The Brucean timberwork of the staircase is perhaps a signal that its late-Georgian cast-iron balusters must have been already subsumed by Victorian joinery. The bedrooms were equipped with a continuation of the series of fine Adamesque chimneypieces, with the most spectacular in what was probably Lord Bute's own bedroom at the front of the house, with its Ionic order, inlaid fluting and porphyry roundel.

Thus transformed, No 5 was fit to be illustrated in John Swarbrick's *Robert Adam and His Brothers* (1915) where it appears as a model of classic

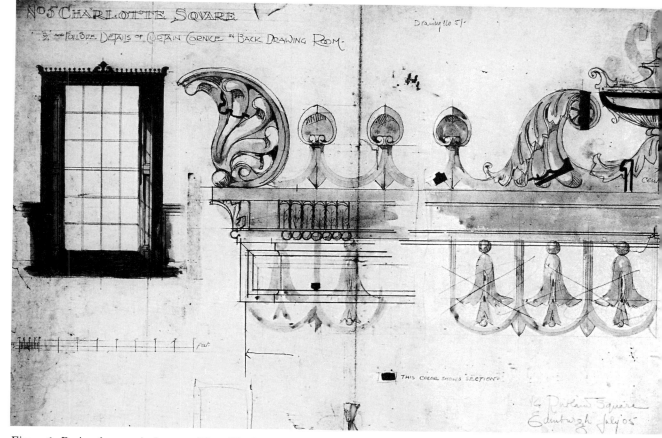

Figure 6. Design for curtain boxes at No 5 Charlotte Square from the Scott Morton collection at Whytock and Reid. (RCAHMS)

Figure 7. Balfour Paul's elevation of Charlotte Square. (RCAHMS, C33061 Edinburgh City architects)

elegance in comparison to its strident neighbours with their plate glass, creepers, window boxes, garish window dressing and an axially placed lampstandard of breathtaking insensitivity (see Figure 3). It is hardly surprising therefore to find Balfour

Paul submitting a planning application in October 1923 for No 6 in the name of Mountjoy Limited, a company not unconnected with Lord Bute.

No 6 was an unusual house by New Town standards because of its centrally placed door and it had

Figure 8. Entrance Hall of No 6 Charlotte Square. (RCAHMS, A 39578)

Figure 9. Drawing Room of No 6 Charlotte Square. (RCAHMS, A39580)

had a chequered history with a phase as an hotel. The fixing for the lettering advertising the hotel may still be seen over the door. Because the house was intended to be let, Lord Bute's internal alterations were not on the same palatial scale as No 5 but they set out to destroy any lingering Victorianisms with no less vigour. The glory of the house is the delicate Neo-classical plaster ceiling in the Front first-floor Drawing Room characteristic of this phase of New Town taste in its etiolated elegance with fans framing an oval field, swags, stylised wheatsheafs and trails of roses as its centrepiece.

Unfortunately, the original plan of the Dining Room flat remains uncertain and the house had been subject to a number of alterations. In May 1867 the architect, David Rhind, submitted plans to build-up the back attic into a full storey, and to add a canted Victorian bay window to the Dining Room at the rear supported on cast-iron columns, one of which penetrated down through the scullery.

In 1889 Thomas Leadbetter carried out a series of alterations for his client who was to become Sir Mitchell Thomas of Cammo, Lord Provost of Edinburgh. The alterations, appropriately for one *en route* to the highest civic office, included a dinner lift, installed in the small slip of a room on the left-hand side of the hall immediately behind the Dining Room, and a top-lit attic Billiard Room. The Dean of Guild collection reveals, as a second thought, a bay window commanding the Forth in this skied Billiard Room to the rear of the house, precariously propped on iron brackets. In 1902 a circular bow was added to balance the Dining Room bay on the rooms on the garden front. At the same time, the service accommodation was extended into a single-storey wing down the west side of the garden faced in glazed white tiles.

These excrescences were all pruned away by Lord Bute whose most substantial contribution was an intricate Neo-Georgian Hall, with a marble fireplace facing visitors on arrival at the front door and an abundance of Adam-revival plasterwork (see Figure 8). This central Hall was designed to ease the transition to the top-lit curved staircase, cantilevered from the eastern party wall at the side of the otherwise typical plan.

In the Front Drawing Room, Neo-Georgian joinery and chaste single doors with carved friezes replaced the standard Edinburgh New-Town, but possibly Victorianised, double-doors (see Figure 9). The Back Drawing Room was no longer connected to that at the Front and, with a screen of columns to improve its long narrow proportions, became a Library. A series of photographs, now in the National Monuments Record of Scotland, copied from a private collection, gives a very complete survey of No 6's subsequent occupation by a tenant with modern pictures but Neo-Georgian furniture complementing Lord Bute's improvements.

Like a line of dominoes going down, No 7 followed in October 1926 when Balfour Paul submitted plans, again on behalf of Mountjoy Ltd, purging the house of any traces of the nineteenth century. Of the three houses, No 7 was perhaps the toughest assignment for this Neo-Georgian team because in 1889 it had become the manse of the celebrated Free Churchman, Alexander Whyte D D, Minister of St George's West. William Scott Morton was a friend of Dr Whyte's and had refitted his earlier manse, at 52 Melville Street, as his biographer G F Barbour recalled in *The Life of Alexander Whyte DD* (1923):

> He had called in the aid of his lifelong friend, William Scott Morton who designed the furniture of the study, and in particular the massive bookcases which in course of time came to fill all the available wall-space. Many a talk the

preacher and the designer had on life and art, on books and personal religion, as the work went forward. In 1889 the same gifted friend was again called in, for the new study was more spacious than the old, and the already large library could be extended further. When all was complete, the high bookcases were surmounted by busts of Homer, Plato, Dante, and other masters of knowledge and imagination, while a lower bookcase, standing close to Dr Whyte's desk and containing many of the books to which he most constantly referred, supported a small cast of the full-length statue of Thakeray [sic]. On the walls on either side of the hearth, portraits of Carlyle and Herschel found a place beside those of Newman already described.

Photographs of the study of this celebrated divine were included in G F Barbour's *The Life of Alexander Whyte DD* (1922) where it appears appropriately sombre with its ranks of books relieved by a Tynecastle Canvas frieze of Italianate swags, beneath a heavy modillion cornice with circular fillets applied to the ceiling (see Figure 10).

The Whytes' architectural alterations were carried out by Watherston and Sons whose plans are dated March and April 1889. The volume of space devoted to the Study installed in the Front Drawing Room was compensated for, to an extent, by enlarging the Back, but now the only, Drawing Room into the 'L'-shaped leg of the Front Drawing Room while Mrs Whyte was awarded a Boudoir behind the staircase on the first floor. The rear attic was built up into a full storey and box-dormers were added to the front, to be copied on No 5. In December 1897 plans were submitted for building a brick workshop of supreme architectural inconsequence against the garden wall.

Dr Whyte's youngest child, Lancelot Law Whyte, wrote a vivid Aldous Huxleyesque description of the life of this unusual Edinburgh household in his autobiography *Focus and Diversions* (1963):

> There were four floors and a basement. On the top floor my eldest sister, a Christian Science

Figure 10. Study at No 7 Charlotte Square from G F Barbour, The Life of Alexander Whyte DD. *(RCAHMS)*

practitioner, earned fees for meditation directed towards clients who, not being Scientists, thought that they were physically ill. On the next floor I only remember two bedrooms: my father's small room, which did not count, and my mother's which most decidedly did. For it was big and full of strange objects, scents, and other mysteries. There was an electric ozone machine to purify the air. There were spirit lamps for midnight meals (in the day-time she preferred, as it were, 'to live off the scent of flowers'), Celtic crosses, scarabs and drawings from Egypt, several Buddhas of dubious sex, eaux de Cologne and lavenders galore, and my mother sitting up in bed writing letters to extraordinary men all over the world: men with dreams to convert mankind (there was nothing sectarian in No 7, everything was universal) to new and better religions and more wonderful ways of living. She did not need to save money, so she gave it away, I imagine, to geniuses and cranks. Patrick Geddes I remember, the cranks are forgotten ... One floor further down was my father's enormous study, a room of dignity with 6,000 books, where he would be writing sermons or letters to simple unhappy men and women everywhere. In retrospect he seems to me, like most of us, to have been a divided person, but with a warm and sensitive nature ... Many of his listeners and readers felt him to be a religious genius ... On the ground floor was a large schoolroom. In an attempt, I suppose, to balance Mary Baker Eddy, the Buddha, Calvin and Boehme, this was devoted to what I call 'muscular Christianity', for it was turned into a gymnasium, complete with parallel bars and what-not, where my father's church assistants used to teach us boys that religion also meant having a healthy body-sex into muscle.

Given these religious atmospheres, it is perhaps less surprising that Balfour Paul's alterations for Lord Bute should have been over-zealous in that, along with so much else, the sideboard recesses in the front Breakfast Room and back Dining Room were swept away, although their Georgian proportions had possibly been too successfully camouflaged by Scott Morton. The Front Drawing room was restored to a rectangle by the expedient of building a partition in front of the existing division. Again single doors were substituted for double sliding ones, with a little Vestibule, flanked by cupboards linking the Drawing Room to the Morning Room behind. The staircase must have been re-balustraded in timber by Scott Morton in a manner which involved shaving away the outer profiles of the steps. These were replaced with cement which by 1995 were, alarmingly, on the loose. A plan rather untypical of the New Town was thus the result. After the completion of this purge, No 7 was subsequently let.

But the prime advantage of possessing No 7 was that it gave him complete control of the exterior of the northern centrepiece and, while his campaign moved westward, its eastern base-camp was not forgotten. The 1925 designs for alterations to No 6 show the Drawing Room windows of No 5 already restored to their true proportions and Adam's masonry belt restored. This alteration was effected ingeniously without disturbing Scott Morton's joinery in the Front Drawing Room of No 5 but creating, in the process, an effect that puzzles many visitors to the house today because the lowest lights of the sash windows are filled in with cedar panels. In November 1927, Balfour Paul presented plans to the Dean of Guild for removing the box dormers on No 5 so that it was once again in harmony with the newly restored No 7.

The final polish was given to the group of three houses when the astragals of No 5 were corrected. In November 1927 Balfour Paul submitted designs to the Dean of Guild for removing the box-dormers of No 5 and giving it a roofline identical to that, so recently restored, at No 7. As a result, all three houses came into an eighteenth-century harmony once more.

The only puzzle in this otherwise careful reinstatement of Adam's original design is why Lord Bute failed to replace the blind Venetian windows in Nos 5 and 7. It may simply have been a result of the way in which the steps in his self-appointed task fell out. It seems unlikely that it was on account of structural problems because areas of the original stonework in the attic of the blind arch in both houses remain undisturbed.

Although Lord Bute was not sanguine about the prospects of the state or the city sharing his architectural enthusiasms, the long Charlotte Square campaign was to be rewarded and given permanent expression when the City of Edinburgh invoked the Town Planning (Scotland) Act of 1925 to effect the Edinburgh Town Planning (Charlotte Square) Scheme Order, 1930.

A substantial bundle of papers relating to the genesis of this Order survives in Edinburgh City Archives but, in this context, they are of particular interest in revealing the lowness of Lord Bute's profile. According to the official version of the facts, many of the Square's proprietors had been alarmed by an unfortunate recent proposal of 1924 to alter No 23 which concentrated their thoughts. Lord Bute, in this list, appeared in the guise of 'Mountjoy Ltd' with their three properties. The delay in invoking the Act in this particular case arose because the proprietors of the corner properties with façades also to adjacent streets were concerned by the potential loss of development potential through a freezing of the eighteenth-century design and were both articulate and required a great deal of persuasion.[9]

This far-sighted, and far-reaching, initiative could not have been possible without the example Lord Bute had set in recreating such a substantial portion of Adam's design from a Victorian free-for-all. Balfour Paul's 1925 design in the collection of the Edinburgh City Architect deposited in the National Monuments Record of Scotland shows the entire north side reinstated. It is impossible to underestimate the importance of Charlotte Square in the subsequent history of the Scottish Conservation Movement. If Lord Bute's efforts reflected the contemporary historiographic re-evaluation o

Adam's place in British architecture, the Planning Order could perhaps only have been invoked because of the groundswell of the general enthusiasm for Adam that Lord Tweedmouth had triggered at Guisachan in the field of the decorative arts.

The foundation of the National Trust for Scotland in 1931 was to be no less important for the future of Charlotte Square than the Town Planning initiatives and was to be a further means by which Lord Bute's private preservation initiatives could be taken up by a public body. Unfortunately, the files of the National Trust for Scotland are not in themselves sufficient to permit a full history as to how this was effected.

The Trust's association with Charlotte Square began with their removal from Gladstone's Land in the Old Town to a new office at No 5 Charlotte Square as tenants of Mountjoy Ltd. They took over an empty house, although one with distinguished interior decoration. There was correspondence with the landlord about the damage that had occurred to the 'tapestry' by the removal of a 'large mirror on East wall of main room facing South' leaving it 'dirty and defective'. Later, at a yet uncertain date, the Trust replaced the sun-damaged and faded lampas with a 'Portsmouth'-design flock paper which preserved at least the character of the silk's pattern and this survived until 1991 (see Figure 11).

The original contents of No 5 had been transferred by the Butes next door to No 6. In 1934, Mountjoy Ltd had let No 7 to Whytock and Reid, then as now Edinburgh's premier cabinetmakers and upholsterers, on a ten-year lease, which was to be renewed.

The offer of all three houses to the National Trust for Scotland by the late Marquess of Bute in 1964 was a consequence of the settlement of the Estate of his father the Fifth Marquess of Bute. Needless to say the negotiations were complicated but there was never the slightest doubt of the architectural importance of Charlotte Square, and the Trust laid particular stress on the educational value that would accrue from the transfer of the properties. Lord Bute made the offer conditional on No 6 being preserved as a 'home' but, because the National Land Fund, which was central to the Treasury negotiations, insisted on a degree of public access to everything they funded, this appeared to be an obstacle to a successful conclusion.

The ultimate decision to establish No 6 as the Official Residence of the Secretary of State for Scotland was the perfect resolution of the difficulty because the house would become a focal point for official entertaining and thus a very large number of Scots and visitors would be enabled to see the house. The transfer of the three houses was completed in 1966. No 6 was leased to the Bute House Trust whose Trustees adapted it to serve its new official function. That story deserves to be written up in detail because it was an important exercise in the patronage of contemporary craftsmen. Three items from No 6 passed to the National Trust for Scotland under the Treasury's arrangements in lieu of death duties. The most important of these was the portrait by Allan Ramsay of John, Third Earl of Bute, the Prime Minister Earl, which was even then valued at £8,000. The other two items were a chandelier installed by Lord Bute's aunt, Lady Flavia, which was valued at £600 [10] and a gilt overmantle mirror at £2,000. In order to hang large pictures in the Dining Room at No 6, Lady Flavia had had the 'astragals' removed from the walls but these had been carefully stored by Bonnar, the Edinburgh decorators.

This gilt mirror, of course, was the Mackie chinoiserie rococo mirror that had been the centrepiece of the Fourth Marquess's Drawing room next door at No 5. From a inventory of the other contents of No 6, drawn up by Sotheby's, the Trust were invited to make further purchases and it is clear that the over-mantle mirror was still accompanied by Mackie's rococo pier glass which it had once reflected in No 5. Although they had been together since 1760 when Mackie supplied them to the Private Drawing room at Duff House, tragically nobody in 1966 knew this history or their significance. Although the Trust must have made some purchases from the Sotheby's list, including the Scott Morton curtain boxes copied from Adam's Luton designs, the Trust cannot have realised that what was on offer was really the contents of No 5. After many years in store, part

Figure 11. Interior of Drawing Room at 5 Charlotte Square, during the occupation of the 4th Marquess of Bute.
(RCAHMS)

of this collection of Charlotte Square furniture, including the glass from Duff House, was offered to the Trust by Lord Bute for Culzean, but this was not taken up and these pieces were subsequently auctioned by Christies.

Although the Trust has long since outgrown No 5, its capacious service accommodation in the basement contained the Trust for a surprisingly long time. Its physical presence as a resident of the Square put the Trust in an exceptionally strong position to campaign for the amenity value of

Charlotte Square in the face of a variety of threats. In 1963 the Trust commissioned John Reid's *The Case for Charlotte Square* in the face of a triple threat. St George's Church had been endangered by dry rot whose eradication threatened to cost £80,000 which was so beyond the resources of the congregation that they entered into union with St Andrew's Church in George Street, leaving a vital component of the Square empty. Secondly, a new building at 130 George Street appeared to herald a change of urban scale which would dwarf the

Street and the right of the Governors and their feuars to use the contemplated street. The Governors however 'would not execute their part of the plan until they found it convenient'. In return the Governors expected that James Hope must have reasonable prospects that the job would be completed by the time of feuing or building, and that the ground was to be used for that specific purpose.[18] These two provisions were the impasse to the completion of any schemes for residential development by the two Trusts. Effectively neither would move until they were sure of an economic return on their outlay.

At this time Gayfield House was not affected as it was not owned by the Hopes. The Erskines had no children and so, by a Trust Deed of 29th November 1784, Lady Charlotte's Trustees seized the lands and house of Gayfield in disposition by her on 17th June 1784.[19] Ten years after her death in 1788, the five acres and three rood lands of Broughton were brought from the Trustees by Agnes Cathcart, widow of Elias Cathcart of Greenfield.[20] The Cathcart family continued to own it until a new era began in 1863 when John Hope WS purchased the property, thereby consolidating his lands of Broughton and Gayfield.[21] The Joint Plan of 1830 had not been taken up but was still in operation, when in November 1863, John Hope asked for ground from the Governors for the access road from Leith Walk to Hope Crescent, and what was necessary for the continuation of London Street. If this request had been granted it would have left the Governors with unusable land producing no income. Hope continually delayed, not wishing to open up ground for building until he was sure it was economically viable to do so, aware that only four feus with expensive houses had been taken up in Hope Crescent. The Governors meanwhile had agreed with the City to build workers' housing on their feus, at fair value.[22]

The eventual development of the Heriot and Hope Trust properties is another story, but because of the indecision between the two parties Gayfield House survived. The unaltered state of Gayfield House is very surprising considering its use from 1873 as a school of Veterinary Medicine.

William Williams, Principal of Edinburgh Veterinary College in Clyde Street, and also Professor of Pathology at Edinburgh University was asked to resign his post on 15 July 1873, after chronic differences became apparent between Williams, his students, and the Governors. He established a new Veterinary School in Gayfield, taking with him over forty students, leaving only nine behind. About ten years later his college moved to Elm Row to the building which eventually became the Gateway Cinema.[23] Eventually, Gayfield House became the property of William Cockburn, manure merchant, thereafter in about 1917, of William Wallace, the owner of ammonia and bleachworks, and eventually in the mid 1930s it became the home of a well-known garage proprietor who built the premises next door.

Today the house is again lived in as a private house having survived the threat of demolition by a developer in 1990, saved by its status as a Category A listed building, and the efforts of the Cockburn Association who fought on behalf of all corporate objectors for its preservation. But, unfortunately, having survived virtually untouched since the 1760s all the original carved wood and gesso chimneypieces were stolen from their positions before the house was boarded up to stop such vandalism (see Figure 6).

The quote in the introduction is from Ian Gow's pioneering study of the Edinburgh villa.[24] He has defined the villa as 'merely a house in a garden, which may graduate by degrees through garden plus field, to garden and farm, and ultimately extend to what in Scotland was called policies'.[25] Evidence on the ground shows that because the countryside was in close proximity to Edinburgh it was possible to have a house in its own grounds, such as Queensberry House and Milton House and other examples along the Canongate, with magnificent views to the Calton Hill and Arthur's Seat. These town houses took on many villa characteristics. The advantages of fresher air and extensive views over beautiful landscapes, combined with the principal element, the garden, outweighed the disadvantages of the filth and unhealthy air of the tightly packed closes, and

appealed to the aristocracy and law lords, who enjoyed a 'half-town and half-villa life' which is 'literally *rus in urb*'.[26]

Gow argues that architectural historians have defined the villa as an architectural type, but as the indispendable component is the garden, any building, even a small country cottage with a garden can take on the aspect of a villa in the eyes of the stressed fugitive from town, many of these simple cottages developed into the status of mansion houses. The steps taken to protect the environs of Gayfield House from encroachment by the growing developments of Broughton and Gayfield suggest that the house built by William Butter was suitably placed as a town house. It was conveniently placed to take advantage of a new North Bridge, projected since the 1750s, as even without the bridge it was only twenty minutes on foot from the Market Cross. The house displays, however, all the characteristics of an Edinburgh villa, and is comparable in layout and planting to many of the

inner ring of villas round the Old Town. Drumsheugh House and pleasure grounds which the Earl of Moray purchased in 1780 was in the meaning of Ian Gow's definition, both urban and country, authentically '*rus in urb*'. In this context Gayfield House, so conveniently close to the town, with its garden, spacious surroundings and prospect views can be considered to be a town house with villa characteristics.

Acknowledgements

I would like to thank the Scottish Record Office for permission to quote from the Mar and Kellie papers, Mr C M Dougan of the Heriot Trust Office, for access to the Records of George Heriot's Trust, and for permission to publish the plan of 1801 copied from John Ainslie, deposited in the National Monuments Record of Scotland. The Trustees of the late John Hope gave permission for the publication of the drawings of the floor plans by Hippolyte Blanc.

NOTES

1. SRO, Register of Sasines, 27 Volume 161, folio 164, 28 Feb 1761.
2. SRO, RS27/Volume 168, folio 163, 1st April 1765, Thomas styled Lord Erskine, born circa 1705, was the son of John, 11th Earl of Mar, who was attainted for his share in the 1715 Rising, when all his honours were forfeited. Thomas Erskine married Lady Charlotte Hope at Hopetoun House on 1st October 1741. He became Commissary of Stores for Gibraltar, and afterwards sat in Parliament as Thomas Erskine of Alloa, for the counties of Stirling and Clackmannan. From exile in France in 1728, his father wrote a letter to his son known as his 'Legacy'. In this prophetic paper he proposed that the valley between the Old Town of Edinburgh and the fields on Multrees Hill and the Bearsford Parks to the north, should be spanned by a bridge, opening up the possibility of development 'where many streets might be built for the inhabitants'. (F C Mears and John Russell, 'The New Town of Edinburgh', *Book of the Old Edinburgh Club*, 22 (1938), p 173, and Charles McKean 'James Craig and Edinburgh's New Town' in Kitty Cruft and Andrew Fraser (eds) *James Craig 1744–1795* (1995), p 48.
3. SRO, GD124/1/1193/1 (Mar and Kellie). John Syme, WS, was the son of Alexander Syme, writer in Edinburgh. He died in June 1790.
4. SRO, GD124/1/1193/2.
5. SRO, GD124/1/1193/3.
6. SRO, GD124/1/1193/3.
7. SRO, GD124/1/1193/5. James Erskine of Alloa (1723–1796), son of Charles Erskine of Tinwald, 3rd son of Sir Charles Erskine of Alva, became Lord Barjarg. He was the owner of 11 acres at the west end of George Street, Young Street and Queen Street, subsequently sold to enable Edinburgh City to complete Craig's plan of the New Town. (Mears and Russell, 'The New Town of Edinburgh', *Book of the Old Edinburgh Club*, 23 (1940), p 5.
8. SRO, GD124/1/1193/6.
9. SRO, GD124/1/1193/7 & 8.
10. SRO, GD124/1/1193/9. Butter's description of Gayfield House 1765, SRO/RHP 11114. Book of architectural plans of Gayfield House, Signed Hippolyte J Blanc, Edinr, 5th March 1870.
11. SRO, GD124/1/1193/11 & 12.
12. SRO, GD124/1/1193/20 & 21.

(OPPOSITE) *Figure 6. Gayfield House in 1982. (Joe Rock Photographer)*

13. SRO, GD124/1/1193/27.

14. SRO, GD/124/1/1193/31.

15. SRO, GD124/1/1193/36.

16. John Kay in his *Original Portraits*, Volume 2 (1838), p 32. gives a biographical sketch of William Butter. He tells us that Charles Butter left his son in possession of considerable property, and was himself a mechanical genius illustrated by the 'building of an additional storey to his dwelling house in Carrubber's Close without taking down the roof. This he accomplished by means of screws'. The fortunes of the Butter family became connected with a number of skilled and successful wrights and merchants, through their own organising ability and advantageous marriages. According to John Kay, Charles Butter originally came from Peterhead. In 1731 he married Ann Reoch, daughter of William Reoch, wright, and Deacon of the Incorporation of Wrights from 1736–37, and it was by right of his wife that he became a Burgess and Guild Brother. In 1731 Charles Butter married, as his second wife, Janet Peter, daughter of James Peter of Chapell, also a wright and Deacon. She was the sister of Alexander Peter, wright, who designed and made furniture from 1757–60 for the 4th Earl of Dumfries, his principal client. In 1754 Charles Butter and his co-wrights, so far unnamed, but probably those wrights with workshops already in Carrubber's Close, set up a co-partnery with James Cullen, the rascally London entrepreneurial upholsterer. they fitted up a large warehouse in Carrubber's Close to display all kinds of household furniture and furnishings in the latest styles; an enterprise which in the end, profited the Edinburgh wrights. (Francis Bamford, *A Dictionary of Edinburgh Furniture Makers 1660–1840* (1983), p 20). In 1755 William Butter married Jean M'Farlane of Gartartan, a small estate in Port of Menteith parish, and in the following year his sister, Anna, married John Biggar, the son of John Biggar of Woolmet. With his brother Walter, John founded a linen manufactory in Sciennes, Edinburgh, noted for its fine and prize winning linens. The Biggar family lived nearby in Sciennes Hill House. In 1821 the heiress Anne Hay-Mackenzie of Cromartie and Newhall, great-granddaughter of John and Anna Biggar, became Countess of Cromartie in her own right, and in 1849 married the 3rd Duke of Sutherland (*Book of the Old Edinburgh Club*, 20 (1935), App 32–5). Kay notes that William Butter worked on Gayfield House, Dundas House and Register House. In the death notice for his wife, Jean McFarlane of Gartarten, Dunbartonshire, in 1800, William is given as an Architect. *Edinburgh Magazine*, March 1800, p 240. He died in 1817.

17. I am grateful to Ian Gow for help with these important features in the house. Information on these subjects can be found in John Cornforth, 'Putting up with Georgian DIY' *Country Life*, April 9th 1992, p 54, and Christopher Gilbert, James Lomax and Anthony Wells-Cole, 'Country House Floors, 1660–1850', *Temple Newsam Country House Studies Number 3* (1987).

18. Records of George Heriot's Hospital, Volume 25, November 1800–April 1832.

19. SRO, PR 284.97

20. SRO, PR 428.101.

21. SRO, PR 2393.167 May 19th 1863.

22. The history of the development of the lands of Broughton and Gayfield from the late eighteenth century, including the Joint Contract of 1867 which would have swept Gayfield House aside, can be found in the Hope Trust Papers, (SRO/253/146), in which is detailed the difficulty the Hope's had in cancelling the Crown's lease of 999 years for the use of ground as a Botanic Garden, and releasing it for building purposes, and the Records of George Heriot's Hospital, held in the Heriot Trust Office, which comprise the Committee Minutes, admirably bound and indexed. The Edinburgh Sasine Registers in the SRO include the development of the feuing and building of the lands of Gayfield belonging to Walter Jolly, and the development of the Hope Trust lands, once feuing had started.

23. D Charnock, *History of the Edinburgh Veterinary College* Facsimile of the 1923 edition (1988).

24. Ian Gow, *The Edinburgh Villa* (1975). Unpublished thesis deposited in the Library of the National Monuments of Scotland.

25. Ian Gow, 'The Edinburgh Villa', *Book of the Old Edinburgh Club*, New Series, 1 (1991), p 35.

26. Gow, *The Edinburgh Villa*. Unpublished thesis.

JAMES MACAULAY

The Demolition of the Western Towers of Glasgow Cathedral

IN THE closing decades of the eighteenth century and with increased momentum in the next, numerous cathedrals in England were subjected to restoration programmes either from necessity, as at Hereford where the western tower collapsed in 1786, or to effect a visual improvement, as at Canterbury where the Norman north-west tower was replaced to conform stylistically with its fellow in 1831. A further impetus came with the publication of *The True Principles of Gothic Architecture* by A W Pugin who favoured thirteenth- and early fourteenth-century Gothic. Henceforth purists deemed it a duty to purge the great ecclesiastical edifices of the middle ages of later additions.

In such a climate the cathedral at Glasgow could not escape attention and the more so as the north transept was unstable and the asymmetrical western towers were seen 'by men of taste and architectural knowledge, as abortive afterthoughts or excrescences, which had no connection with the pristine designs of the Cathedral'.[1] Their consequent removal was the more unfortunate since Glasgow, alone on the Scottish mainland, had survived intact from the middle ages.

The first recorded view of the architecture of Glasgow is by John Slezer at the close of the seventeenth century. The most prominent feature is the cathedral with its central spire and two western towers and beyond the roofs of the bishop's castle. With the permanent establishment of Presbyterianism after the revolution of 1689 the castle no longer had a use and became ruinous. A hundred years later the remains of the castle were cleared to make way for Robert Adam's Royal Infirmary. Until then the western towers of the cathedral were integral parts of a varied architectural and topographical ensemble (see Figure 1). The cathedral was approached from the south-west with both vista and route prescribed by the castle to the north with its southern limits marked by the defensive tower at the south-west angle, then by the precinct wall (such as survives still at St Andrews) with the view closed by the cathedral's towers giving presence and dignity to the west front. In that scene much of the contrast, the play of forms, the changing scale was lost with the disappearance of the castle. Thereafter the cathedral was isolated and more exposed for, lacking an architectural foreground, it was brought into more prominence. Early nineteenth-century depictions show the infirmary to the north, the cathedral to the east and to the south the Barony Church whose congregation had worshipped in the cathedral's crypt which on their departure then became a place of sepulture. Given the disposition of public buildings around the cathedral and the laying out of a paved square it was perhaps inevitable that interested attention should focus on the cathedral. Questions about its use, condition and appearance came to be asked by the antiquarians prompted in part perhaps by the contemporary building programmes on the truncated remains of Paisley Abbey and at St Giles' Cathedral in Edinburgh. At the former, where the roof of the nave (the only part of the medieval abbey then in congregational use) needed repairs in 1825, the heritors and others

Figure 1. Joseph Swan, Archiepiscopal Palace and Cathedral as they stood in the year 1790.

were becoming aware of the antiquarian worth of the abbey whereas a generation earlier there had been a desire to pull down the surviving parts using the stones to build a parish church.[2]

More importantly, in view of subsequent attitudes in Glasgow, may have been the remodelling, externally as well as internally, of St Giles' Cathedral by William Burn between 1829 and 1833. Once the surrounding Krames had been demolished the exterior of St Giles, according to William Chambers, 'had a very ragged appearance' which was remedied by Burn's demolition of side chapels, the erasure of idiosyncratic excrescences and the imposition of a fictitious symmetry over the fabric now clad with polished ashlar.[3]

Indeed, it cannot be coincidence that in 1833 there appeared an *Essay on the Cathedral Church of*

Glasgow published at his own expense by Archibald McLellan, one of the city's richest merchants, a noted art connoisseur and a member of the town council. McLellan provides valuable information about recent changes to the fabric of the cathedral, such as the unblocking of the west window in 1812, although in 1833 the west doorway and the south porch were still blocked so that the entrance to the cathedral was by a doorway in the eastern portion of the nave.[4] That led into a no-man's land between the two congregations with one occupying the western arm of the nave and the other the choir, a physical separation still to be seen in the church of St Nicholas in Aberdeen.

The aim of the *Essay* was to promote the improvement of the cathedral especially in the nave where 'the grandeur of its appearance, however, is

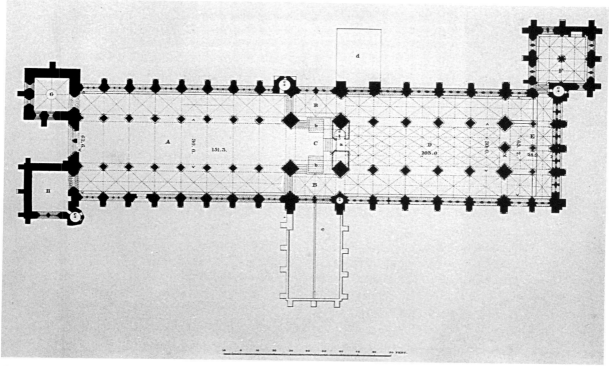

Figure 2. Plan of Glasgow Cathedral by James Collie, 1835.

completely destroyed by a partition wall of rough masonry ... and the necessity of the removal of which it is one of the principal objects of this essay to illustrate.' As for the western towers, however, 'Little time may be answered in describing these portions of the structure' since to McLellan they were 'ungainly forms ... they have not even the merit of antiquity.'[5] That most damning statement in an age of antiquarianism seems to have been accepted without debate by subsequent commentators. With the unquestioning optimism of his age and, possibly, with the radical overhaul of St Giles in mind, McLellan saw 'no limit to the extent of our operations in improving the Cathedral. We may live to see two magnificent transepts, in the fulfilment of Bishop Blackadder's original design, completed – the unsightly buildings which deform the western front removed, and their places supplied by such an elevation as the grand western front at York.'[6] Thus, were the seeds sown for the destruction of the western towers.

In the Prefatory Notice to his *Essay* McLellan

deponed that it had originally been a lecture delivered 'to the members of the Glasgow Dilettanti Society' several of whom had suggested its publication. In doing that McLellan took the opportunity to call for 'a more complete and detailed history of the See of Glasgow.' Such 'an extended work' might be accompanied 'by an architectural description of the edifice illustrated by external and internal views, with accurate ground plans and sections of the principal parts' on the model 'of Dodsworth's Salisbury or Britton's English Cathedrals.'[7] Or, he might have added, of Paisley Abbey and the publication by James Russell, a local architect, of the first measured survey of both the exterior and the interior with accompanying notes 'in an effort', he wrote, 'to counter balance the lack of published material on Scottish ecclesiological architecture when compared with that available in England.'[8]

McLellan's plea did not fall on deaf ears for almost immediately the suggested task was undertaken by James Collie, an architect practising in the eighteen twenties in Aberdeen which he subsequently quitted [9] doubtless because of the monopoly of architectural commissions held by the local men, John Smith and Archibald Simpson. Collie went to Glasgow and in 1835 published *Plans, Elevations, Sections, Details and Views of the Cathedral of Glasgow* which was the first measured survey of the cathedral. The plates included elevations of the western towers as well as their ground plans which, being the only recorded ones, have been utilised by every historian since (see Figure 2). It is the plan of the north-west tower which shows the ribbed vault, the south-west tower has its staircase while both plans show the entrances from the nave aisles. Collie followed McLellan in supposing Bishop Bondington 'to have erected the north-western tower and the consistory house' of which 'there is nothing worthy of remark'.[10] In delineating the cathedral Collie also harked back to McLellan's unillustrated *Essay* with its list of suggested improvements. Thus, Collie not only shows the nave uncluttered by internal partitions but he provides pictorial evidence as to now vanished roofs and the evident cracking of the structural framework in the west wall of the north transept.

As a result of awakened interest in the cathedral proposals for its repair and for additions were published in 1836 by a local committee, motivated by McLellan,[11] whereupon several interconnected and contending issues appeared over the rôles of the Lords of the Treasury, as the owners of the cathedral, of the Edinburgh architects George Meikle Kemp and James Gillespie Graham and of McLellan himself.

The main thrust of the argument as put forward by Kemp was that the cathedral, as it stood, was incomplete for 'it wanted transepts ... nor was its western front at all suited to the grand and impressive character of the rest of the structure.'[12] Having accepted that the building was not in good repair, with the north transept, for instance, 'fully two feet off the perpendicular', the Lords of the Treasury had asked Robert Reid as head of the office of works in Scotland to make a survey and cost the necessary repairs with the proviso that any improvements 'they leave to the good taste and

right feeling of the community' for whom additions had been drawn up 'by a professional Gentleman of great eminence and experience in Gothic architecture.'[13] That was Gillespie Graham. It is at this point that the controversy begins since the prospectus for the beautification of the cathedral had included drawings by Kemp but without acknowledging the artist alongside the 'Western Front by James Gillespie Graham Esquire; as approved by the Right Honourable the Lords of the Treasury.'

Kemp had been collecting material for an aborted work on *Scottish Cathedrals and Antiquities* on the lines of those published by John Britton in England. He decided to supplement his studies of Glasgow Cathedral with a perspective showing 'the probable plan of the original architect for the completion of the building' with supporting drawings and with costs obtained from an Edinburgh surveyor. Eventually, there was a wooden model, 'about 12 feet long, by 6 feet broad, and the central spire rises about 8 feet from the ground', which Kemp opined 'may last a thousand years.' As its construction took more than two years it was not until 1839 that it could be despatched to Glasgow for public viewing. The cost was to have been borne by McLellan but at the halfway mark his advice to Kemp was not to continue 'for Mr. Graham had got up a design, and that it was useless for us to contend with him, because he had the ear of the Lords of the Treasury'.

Like others before Kemp considered that the transepts 'bear evident remarks of an unfinished condition; while the great western front appears to considerable disadvantage from its want of detailed finishing'. For him the north-west tower was 'clumsy' and its companion 'a building of a peculiar and unseemly character'. Kemp wished to extend the nave to the line of new symmetrical towers to be only slightly lower than Bishop Cameron's spire (see Figure 3). Kemp's proposal were criticised for the 'diminutive central pinnacle on the western towers' and because his south transept only partially covered Blackadder's Aisle. As Kemp wrote to McLellan, 'You have corrected the one error; the plans of Mr. Gillespie Graham correct the other.'[14]

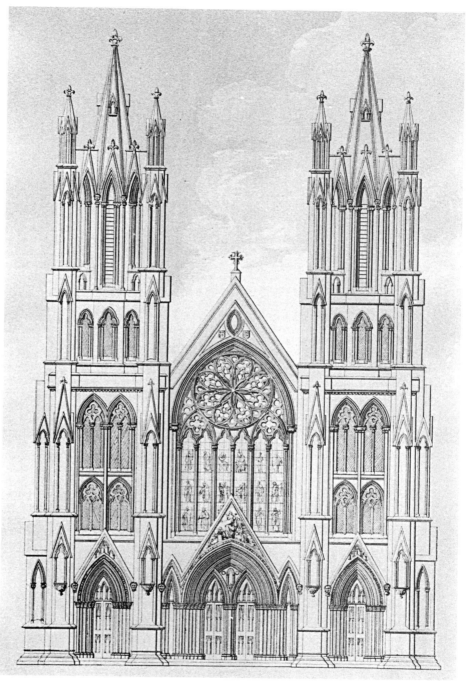

Figure 3.
J M Kemp's proposed western towers, taken from A McLellan, Plans and Elevations of the Proposed Restoration and Additions to Glasgow Cathedral, 1836.

Why were Kemp's proposals jettisoned? Mc-Lellan was ready to blame the Lords of the Treasury who since 1836 had been discussing with Gillespie Graham a scheme to restore the remains of Holyrood Abbey as the meeting place of the general assembly of the Church of Scotland.[15] If Glasgow Cathedral was to receive embellishments there would be no objection provided they were in keeping stylistically and by a government appointed architect.[16] However, when the Glasgow

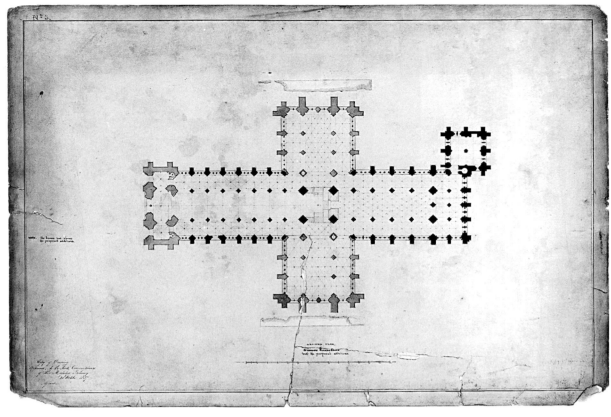

Figure 4. A W Pugin, Plan of Glasgow Cathedral showing proposed additions. (RCAHMS)
Figure 5. A W Pugin, Plan of Glasgow Cathedral in its present state. (RCAHMS)

Figure 6. The south front of Glasgow Cathedral showing A W Pugin's proposed changes. (RCAHMS)

town council appointed Gillespie Graham that was accepted.[17]

The true reason why Kemp lost out was because, despite his superior knowledge of medieval Gothic, he had built nothing of any import, whereas Gillespie Graham had not only some fifteen Gothic revival churches to his name but had worked on the medieval churches of Linlithgow, Stirling and Perth as well as Dunblane Cathedral. Yet how did the connection between Gillespie Graham and McLellan come about? Probably, through the surveyor William Kyle who had worked for many years with the architect and had contributed a section to McLellan's *Essay*.

Early in 1837 the Glasgow Dean of Guild court, of which McLellan was a member, ordered the north transept to be shored 'to prevent danger to the lieges'.[18] Some months later, 'As the Designs for our Cathedral are now finished', Gillespie Graham was instructed to forward them to the Treasury. 'I have no doubt,' wrote Baillie Henry Paul, 'that we shall be able to raise in Glasgow a subscription that may be sufficient to build the West Front and Spires and therefore I do hope that the Treasury will proceed this summer to build the Transepts.'[19] Gillespie Graham did as requested and appended a note saying that the north transept should be dismantled and rebuilt 'which will not probably exceed £7,000'. He also enclosed a report on the 'Lithographic Plans'. Referring indirectly to Kemp's proposals he advised that 'the contemplated additions are, in my humble opinion, somewhat at variance with that decided simplicity of outline which characterises the Venerable Minster of St Mungo'. He rested his case for the acceptance of his own designs on an analogy with Lichfield Cathedral with its triple spires with the central one similar to that at Glasgow 'and warrants on high authority the restoration of the others ...' Unlike Lichfield and other cathedrals, however, Glasgow 'is well seen from many parts of the surrounding country, and with its group of three spires, could not but have a peculiarly picturesque and magnificent effect'. To demonstrate the affinity between all three towers, 'as a perspective view alone is very inadequate for such a purpose', he enclosed new drawings of the west and south elevations and a plan showing the south transept extending laterally beyond Blackadder's Aisle.[20]

What Gillespie Graham did not say, and what was not known until recently, was that the three new drawings had been prepared by the twenty-four year old A W Pugin[21] who had just been converted to Catholicism. What would the brethren of the kirk have said if they had known! Since 1829 Pugin had been paid by Gillespie Graham to supply drawings for schemes as diverse as the new castle at Murthly, Perthshire, and St Margaret's convent in Edinburgh, the first in Scotland since the Reformation. Pugin was no doubt the 'high authority' who made the comparison between the cathedrals of Glasgow and Lichfield. The Glasgow drawings intended for publication are probably those referred to by Pugin in his diary early in 1836[22] and would have been based on Collie's survey, a copy of which Pugin possessed.[23] A further diary entry by Pugin in May 1837 records: 'Finish(?) churches for Mr. G. 6 drawings' which were later priced as '3 drawings ... of Glasgow £10:10:0' and '3 ditto altered £15:15:0.'[24] Three of these survive, a plan with expanded transepts and before and after south elevations, and show evidence of Pugin's hand in lettering, in the impressionistic rendering of window tracery and in the vigour of the architectural presentation (see Figures 4, 5 and 6).[25] These conform to the published west elevation which was more elegant than Kemp's four layered composition. In his rival's scheme the aisled transepts and the acute west gable set between thin towers, which read as high bases for the spires, imitate Lichfield although the slenderness and details of the spires seem to correspond to a foreign source, namely the church of St Elizabeth at Marburg in Germany.

Approval came from the Treasury 'both as re-gards the harmony of style preserved in the proposed restoration and the general beauty of the designs'.[26] Although it was accepted that, 'The second object is to substitute buildings of a style and character worthy of the Grandeur of the ancient Edifice, in place of those which at present deform the Western Front' and that a new west front, costing £10,296 over two years according to Gillespie Graham,[27] was Glasgow's burden, the Treasury still would not meet the cost of extending the transepts, which were intended in part to secure the stability of the central tower. The Treasury saw its liability as the repair of the existing fabric only.[28]

Early in 1840 Edward Blore, the surveyor of Westminster Abbey and a well known, if uninspired, authority on medieval architecture, was ordered 'to proceed to Glasgow and make a careful survey of the Cathedral in that City ...' While accepting that the north transept was indeed unstable he saw no need for its enlargement doubting 'whether the Tower derives any effective support from the Transept.' Blore included the western towers in his report but, despite his knowledge of Scottish medieval architecture, could see little merit in them. The upper portion of the north-west tower had fractured because of decayed timbers and the weight of the lead spire and his recommendation was that it should be rebuilt; its fellow he condemned as dilapidated, unsightly and of no use 'and the inside a scene of great neglect and desolation'. By removing that tower the west front could be restored to its original design 'so far as it has been damaged, or disfigured, by the addition of this excrescence ...'[29] In June the Treasury yielded sufficiently to promise £10,000 towards the cost of Gillespie Graham's scheme provided the balance was guaranteed by the town council[30] which had opened a subscription the year before with £1,000.[31]

Four years later and with little progress on the cathedral two papers summarised the situation. In the first it was calculated that £29,563:15:11 would pay for a new west front and new transepts. Against that the local committee had failed having raised £5,000 only which was half the sum required. The recommendation, therefore, was for the government to rebuild the north transept in its existing form for £3,105.[32] Blore had further reported that 'as regards the designs furnished by Mr. Gillespie Graham ... I think them extremely objectionable inasmuch as they would be utterly destructive of the unity and simplicity of the original design' and 'completely at variance with its spirit and proportions'. By now he had changed his mind about the north-west tower which he wanted replaced with 'one of better and more ornamental design'[33] which for him meant a Scottish corona of pinnacles.[34] Blore's scheme of repairs was fully sanctioned which meant the early disappearance of the south west tower. *The Builder* in an account in 1847 of the repairs underway in the cathedral merely said, 'The south-east corner, near the great western door, where formerly stood the Consistory Court, has also been completely rebuilt, ...'[35] Within a year its companion had been felled[36] although not without a signed protest from 'twenty gentlemen ten of whom are architects' that the cathedral would be diminished by the subtraction of a feature as old as any part of the building, a plea which was not supported by Archibald McLellan 'of which there was none had a more thorough knowledge'. His stance provoked 'Groans from the Auld Bell Tower of the Hie Kirk ... but I ken I'm at least sax hunder; and this is admitted even by that crouse chield that's sair on me in the bonnie beuk he wrote on the Hie Kirk — I mean him that mak's coaches ...'[37] Thus perished Glasgow's unique assemblage of towers. A sorry tale perhaps best summarised by a later commentator. '... what followed all the enthusiasm of the (Local) Committee? A change of architects, and the utter disappearance of the feature it was their main object to preserve.'[38]

Acknowledgements

The author is indebted to Dr Ronald Cant, to Dr John Durkan and to Dr Richard Fawcett for reading the typescript of this article whilst it was in preparation and for much helpful comment; and to Dr Philip McWilliams for allowing excerpts to be quoted from his unpublished thesis on Paisley Abbey.

NOTES

1. James Pagan, *History of the Cathedral and See of Glasgow*, 2nd edn (Glasgow, 1856), p 77.
2. Philip McWilliams, *Paisley Abbey*, chp 4. An unpublished thesis for the University of Glasgow.
3. George Hay, 'The Late Medieval Development of the High Kirk of St Giles, Edinburgh', *Proceedings of the Society of Antiquaries*, vol 107 (1975–76), p 246.
4. Archibald McLellan, *Essay on the Cathedral of Glasgow and Plan for its Repair and Restoration* (Glasgow, 1833), pp 47, 50.
5. McLellan, *Cathedral of Glasgow*, p 62.
6. McLellan, *Cathedral of Glasgow*, p 90.
7. McLellan, *Cathedral of Glasgow*, p vii.
8. McWilliams *Paisley Abbey*, ch 4.
9. Howard Colvin, *A Biographical Dictionary of British Architects, 1600–1840* (London, 1978), p 230.
10. James Collie, *Plans, Elevations, Sections, Details and Views of the Cathedral of Glasgow*, (London, 1835), pp 1 and 4.
11. In a letter Kemp mentions McLellan's 'claim to priority in originating the idea of restoring Glasgow Cathedral'. Quoted by Thomas Bonnar, *Biographical Sketch of George Meikle Kemp* (Edinburgh and London, 1892), p 76.
12. Bonnar, *Sketch of Meikle Kemp*, p 67.
13. *Plans and Elevations of the Proposed Restoration and Additions to Glasgow Cathedral with Explanatory Address by the Local Committee* (Glasgow, 1836), pp 5 and 6.
14. Bonnar, *Sketch of Meikle Kemp*, ch III.
15. James Macaulay, 'The Architectural Collaboration Between J Gillespie Graham and A W Pugin', *Architectural History*, vol 27 (1984), pp 410–11.
16. Copy of Treasury Minute, 1 Nov, 1836. SRO, W/1/188/Pt I and hereafter.
17. R Reid, Office of Works, Exchequer Buildings, Edinburgh to H H Seward, Office of Woods, 3 Jan, 1837.
18. J Gillespie Graham to H H Seward. Edinburgh, 9 Aug 1837.
19. Henry Paul to J Gillespie Graham, Glasgow, 30 May 1837.
20. Paul to Gillespie Graham, 30 May 1837.

21. See Macaulay, 'The Architectural Collaboration ...' for an analysis of the working relationship between Gillespie Graham and Pugin, pp 406–22.

22. The relevant Pugin diary is in the Victoria and Albert Museum, MS 86 MM55 and 56. See also Alexandra Wedgwood, *A W N Pugin and the Pugin Family* (London, 1985) for transcriptions of Pugin's diaries.

23. *Sale Catalogues of Libraries of Eminent Persons*, vol 4, *Architects*, introduction by David J Watkin (London, 1972), p 254.

24. V and A, MS 61. See note 22.

25. Ministry of Works MSS, Glasgow Cathedral.

26. Ministry of Works, Glasgow Cathedral 1. 'Copy of a Treasury Minute, 29 Septr. 1837.'

27. Lord Provost of Glasgow to the Treasury, nd.

28. Copy of a Treasury Minute, 4 Feb 1840.

29. E Blore, 'Report on the State of Glasgow Cathedral, 29 March 1840.'

30. Copy of a Treasury Minute, 10 June 1840.

31. 'Extract from a letter of the Lord Provost of Glasgow to A Y Spearman, Esq, Dated 1st March 1839.'

32. W Nixon, Office of Works, Edinburgh to the Commissioners of Woods, 3 Feb 1844.

33. E Blore to the Office of Woods, 19 March 1844.

34. Victoria and Albert Museum, drawings collection.

35. *The Builder*, vol V, (1847), p 187.

36. George Eyre-Todd, *The Book of Glasgow Cathedral* (Glasgow, 1898), p 286. In a text published fifty years after the demolition of the north-west tower it is stated that a stone, bearing the arms of Bishop Wardlaw, was found on the floor. His arms also appear on the western vault of the north aisle. Fairbairn, *Relics of Ancient Architecture in Glasgow* (Glasgow, 1896).

37. *Scotch Reformers' Gazette*, 19 and 26 Aug, 2 and 16 Sept 1848. The protest was got up by Charles Hutcheson who sketched the partially demolished north-west tower. NLS, MS 2773, f8. Information from Dr J Durkan.

38. R W Billings and J Hill Burton, *The Baronial and Ecclesiastical Antiquities of Scotland*, vol III (1901), p 9.

ANDOR GOMME

An American Influence on Alexander Thomson

FOLLOWING a handful of late eighteenth-century prototypes, neo-Greek took over in England as the *de facto* official style for public buildings soon after 1800. Its formal adoption in Scotland came slightly later but with impressive confidence and completeness; and it lasted in various individual interpretations much longer than in England. The portico of William Stark's Justiciary Court in Glasgow (designed 1809) was the first, and remains perhaps the purest, Greek Doric in Scotland, but thereafter the impulse passed to Edinburgh, where a magnificent sequence of Greek Revival public buildings was initiated by Robert Reid's uncompromising Custom House in Leith (1810). The young William Burn went no further at Edinburgh Academy (1823) and John Watson's School (1825) than refining the manner of his master Robert Smirke in adding severely correct porticoes to long late Georgian elevations; but with the emergence of Thomas Hamilton and Stark's pupil William Henry Playfair, the Scottish Greek Revival – notable in its earlier decades for strong reliance on Doric – became an increasingly athletic medium, not only adaptable to a wide range of institutional and public needs but revealing remarkable plastic qualities as architects used porticoes and colonnades, sometimes contrasting in scale, to articulate entire façades. Playfair's deeply modelled Royal Institution (begun 1822) shows how rich an interplay of volumes and chiaroscuro is possible within one single order, and the brilliant inventiveness of the intersecting and interlocking locks of Hamilton's Royal High School (1825) turned neo-Greek at a stroke into something vibrantly picturesque.

The younger Archibald Elliot (son of the

designer of Waterloo Place, which makes so impressive an introduction to Edinburgh's Athenian climax on Calton Hill) brought the Greek Revival back to Glasgow in his Royal Bank of Scotland (1827), soon to be upstaged by David Hamilton's Soanian transformation of an eighteenth-century mansion into the Royal Exchange, whose superb colonnaded and barrel-vaulted newsroom owes much to Playfair's Upper Library at the Old College in Edinburgh. This was late for a new infusion of the formal neo-Greek which never dominated Glasgow as it did Edinburgh: the intermittent appearances of portico or colonnade in churches or such prominent public works as the City and County Buildings and the Merchants' House (1845) are incidents within a general shift into more relaxed and flexible Renaissance ways in the early Victorian years – until, that is, the extraordinary phenomenon of Alexander Thomson.

Thomson took neo-Greek by the throat and transformed it into a style wholly his own,[1] so much so that his buildings are among the most readily recognisable of his or any other time. No architect indeed, however original, is entirely author of himself, and the ultimate sources on which Thomson drew are often not difficult to spot; but more specific and later influences are elusive and have been much argued over.[2] The aim of this paper is to offer evidence of the architectural debt which, it is suggested, Thomson owed to the early nineteenth-century architect, Minard Lafever.[3] Consider the twin doorcases on the entrance front of Caledonia Road Church in Glasgow, which have always appeared so quintessentially Thomsonesque (see Figure 1). Their outer frames derive unquestionably

Figure 1.
Doorcase, Caledonia Road
Church, Glasgow, Thomson,
1856. (RCAHMS)

from the north door of the Erekhtheion on the Athenian Akropolis – the door which leads to the section of the temple referred to in the old texts as that of Athena (or Minerva) Polias. How did Thomson, who never went to Greece, come to know it? Did he know it directly at all? He certainly knew Stuart and Revett's *Antiquities of Athens*; but they give no illustration of the door, which was apparently first engraved in full in 1833 in T L Donaldson's *Collection of the Most Approved Examples of Doorways from Ancient Buildings in Greece and Italy*.[4] Among its most striking features are the rosettes in the delicately battered architrave frame (closely reproduced by Thomson) and the enriched anthemion cornice, which reappears in Caledonia Road in a slightly simplified form in which the palmettes are divided from the lotus by

a skimpy scrollwork. Thomson very likely knew Donaldson's book (though it was apparently published only in a small edition), but his simplified cornice reproduces not that shown by Donaldson but that of a doorcase design (see Figure 2) included in Lafever's *Modern Builder's Guide*,[5] which, though (like the Erekhtheion door) it lacks Thomson's characteristic lugs, has the same battered frame with rosettes. Battered window frames were nothing new: Thomson would have seen Stuart and Revett's engraving of the lugged windows flanking the door in the Polias porch,[6] and, if from nowhere else, might have been moved to use them himself by the nearby example of Arthur Lodge, the Edinburgh villa almost certainly by Thomas Hamilton, one of Thomson's heroes.[7]

Lafever, however, *must* have known Donaldson's

Figure 2. Design for a doorcase from Lafever's Modern Builder's Guide, *plate 60.*

Figure 3. Doorcase design from Lafever's The Beauties of Modern Architecture, *plate 14.*

work: it is his only possible source. And, especially since (on the page opposite the doorcase with the critical cornice [8]) he gives large-scale details, usable when scaled up as working templates, of the rosettes and the particular lotus form which Thomson also used, Thomson's dependence on the older architect's work seems certain.[9] As for the palmette standing at the apex of the ever-so-slightly raked blocking course, a closely similar one (whose scrolls run off either side into little rinceaux) crowns a doorcase (see Figure 3) – with lugs and an outer moulding exactly as at Caledonia Road – illustrated in Lafever's later book, *The Beauties of Modern Architecture.*[10]

Lafever, little-known in this country, was, especially through his books, once widely influential in the eastern USA.[11] He was born in 1798 and trained as a carpenter but was calling himself 'architect' by 1830, a year after the publication of his first book, *The Young Builder's General Instructor*, which was largely derived from Peter Nicholson and which Lafever later withdrew. In 1833 he produced the much more mature *Modern Builder's Guide*, which was reprinted six times between 1841 and 1855.[12] It was followed in 1835 by *The Beauties of Modern Architecture* (also several times reprinted [13]) – the most finely executed and best-considered of Lafever's books, in which designs for doors, windows, chimneypieces and so forth are accompanied both by descriptive explanations and by large-scale details giving 'all the particulars necessary to render [their] execution ... intelligible to the understanding of every workman'.[14] These are thought through with the understanding of a true craftsman; and the designs themselves, in the words of Lafever's editor, D P Myers, show 'mastery of proportion and [an] ability to combine restrained simplicity with delicate exuberance'.[15] In the later years of his life (he died in 1854) Lafever gave up neo-Greek, designed a number of Gothic churches, and for cottages and villas turned to the widely fashionable and less

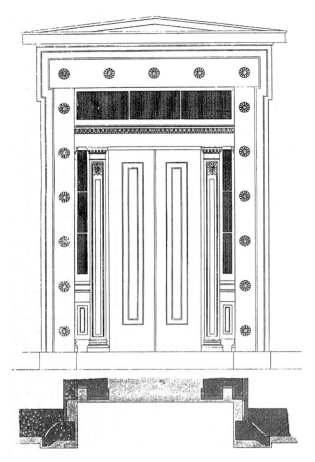

Figure 4. Lafever's design for a doorcase from The Modern Builder's Guide, *plate 80(I).*

demanding Italianate which he illustrated in his posthumously published *Architectural Instructor*, a latter-day swim-of-the-tide book of no special distinction and lacking the thoughtful refinement which so strongly characterizes Lafever's Greek work.

By the mid-1850s Thomson must have owned or had access to both *The Modern Builder's Guide* and *The Beauties of Modern Architecture*. While no single large feature of a Thomson building appears exactly to replicate a Lafever engraving, such examples as the doorcases in the dining room at Holmwood and those at the foot of the main staircases in the high pavilions of Great Western Terrace

are remarkably close reworkings of the Caledonia Road theme, reduced (as in Figures 2 and 3) to the scale of domestic interiors. Thomson's method – taking advantage of the mature artist's privilege of theft from others and making something new of what he stole [16] – was characteristically to play variations on several Lafever designs, mixing motifs and adding fresh ones to create an 'invention' which now seems the essence of Thomson. Thus Lafever, though he offers a couple of complex meander frets,[17] does not use them in lintels, nor flank doorcases with subsidiary antae as at Caledonia Road; nor again, as within closely similar 'pylons' at the end of the galleries at St Vincent Street Church, does he split his windows by square pilaster-like mullions under a massive transom, a motif that Thomson adapted from Stuart and Revett's illustration of the elevation of the choragic monument of Thrasyllus.[18] Transom lights are common features of Thomson entrance doors ,[19] though rarely accompanied by the sidelights which Lafever added to enrich his larger examples.[20] The Sauchiehall Street doorcase of Grecian Chambers, for example, suggests plate 80 (i) in *The Modern Builder's Guide* (see Figure 4) with the sidelights removed, the architraves battered and brackets (taken from plate 66 (i) in the same book) added to carry a characteristic Thomson cornice with its slightly pointed corona (too shallow to count as a pediment) crowned with his favourite acanthus akroterion – the last a feature appearing any number of times in both of Lafever's chief books. The frontispiece of Queen's Park Church (see Figure 5), with its main architrave carried on two great antae, through which the subsidiary entablature is threaded, could be seen as a magnificent enrichment of several Lafever designs based on the same formal skeleton, for example, plate 64 in *The Modern Builder's Guide* (see Figure 6), surmounted once again by the Erekhtheion cornice. On the same façade the Egyptianesque windows at gallery level again reproduce very faithfully the doorframe of Figure 2, with the Thrasyllus theme added within. At Westbourne Terrace, on the other hand, the front doors – which

(OPPOSITE) *Figure 5. The front elevation of Thomson's Queen's Park Church, Glasgow, 1867 (now demolished).*

Figure 6.
Plate 64 from Lafever's
The Modern Builder's
Guide.

have sidelights – are recessed within a shallow porch behind Ionic columns in antis (see Figure 7), which together make up a simplified paraphrase of plate 80 (ii) of the *Guide* (see Figure 8), superimposed on an inner frame adapted from Plate 66. The framing doorcase antae, missing from Westbourne Terrace, are however present, though without decorated necking, on the pavilion porches of Great

Western Terrace, with a full entablature above the Ionic columns identical with that in plate 80 (ii).

The lesser antae which typically flank Thomson front doors (as for example at Moray Place) could, though they need not, come from those included in numerous Lafever designs, sometimes shown with enlarged details for capital and base moulds. Such details are at times remarkably close; the base moulds of the antae which act as mullions to the great ground-floor windows on the Double Villa in Mansionhouse Road are identical with those shown in large scale in plate 16 of *The Beauties of Modern Architecture*, an engraving which also gives fully worked-out detail for anta capitals decorated with anthemia in a form which appears whole or in part in close replica on many and varied Thomson buildings – among them Holmwood, Moray Place, Caledonia Road, terraces or tenements in Oakfield Avenue and Norfolk Street, and the Dunlop Street warehouse. The ultimate source of all

such ornament is yet again the Ionic of the Erekhtheion, where bands alternating in Lafever's and Thomson's way form the necking of the capitals. These, unlike the doorcase details discussed earlier, are shown in large scale in *The Antiquities of Athens*,[21] from which Lafever gives a selection of redrawn examples in *The Beauties of Modern Architecture*, together with some fresh variations of his own. There is clearly no need for Thomson to have gone to Lafever for things he could find in Stuart and Revett, but he may have found Lafever's scale drawings useful short cuts.

Once one has accustomed oneself to the idea of Thomson's having used Lafever's books, it is easy to notice parallels and likenesses which may be no more than coincidences. The elevation of the fireplace wall in drawing rooms in Great Western Terrace is divided in three by thin pilasters exactly as shown in an only slightly more enriched form in *The Modern Builder's Guide* (plate 68). So, very

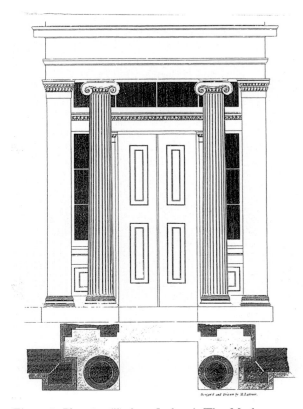

Figure 7. Doorcase at Westbourne Terrace, Glasgow, by Thomson, 1871.

Figure 8. Plate 80 (ii) from Lafever's The Modern Builder's Guide.

likely, are many other Victorian drawing-room walls. Or as a curiosity one might guess that Thomson's shift from dadoes or high skirting for principal rooms at Holmwood and the Double Villa to a preference for low skirting boards in Great Western Terrace, with Moray Place occupying a slightly ambiguous halfway position, could follow his reading of the note to plate 19 in *The Beauties of Modern Architecture*:

> The present and former custom of executing high skirting and bases in parlours being fixed

in the minds of almost every workman as unavoidably necessary, it may be well to remark ... that no one branch of finishing more requires a reform from the old school system. The writer is aware of the prejudices against new designs in the architectural department; he nevertheless resolves to carry into effect, as far as his abilities will permit, a change in designs and proportions of interior finishings for private residences. He would therefore recommend to those concerned, to duly consider all subjects of the above importance, prior to the execution thereof.

Figure 9.
Section of a gallery front and capital taken from Lafever's The Beauties of Modern Architecture, *plate 48.*

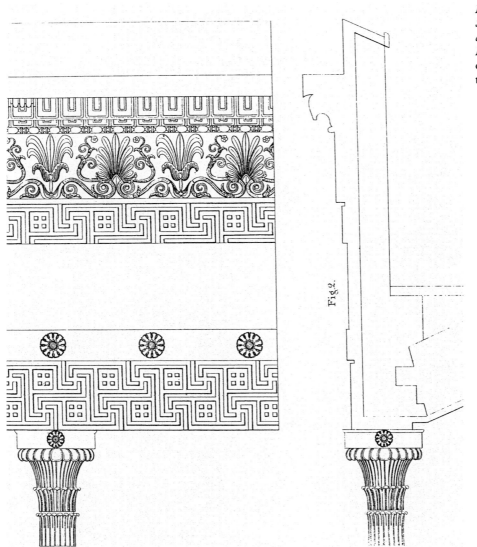

Figure 10. Plate 47, Lafever, The Beauties of Modern Architecture.

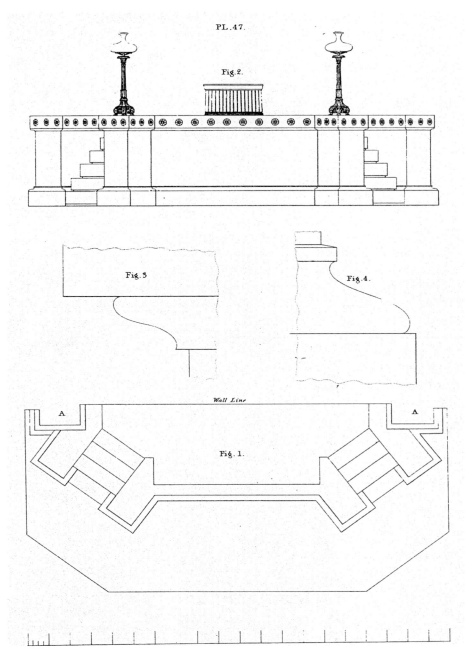

It seems likely that Lafever effected such changes on his own.

Like all great artists, Thomson helped himself to whatever he found that was useful to him, and his debt to Lafever – limited, but real and continuing – is a small aspect of the growth of his own architectural imagination, which far outstripped any detailed thefts and borrowings. Lafever is a minor master of real interest and individuality, but his distinctive talents seem to run essentially towards detail: in a larger view none of his work appears to go beyond the ordinary competence of many neo-classical (or early Gothic Revival) architects of his time on both sides of the Atlantic. There is for example nothing whatever to suggest that he had the innovative power to conceive anything like Thomson's whole-hearted reworking, or thinking out *ab initio*, of the architectural opportunities represented in his great series of warehouses [22] – or the briefer but equally comprehensive re-invention of the basic physical form of the church, for congregations with specific and newly identified requirements. Lafever's church designs were for decent neo-Greek temples [23] (at best no more inventive than, say, John Burnet's Elgin Place), for a Victorianized Palladian which makes notably little distinction between the façade of a reformed church and a bank,[24] or for carefully detailed but rather sterile Gothic: in *The Modern Builder's Guide* he gives the plan and front elevation of a Gothic church which, he ingeniously announces, 'is in its Elevation very similar to the New National Scotch church, London' – ie, the Presbyterian church in Regent Square, St Pancras, copied with all the pasteboard meagreness with which Sir William Tite had depreciated his own grander source in the west front of York Minster.[25]

Nevertheless Lafever perhaps gave something not only to the exteriors of Thomson's three great Glasgow churches but – again in detail rather than layout or overall design – to their interiors as well. The last plate (48) in *The Beauties of Modern Architecture* shows the section and part elevation of a 'gallery-front' supported on a three-decker palm-leaf capital (see Figure 9). The capitals of the columns which carried the clearstorey of Queen's Park Church [26] were simpler single-decker versions, with an almost identical profile.[27] (The capitals in St Vincent Street are fantastically elaborated forms of the same.) Even more interesting is the previous plate (see Figure 10), showing the plan and elevation of a pulpit – not one of the simple old-fashioned tubs but a large stage, twenty feet wide, approached on each side by a diagonally set flight of steps. It is not clear where this kind of stage – a development possibly of occasional layouts in eighteenth-century England – first became formalised in Britain, though its use was widespread in various branches of the reformed church from the 1860s onwards. Perhaps it did in fact originate in the United States. Lafever's pulpit design is not closely similar to any of Thomson's but it is at least conceivable that the initial idea came from him.

NOTES

1. For Thomson generally see Ronald McFadzean, *The Life and Work of Alexander Thomson* (London, 1979), *passim*, and Andor Gomme and David Walker, *The Architecture of Glasgow*, 2nd edn (London 1987), especially pp 123–52.
2. One forerunner which has not received due acknowledgement is the starkly impressive pylon façade of the former St Jude's Episcopal Church in West George Street, Glasgow (1838–39) by John Stephen.
3. The similarities between Lafever and Thomson were mentioned in passing in *The Architecture of Glasgow*, p 134n, though neither at first nor in the second edition did the authors consider the direct influence likely. Recently, in a paper written jointly with Gavin Stamp ('An American Forerunner? Minard Lafever and Alexander Thomson', in *'Greek' Thomson*, Stamp and S McKinstry (eds) (Edinburgh University Press, 1994), pp 199–206), the present author has briefly outlined the argument given in more detail here. Dr Stamp suggested that

Thomson may have received copies of Lafever's books from cousins who had settled in the United States, but the precise family relationship is still obscure.
4. This was pointed out by Talbot Hamlin in *Greek Revival Architecture in America* (1944): see the reprint (Dover, 1964), p 35n. Hamlin was the first historian to appreciate Lafever's distinctive qualities.
5. First published in 1833: see plate 60.
6. Stuart & Revett, *The Antiquities of Athens*, vol II, ch ii, p lxv, fig 1.
7. A pleasant coincidence – evidently nothing more – is the use of inverted anthemia both by Lafever (eg *Modern Builder's Guide*, plate 81) and on the entrance front of Arthur Lodge.
8. *Modern Builder's Guide*, plate 61.
9. Cf *The Beauties of Modern Architecture*, plates 19 and 20, and the accompanying text.
10. *The Beauties of Modern Architecture*, plate 14. Lafever's career is discussed at length in Jacob Landy's

The Architecture of Minard Lafever (Columbia University Press, New York, 1970).

11. Cf Hamlin, *Greek Revival Architecture in America*, pp 349–55.

12. A facsimile was published by Dover in 1969, with an introduction by Jacob Landy which includes a useful summary of Lafever's career.

13. A facsimile, with an introduction by Denys Peter Myers, likewise including a brief account of Lafever's career, was published by Da Capo Press (New York) in 1968. A great part of the book is taken up by extracts lifted from *Elme's Dictionary* [sic], ie James Elmes' *General and Bibliographical Dictionary of the Fine Arts* and a glossary of architectural terms copied from the *Encyclopaedia Britannica*. These, Lafever tells us, were afterthoughts added 'after a more mature consideration' with the intention of giving the practical workman 'more magnified and pleasing ideas of his profession'.

14. Descriptive note to plate 17.

15. See facsimile, Myers (ed), p viii.

16. Cf Andor Gomme, *On Theft as a Principle in Architectural Design*, an inaugural lecture delivered at Keele University (Keele, 1985).

17. *Beauties of Modern Architecture*, plate 48 (I).

18. *Antiquities of Athens*, vol II, chp iv, plate iii.

19. Each of the front doors at the Double Villa in Mansionhouse Road is itself a miniature of this formula set within a frame underneath a broad transom.

20. *Modern Builder's Guide*, plates 63–6, 80, 81; small front doors within transom light but no sidelights are shown on plates 85, 86.

21. Vol II, chp ii, plate viii, ix, xii.

22. Cf Gomme & Walker, *The Architecture of Glasgow*, pp 143–52, especially 150f.

23. See the first Dutch Reformed Church, Brooklyn (1834–35), illustrated in Landy, *Minard Lafever*, p vii, fig 1.

24. Cf Reformed Church on the Heights, Brooklyn (1850–51) and Brooklyn Savings Bank (1864–67), both now destroyed: see Landy, *Minard Lafever*, p xi, fig 7 and p viii, fig 6.

25. *Modern Builder's Guide*, plate 55. When Lafever actually built this design in 1839–40, for the (long demolished) Dutch Reformed Church in Washington Square, Manhattan, he does seem to have given it some added sturdiness: see Landy, *Minard Lafever*, p vii, fig 2. Another close crib, this time unacknowledged, appears in the elevation of a church 'designed in the Grecian Ionic order' – out of Smirke's St Mary's Wyndham Place, with the portico flattened into a conventional rectangle. Lafever's information in both cases probably came from Shepherd and Elmes's Metropolitan Improvements of 1829.

26. Preserved in measured drawings by John Jeffrey, now in the National Monuments Record of Scotland.

27. The same capitals appear in plate 17 – a design for sliding doors which, 'if executed in every particular suggested, would eclipse everything of the kind yet introduced'. The doors would slide between two pairs of palm columns.

13

DEBORAH MAYS

'A Taste of Haven': Some Picture Books for the Developing Victorian Suburb

THE nineteenth century was a boom period for domestic architecture but the dull sameness of much of the speculative development which resulted, as in the pockets of mediocrity around Edinburgh and Glasgow, aroused adverse comment. The attempts at romantic individualism, born in reaction, invariably showed lack of direction. Sir George Gilbert Scott showed that this waywardness was apparent in the mid-nineteenth century. Writing in 1858, he lamented that the 'vernacular Domestic architecture of our day is wholly unworthy of our state of civilisation, and requires a thorough reformation'.[1] Evidently, the three score of books produced between 1790 and 1835 illustrating designs for small to medium sized houses and informing the creation of the suburbs, had failed to educate popular taste sufficiently or to reach the offending audience,[2] and their picturesque variety embodied the prevailing confusion.

John Archer has provided an excellent catalogue and critique of such architectural publications up to the birth of the periodical press, specifically the creation of *The Builder* in 1842. He curtailed his studies in this year as he considered that the demand for individual monographs was negated by the arrival of a wider, more accessible outlet.[3] In terms of numerical output this is certainly true, as fewer 'pattern books' were published after the start of Queen Victoria's reign. However, a number of influential pictorial monographs dated from this period, and while far-removed from such seminal and weighty tomes as Loudon's *Encyclopedia of Cottage, Farm and Villa Architecture*, Kerr's *The*

Gentleman's House and Stevenson's *House Architecture* which divide the decades,[4] they are all the more valuable nonetheless for their rarity. A representative selection of these key volumes is here set in context to demonstrate their evolution under changing circumstances.

Along with the growth of an architectural profession and the burgeoning of the British middle classes, the market for such publications was changing through the century. Many of the volumes produced early in the century had contained exemplars for labourers' houses and were aimed at the provincial builder and operative mechanic and more rural than suburban locations. Peter Nicholson was particularly prolific in this field. George Jameson's *Thirty-three Designs with the Orders of Architecture* of 1765 would be reprinted as *The Rudiments of Architecture* in 1772 and continue in circulation (with two further editions and a reprint) up to the 1840s as an incomparably influential text, an indispensable handbook for many, providing designs which shaped a notable number of early suburban villas.[5] The need for these technical tomes lessened gradually with the evolution of a structured architectural education, though their usage continued through to the 1860s.[6]

A significant class of the early nineteenth-century volumes had focused on picturesque designs for cottage villas and were pitched at potential clients. These included works by such Scottish architects as Robert Lugar, but were mostly by English authors such as P F Robinson or Edward Jones.[7] It was this vein which survived and evolved:

the continuing need was identified by a reviewer in *The Builder* in 1866, who wrote that 'We are constantly asked by "persons about to build", sometimes indeed by "persons about to marry" for the name of a book containing designs for small houses to assist in settling their ideas, and enabling them to instruct their architect properly'.[8]

The reasons for the predominance of domestic design in these years are perhaps familiar but can usefully be outlined here. The essential demand for the growth and development of outer residential areas was caused by the ever-growing numbers of middle class professionals. With the rise in their real incomes (particularly in the Great Depression of the 1880s) they could afford the privacy and social superiority of the suburb. In addition, the arrival of street lighting and cheaper transport opened up new tracts of land, prerequisites to such developments. While keeping a horse and gig would be beyond the average salary, the appearance of cheaper transport made it possible for those with middle incomes to live at a distance from the office, to enjoy the best of city and suburb. First came the horse-drawn omnibus in the 1820s, and then the suburban train from the 1840s – which was made still more available by the Cheap Trains Act of 1883 [9] – and then the electric tram. These answered the demand for access to semi-rural locations and fueled the pressure for middle-class, suburban housing.

The authors were not without motives of self-interest in producing illustrated volumes. As in the eighteenth century, self-advertisement remained a key reason for publishing, with the monograph offering a different and superior way by which an architect could display his credentials and catch the eye of a prospective client. Such a publication was the equivalent of a portfolio giving evidence of applied interest and study of domestic design, demonstrating skills of draughtsmanship and knowledge of a range of styles. Then as now, architectural designs rarely graced the walls of art galleries, buildings were not signed on site, and an alternative form of advertisement was required. In 1859, the reviewer of Samuel Hemming's *Villa and House Architecture* explained the predicament facing architects: 'They are ... accused of not sufficiently valuing the printing-press as a means of spreading their fame abroad, and for disseminating a knowledge of their work. Not a noticeable fraction of those whose approbation he most desires to win can he hope will see his work. It cannot be transported to suit the convenience of amateurs, and they have not the means or the leisure to journey to see it. The mountain will not go to Mahomet, neither will Mahomet go to the mountain'.[10]

At the height of the fashion for historicist revival designs, in the later nineteenth century, sketching the built heritage of yesteryear and assimilating source books became a crucial part of an architect's education. Superb record volumes were produced by the various architectural associations (notably those of Glasgow and Edinburgh) and by winners of bursaries, such as the Pugin Studentship offered by the RIBA. This specifically late nineteenth-century genre can be linked to the publication of idea books asserting the place of architecture in the realm of art and demonstrating the architect's prowess.[11] Hemming's reviewer was especially mindful of the architects' need to record their intentions as engraved evidence was necessary 'to prevent their reputation from being damaged by subsequent travesties and mutilations' by future owners or by the critics of the architectural press.

A more altruistic motive for publishing designs can be found in the reaction to the monotonous, poor quality work of the 'jerry-builders'. The authors considered that swathes of British countryside were being besmirched at the powerful hand of speculative developers, with housing for the middle classes as well as for the working classes. Robinson stated with missionary righteousness that his aim was 'to reform the absence of taste and good feeling which is so manifest in most of our modern buildings, where the aid of an architect has not been sought in creating them'.[12]

John White's *Rural Architecture*, published in 1845 and again in 1857, was intended to conjure up ideas of retirement and retreat from the pressures of city life.[13] While the majority of the designs are essentially 'suburban', he evidently wished to evoke through the title an association with the rural idyll, and to exaggerate the more rustic dimension of a town's periphery in contrast to its core. The Victorian search for intellectual regeneration in beautiful surroundings encouraged the growth of such early suburbs in pastoral locations such as Birnam, yet as they grew, many destroyed the very thing they desired. The author accounted for the variety of the cottage villa designs illustrated (Gothic, Grecian, Italianate, Castellated, typical of the early Victorian period) on the grounds of market demand for each style. *Rural Architecture* was

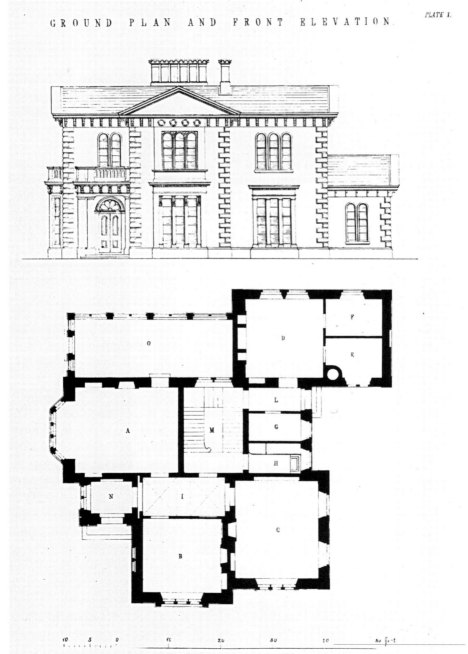

GROUND PLAN AND FRONT ELEVATION.   PLATE I.

Figure 1.
Design for a villa in the 'Italian style' by John White, from Rural Architecture, 1845, *plate xxv, a villa style which he described as 'best adapted for suburban situations where the surrounding scenery is generally more improved by cultivation'.*

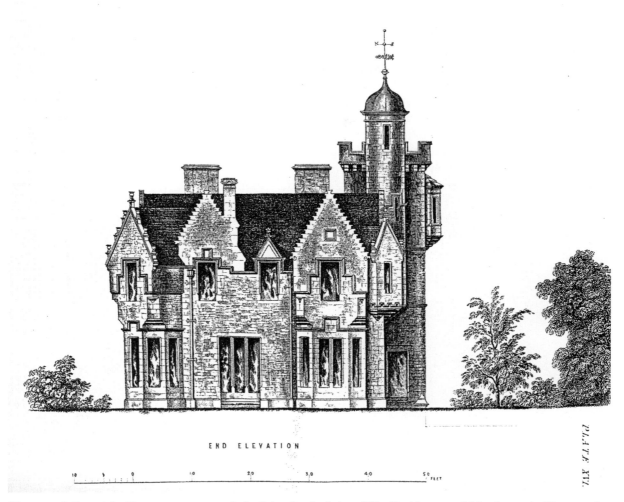

END ELEVATION

PLATE XVI.

Figure 2. A Baronial villa on a generous scale by John Starforth from Villa Residences, 1866, *plate xvi. (Trustees of the National Library of Scotland)*

a transitional work in terms of the breadth of intended audience defined by White, who included himself the author in the definition, as 'Architect and Builder'. It was geared to provide as much information as possible to the operative classes, all offered in plans, elevations, sections and details. The designs were the author's own and, he modestly stated, they were 'not to be less worthy of notice on that account'. He hoped 'to instruct the ignorant and assist the intelligent, in the promotion of a science which has been ever conducive to the comforts and happiness of mankind'. Evidently he was successful in inspiring others, as the influence

of his designs appeared in similar monographs by Gervase Wheeler and Calvert Vaux in America in the 1850s.[14] White advocated the Italianate style for the suburb (see Figure 1), a recommendation seized by many across Scotland, from the Grange district of Edinburgh to Dalkeith's Eskbank and Glasgow's Kelvinside.

Villa Residences, by John Starforth, published in 1866, contained only six designs but these were thoroughly illustrated across forty plates.[15] In contrast to the sixty pages of descriptive text in White's volume, Starforth was brief. It appears that he did not entirely approve of some of the designs he chose to include, noting perhaps disparagingly that they were typical of a client's taste. The fourth design for 'a square house', was described as 'favoured by many to obtain the greatest amount of convenience and comfort at the least cost'. This may be one advantage of the classical form but not necessarily the paramount factor in its favour, as political affiliations may also have had a hand: Gothic was High Tory and High Church, whereas classical was embraced by Whig and Liberal. Nonetheless, such ergonomic considerations showed a farsighted view of the future diminution in scale of suburban design, in sharp contrast to the segregated, sprawling designs advocated by Kerr in his *Gentleman's House*, produced just two years earlier.

In contrast to the reservations on the classic, Starforth's Gothic design was given greater praise, the style commended for producing a highly pleasing picturesque effect. Sympathies with Sir G G Scott's rhetorical question 'Shall we ever have an architecture of our own day?' [16] can be found in Starforth's words accompanying the Scotch Baronial design, '. . . to what extent such a modernising of a style is proper for the advancement of architecture is not within the province of the present work to discuss' (see Figure 2). Yet he continued to 'recommend' the style a quarter of a century later, including it freely in *The Architecture of the Park*.[17] W and G Audsley wrote with similar hesitancy on the Baronial two years later in their book

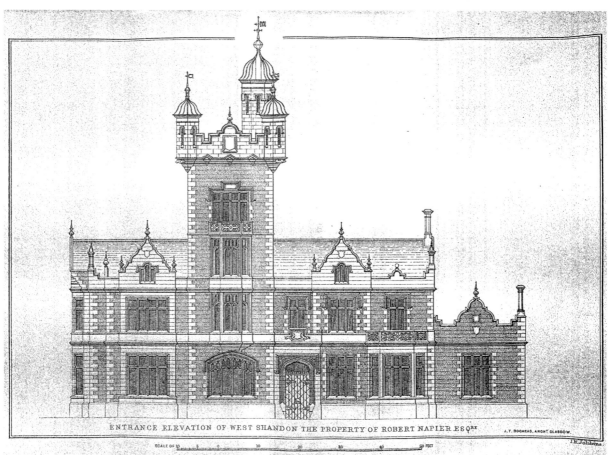

Figure 3. West Shandon House, Gareloch, J T Rochead, from Scott's Executed Examples, *1858, plate xv. Built for Robert Napier Esq. Comparison with Figure 2 proves that the essential form of the villas differed little, as in so many cases, and that the outer clothing, be it Baronial or Tudor Gothic, was purely superficial. (Courtesy of the British Library)*

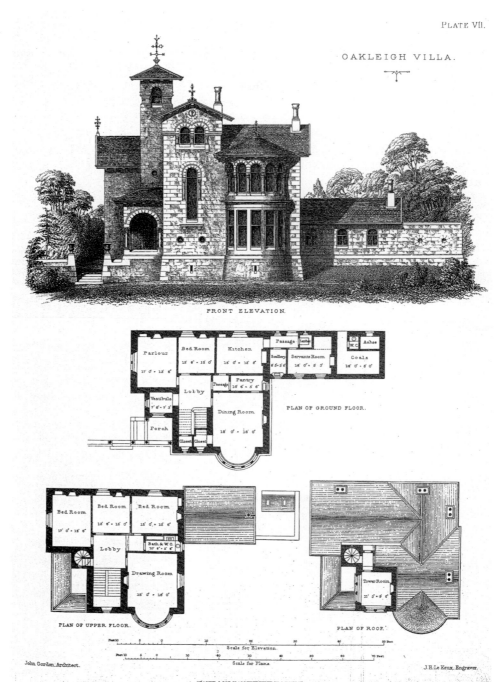

PLATE VII.

OAKLEIGH VILLA.

FRONT ELEVATION.

PLAN OF GROUND FLOOR.

PLAN OF UPPER FLOOR.

PLAN OF ROOF.

Scale for Elevation.

Scale for Plans.

John Gordon Architect.

J.H. Le Keux, Engraver.

of domestic designs, stating that its 'tendency to Classic forms and details is frequently to be observed, but it may be questioned whether this must not be considered rather as an imperfection than as a beauty'.[18] As fellow Goths, this dismissive assessment is not surprising.

Sir George Gilbert Scott provided a turning point in the form of the idea book in his *Executed*

Examples, published in 1858, though this advance was overlooked by Starforth.[19] It was the first of a new kind of higher-minded monograph which gradually assumed the lead in subsequent years. The contents were collated by Sir George Gilbert Scott and comprised carefully chosen designs by a variety of architects, including the author, together demonstrating the vogue for eclectic composition. Scott justified the production of yet another book of designs by explaining that the inclusion of executed designs distinguished his from any previous and made it worthy of consultation. Evidently, the intended audience was the student and the professional library.

Scott's passion for Gothic, particularly Middle Pointed, was given voice in this volume. The suitability of Gothic to domestic design, ecclesiastical by association, was defended energetically. He warmly described J T Rochead's West Shandon House, on the north bank of the Gareloch – which is a pure derivation of Abbotsford – as an 'admixture of Gothic, Tudor and Elizabethan', producing an effect enhanced by its picturesque setting and the freestone from the Kenmure Quarry (see Figure 3). In striking contrast to the earlier technical volumes of the later eighteenth century, the educational remit in this new brand of publication was more cerebral. Scott aimed to make the budding architect aware of the quality of the subjects illustrated, and mindful of their 'character, design and treatment', all of which he considered exemplary and singularly instructive.

Following Scott's lead but aiming at a wider audience, Blackie's *Villa and Cottage Architecture* developed further the educational orientation as this began to take the place of the self-advertising portfolio volumes of earlier years.[20] Published in twenty instalments between 1865 and 1868 on a subscription basis, it was ingeniously financed with controlled print runs matching demand.[21] The compendium volume was one of the most commonly found in the library of an architectural practice in the closing years of the century.[22] It certainly received more reviews than any comparable volume in the field for many years, and while *The Building News* was unduly critical, *The*

Builder was more favourable.[23] The latter welcomed the volume which it could warmly recommend in response to the constant requests from their readership for 'the name of a book containing designs for small houses to assist in settling their ideas, and to enable them to instruct their architect properly'.

Seven of the nineteen practices represented in Blackie's volume came from Scotland, and it is interesting that these contributions particularly caught the eyes of the reviewers. The plan of John Gordon's Italianate Oakleigh Villa (see Figure 4) is met with moderate acceptance by *The Building News*, but the elevations do not fare so well: 'there is one column in the porch which could have got there only out of malice' while the details 'are much too fine for a house of this humble class'. Its popularity could not be denied as this was the design seized by the owner of an iron foundry in Banff as a template for his home, South Colleonard, which followed Gordon's published design closely, down to the plasterwork details of the interior (see Figure 5). The critic's dismissive words on the 'excessive detail' in A and G Thomson's Seymour Lodge

Figure 5. South Colleonard, Banff, taken directly from Gordon's Oakleigh Villa, no doubt seen in Blackie's publication, by the owner of the Banff Foundry who chose to erect the tower in cast-iron plates. (Nicholas Haynes, courtesy of Mrs Laura Wilson)

(OPPOSITE) *Figure 6. Heathery Park, Wishaw, by Alexander Cullen, plate 17 in Nicoll's* Domestic Architecture in Scotland *(1908). Showing the diminutive scale which would populate the later suburbs. It possessed good plasterwork and fine leaded glass to the staircase windows.*

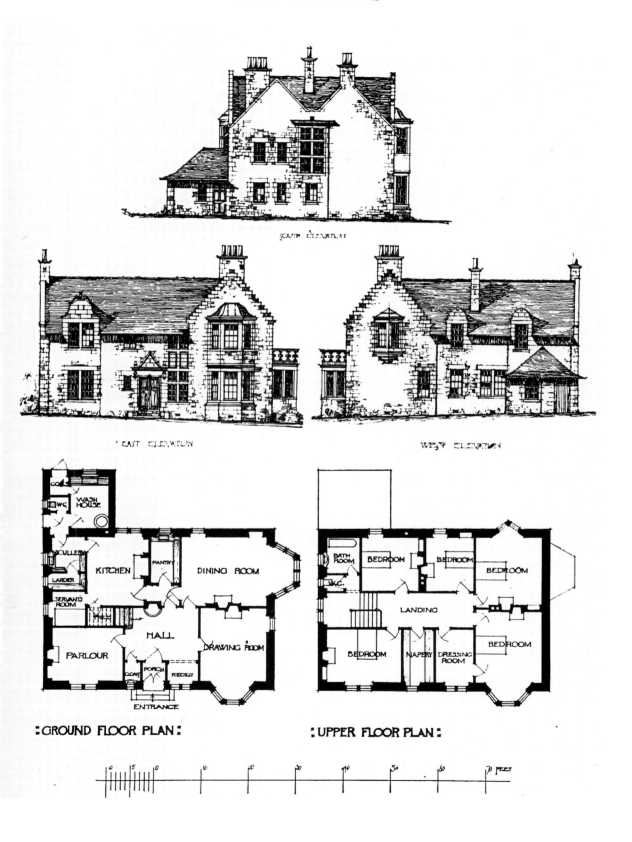

SOUTH ELEVATION

EAST ELEVATION

WEST ELEVATION

:GROUND FLOOR PLAN:

:UPPER FLOOR PLAN:

WC

COALS

WASH HOUSE

SCULLERY

LARDER

SERVANT ROOM

KITCHEN

PANTRY

DINING ROOM

PARLOUR

HALL

DRAWING ROOM

CLOAK

PORCH

RECESS

ENTRANCE

BATH ROOM

WC

BEDROOM

BEDROOM

BEDROOM

LANDING

BEDROOM

NAPERY

DRESSING ROOM

BEDROOM

FEET

foreshadowed first principles of design to emerge in later publications, as encapsulated in C H B Quennell's *Modern Suburban Houses*, with the plan as the prime consideration in conjunction with economy of accommodation and avoidance of unnecessary ornamentation.[24]

That the evolution of this developing kind of 'picture book' was complete by 1908 is evidenced superbly in the publication *Domestic Architecture in Scotland*, edited by James Nicoll.[25] By this date, the rise in living standards meant that more sought and more could afford their own tailored, architect-designed home. In illustrating recent domestic work in Scotland, Nicoll hoped to educate tastes and urge that the traditional, national architecture should not be lost in the wealth of foreign styles and materials then available. He recognised that the passion for individuality in the preceding decades had been a reaction to the speculative builder's excesses, yet warned that it could be at the expense of restraint and good design. While an exponent of Arts and Crafts work, he was not a hard-liner, and tolerated imported materials and modern advances so long as the work harmonised with its surroundings. He acknowledged the realities of the 'servant problem', yet warned against 'anglicising' buildings, perhaps making an obliquely critical reference to Lorimer's aptly named Rustic Cottages in Colinton. Nicoll's introduction discussed technical issues, dismissing the dishonest, such as blinded windows and the lining of render as ashlar, with Puginian conviction. The works illustrated range from smaller suburban country houses such as Fairnalie, to lodge style residences such as Heathery Park (see Figure 6). It is both an admonitory and a thoroughly forward-looking collection of designs, plans and elevations all frequently combined on one page. The majority adhere to sensible tenets akin to those expounded in volume two of Stevenson's *House Architecture* in 1880, together with more contemporary advances, such as the appearance of a cycle shed in several of the houses. This practical focus indicates that the volume was pitched more towards the functional needs of the prospective client than the aesthetic concerns of the professional, or to fill the educational gap in their library as in Scott's case.

By 1914, the building trade faced a restricted economy and the dominance of residential work had given way to public architecture. After the Great War, suburban design and development was influenced more by texts such as Hermann Muthesius's *Das Englische Haus*, 1904–5, and the planning principles of the Garden City movement, than by the picture books of preceding decades. The interest of these volumes, however, remains undiminished by their passing: they reflect the intellectual, recreational and social aspirations of their time and provide a welcome visual record of the realisation of the same. Their role in shaping the character of the suburbs was admittedly more inspirational than seminal – the read-across seen at South Colleonard being exceptional – but it is no less important for that. Their *raison d'être* evolved across the century: the author's self-advancement was undeniably paramount in the picturesque pattern books which continued on from previous generations at the start of Queen Victoria's reign, but this individual motivation gave way gradually to the instructive goal of later monographs which appeared – or wished to appear – to be born rather from a polemical remit, their compilers eager to inform the taste of contemporaries. As photographic illustration increasingly took the place of draughtsmanship in publications such as Shaw Sparrow's *The British Home of Today* and Lawrence Weaver's monographs for *Country Life*,[26] the design concept was distanced from the drawing board in the eyes of the public, an important and accessible outlet for architecture as an art was lost, and there is further cause to regret the demise of the nineteenth-century picture book.

Acknowledgements

The evolution of this article has been assisted invaluably by John H G Archer, Nicholas Haynes, Seán O'Reilly and Anne Riches.

NOTES

1. Sir George Gilbert Scott, *Remarks on Secular and Domestic Architecture* (London, 1858), Preface.
2. Michael McMordie, 'Picturesque Pattern Books and Pre-Victorian Designers', *Architectural History*, vol 18, 1975, pp 43–59.
3. John Archer, *The Literature of British Domestic Architecture* (MIT Press, 1985). Frank Jenkins, 'Nineteenth-Century Architectural Periodicals', in *Concerning Architecture: Essays Printed to Nikolaus Pevsner*, Ed John Summerson, (The Penguin Press, 1968), pp 153–60.
4. John Claudius Loudon, *Encyclopedia of Cottage, Farm and Villa Architecture and Furniture* (Longmans, in 11 or more editions between 1833 to 1883); Robert Kerr, *The Gentleman's House; or how to plan English residences from the parsonage to the palace; with tables of accommodation and cost and a series of selected plates* (1864, 1865 and 1871); John James Stevenson, *House Architecture* (London: Macmillan, 1880), 2 volumes (1 Architecture, 2 House Planning).
5. *The Rudiments of Architecture* was reprinted by Robert Mundell in 1772, with a 3rd edition in 1773, reprinted in London in 1775 , taken over and reprinted by James Dickson and Charles Elliot in 1778 and with a third edition from Dundee in 1799. David Walker charts its history and importance in his introduction to the reprint by Black and Harris, 1992.
6. Howard Colvin, 'The Beginnings of the Architectural Profession in Scotland', in *Architectural History*, vol 29, 1986, pp 168–82. Henry-Russell Hitchcock, *Early Victorian Architecture in Britain*, vol 1 (Yale, 1954), p 425.
7. For example: Lugar, *Villa Architecture* (London, 1828); P F Robinson, *Designs for Ornamental Villas* (London, 1827); E Jones, *Athenian or Grecian Villas* (London, 1835).
8. *The Builder*, November 3, 1866, Books Received, p 822.
9. For the Act, see 46 and 47 Victoria Cap 34, and G Alderman *The Railway Interest* (1973); information courtesy of Dr Malcolm Reed.
10. *Building News*, February 25, 1859.
11. Following this fashion, David M Walker's *Nineteenth Century Mansions in the Dundee Area* (Dundee College of Art, 1958), provided an excellent portfolio of this artist-historian's skills of draughtsmanship and perspective, as well as a valuable record, evidence and inspiration for the future historian, conservation architect or historicist designer.
12. Robinson, from the opening Address in *Ornamental Villas*.
13. John White, *Rural Architecture, Illustrated in a New Series of Designs for Ornamental Cottages and Villas* (Blackie & Son, Glasgow, London, Dublin, 1845, 1857). 90 plates.
14. Hitchcock, *Early Victorian Architecture*, pp 426–7.
15. John Starforth, *Villa Residences: designs for villa residences with descriptions*, (William Blackwood and Sons, Edinburgh and London, 1866). 40 plates.
16. Sir George Gilbert Scott, *Remarks on Secular and Domestic Architecture* (1858), Chapter xii, 'The Architecture of the Future'.
17. Starforth, *The Architecture of the Park* (Edinburgh, 1890), and very much following the form of the earlier *Villa Residences*. 100 plates.
18. W and G Audsley, *Cottage, Lodge and Villa Architecture* (William Mackenzie, London: 1868), p 11.
19. *Executed Examples: of Ecclesiastical and Domestic Structures From the Designs of Modern Architects* by George Gilbert Scott, Architect, and Others, (Atchley & Co, London: 1858). 26 Plates.
20. *Villa and Cottage Architecture: Select Examples of Country and Suburban Residences recently erected by various Architects* (Blackie & Son, London, December 1865–May 1868). 80 plates.
21. Colin MacKellar, 'Printing by Numbers', *The Alexander Thomson Society Newsletter*, No 15, May 1996, pp 8–9.
22. David Walker, 'Scotland and Paris 1874–1887', in *Scotland and Europe: Architecture and Design 1850–1940*, from the series St Andrews Studies in the History of Scottish Architecture, 1991, p 15.
23. *The Builder*, November 3, 1866, pp 822–3. *The Builder*, July 4, 1868, pp 482–3. *The Building News*, September 28, 1866.
24. C H B Quennell, *Modern Suburban Houses* (B T Batsford, London, 1906), Preface.
25. James Nicoll (ed), *Domestic Architecture in Scotland* (Daily Journal Offices, Aberdeen, 1908). 66 plates.
26. W Shaw Sparrow *The British Home of Today* (London, 1904); there are many relevant volumes by Lawrence Weaver, but particularly of note is *Small Country Houses of Today* in various editions from 1910.

14

JOHN R HUME

Building for Transport in Urban Scotland

SINCE the middle of the eighteenth century public transport, and public infrastructure for
privately-owned vehicles, have completely transformed the way we live. As with most
socio-economic changes, this revolution has found
physical expression in new and improved routes,
often carved out of existing urban fabric, or gener-
ating new urban growth. Improved transport,
together with better systems for supplying water
and fuel, and dealing with waste, have been critical
to the development of the modern city. Leaving
aside the routes themselves, with their embank-
ments, cuttings, bridges and viaducts, transport
improvement has been accompanied by the development of specific building types, some rooted in
tradition, others new creations, which have been
designed to accommodate vehicles, passengers and
goods, and the interfaces between them. Such
buildings have featured in much published work,
but generally as part of a broader theme, such as
railway or tramway operation, or the architecture of
a city or region. This article aims to draw together
references to buildings created or modified for use
in connection with transport and to provide an
overview of their evolution.[1] To render the subject
manageable, bridges and viaducts have been excluded, as have buildings connected with shipping.
For clarity, a thematic treatment has been adopted.

Before 1750 wheeled vehicles were rare in Scotland, because of the condition of the roads. The
first stage-coach services started about then, but it
was not until later in the eighteenth century that
more efficient parish administration and turnpike
trusts improved roads sufficiently for coach
services to become widespread. Improved roads
also allowed heavy and bulky goods to be transported efficiently, and thus encouraged agricultural
improvement and industrial growth. Extended systems of cartage allowed a dispersed cotton industry
to grow, between 1780 and 1800, and made it
possible to exploit iron ore resources in relatively
remote places like Wilsontown, Muirkirk and
Shotts. The creation of effective economic hinter-
lands for the more important Scottish settlements,
together with the exploitation of overseas markets,
were powerful forces operating in eighteenth-century Scotland. The built expression of developing
road systems was most obviously seen in the regional centres – the four major cities, plus places
like Stirling, Perth, Dumfries and Ayr – but also
in important intermediate points on major routes,
such as Moffat, Thornhill, Dunkeld, Montrose.
These places all became nodal points on the coaching networks, with inn and stabling accommodation, often provided in the smaller burghs with
landowning support. In Glasgow, the first purpose-
built coaching inn was the Saracen's Head, built
in 1755. The Buck's Head and the Tontine Hotel
(converted in 1781 from an earlier building) followed, and the area round Glasgow Cross became
the focal point for coach services. Equivalent developments included the Tontine Hotel in
Greenock, the Salutation Hotel in Perth and the
Buccleuch Arms in Thornhill, to name only a few.
The first edition large-scale plans of, for instance,
Dumfries, show inns and stabling crammed into
the town centre.

The other characteristic building type of the
coaching era was the tollhouse. This was not in
essence an urban phenomenon, but a few were

Figure 5. The Booking Hall of Waverley Station, Edinburgh, as built in mid-1890s. The hall itself survives, altered at ground-floor level, but the timber booking office and mosaic floor have gone. (RCAHMS)

1880s and 1890s had seen a remarkable rise in the use of railways by the less well-off, and suburban and short-haul services had become very popular (see below). There were not enough platforms in central locations to accommodate this traffic, so only a few years after it had completed a new Bridge Street, the Caledonian radically revised and extended Central Station in Glasgow (1899–1905, Donald Mathieson & James Miller, engineer and architect), and the Glasgow and South Western Railway extended St Enoch (1898–1902, William Melville, engineer). In both these cases, the style of the extension matched the existing station, but Central had a radical revision of its circulating areas, including links with the underground lines.

To increase the capacity of the through lines at Waverley, and the suburban underground systems in Queen Street and Central stations, Glasgow, large inner-suburban terminals were built to accommodate trains used mainly at rush hours. One of these, Leith Central (1898–1903) rivalled the city centre stations in scale and architectural treatment, with its ridge and furrow roof and wrap-round offices and shops. Comparable stations in the Glasgow area, such as Maryhill Central (1896, Robert Wemyss architect), Hyndland (circa 1886, prob J Carswell, engineer) and Bridgeton Central (front 1897–98, Thomson & Turnbull, architects) were less elaborate.

While all these changes were taking place in Edinburgh and Glasgow, Dundee and Aberdeen were being left behind. Dundee's growth as a city slackened after the 1860s, and Aberdeen, compact, at the end of the main trunk system, and not much industrialised, did not experience intense suburbanisation or inter-railway competition. Dundee never got its 'Edwardian' station, and it was not until the second decade of the twentieth century that Aberdeen got its, with the rebuilding and enlarging of the joint station. The clarity and spaciousness of the new station is still striking, all glass and steel behind a low-profile sandstone front (1913–16, J A Parker, engineer). As at Waverley, the booking office was notable for its grandeur.

By the time the Scottish railway companies ceased to exist, in 1923, the country had some of the finest urban stations in Britain, with a sophistication of architectural and functional design all their own. Though reduced in numbers, they still work well in today's much-changed circumstances. The great urban stations, however, did not represent by any means the totality of railway architecture in the cities. Both subsidiary and suburban stations were built in large numbers in Glasgow and in smaller numbers in the other Scottish cities, and railway workshops, goods stations and offices, though not particularly numerous, were often distinctive and conspicuous buildings. Bridges and viaducts, too, formed part of the urban fabric, and were often given care in design beyond technical necessity. Once one moves outside the centres, of course, account must be taken of urban expansion, so that a station or structure may now have a visual context very different from that originally envisaged.

Taking smaller stations first, these were at first rare within present city limits. Current survivors, Pollokshaws West in Glasgow (1847, Neil Robson, engineer) Trinity in Edinburgh (1846, Grainger & Miller, engineers) and West Ferry in Dundee (1838) are basically country stations swamped by urban sprawl. All exhibit limited architectural pretension, and incorporated houses for the agents. In Leith, the Citadel station, in its classical detailing (1846, Grainger & Miller, engineers) is an example of small urban station comparable with, for example, Burntisland. The now-demolished Maryhill Park (1858), with surviving parallels at

Kilpatrick and Cardross, was a very simple building, significantly with a separate house for the agent. It was not really until the 1880s that suburban growth began to generate new railways and new stations, mainly in Glasgow.

On the North side of the Clyde the North British Railway promoted the Glasgow City and District Railway, (opened 1886) underground through the city centre. Its stations had platform buildings of wood, in style distinctive to the parent railway, but surface buildings were stone-built, simple single storey buildings, though the High Street station was slightly more elaborate, and the Hyndland and Bridgeton termini (already mentioned), were Italianate in design. On the south side, the Cathcart District Railway, originally a branch (1886), but turned into a circle in 1894, featured island platforms, suitable for handling short-distance passengers, and economical in staff, with neat wood and glass buildings most were single storey, but two in cutting had footbridge access through an upper floor. Extensions of the Cathcart line to Kirkhill and, ultimately to Ardrossan (strictly the Lanarkshire and Ayrshire Railway) had a mixture of island and two platform stations. The most elaborate minor stations were those on the Glasgow Central and Lanarkshire and Dumbartonshire railways, featuring original and outstanding designs by Sir J J Burnet, James Miller and Robert Wemyss (see Figure 6).

Architectural style was important both for private and public concerns investing in transport improvement in the eighteenth and nineteenth centuries. The intention varied according to location and purpose. In town centres there was some pressure to fit into existing streetscapes so, for example, coaching inns and horse bazaars generally hid their purpose behind unexceptional facades. In other cases the intent was clearly to signal the arrival of a new mode of transport. The classical style was adopted in Glasgow, Greenock and at Edinburgh Haymarket by railway companies between 1840 and 1842. In Paisley a civic tudor style was used, and at Ayr a more losely 'tudor' station was opened in 1839. During the mid and late 1840s railway stations were built in a wide range of styles.

Figure 6. Kelvinside Station, Glasgow, built for the Glasgow Central Railway in 1896, and designed by Sir J J Burnet. This was designed to harmonise with the buildings of Glasgow's most select residential suburb. (John R Hume)

Italianate stations were built on the Edinburgh and Glasgow Railway, the North British Railway, the Edinburgh and Northern Railway and the Highland Railway, and were planned for Caledonian Railway terminals in Glasgow and Edinburgh (see Figure 7), while a vaguely Scottish style was used for stations at Beattock and Lockerbie, and between Larbert and Perth. Simple Italianate styling was also used in some tollhouses, though most of these were more consciously vernacular in construction. As the new modes of transport became more generally accepted, specifically 'railway' or 'tramway' buildings became more general. In the 1880s, and later, timber brick and steel stations became common (see Figure 8). Though many of these were simple structures, some were very elaborate, the apogee being Greenock (Princes Pier) Station. In others, for instance at Troon and

Wemyss Bay, English Arts and Crafts influence was evident. In the large town and city centre stations of the later nineteenth and early twentieth century more explicitly architectural statements were made. Edinburgh Princes Street Station's blowsily French treatment has already been mentioned, and Glasgow Central Station was heavily North European. Glasgow St Enoch was mildly Gothic and Aberdeen Joint was in a simple Beaux Arts style. A clearly industrial aesthetic was developed for tram depots, many of which, in Glasgow, were of brick. Haulage contractors' depots, too, were often 'industrial' in character. The most elaborate, the Kinning Park Cooperative Society's deport in Stanley Street, was heavily Ruskinian in inspiration, but had an 'over the top' charm all its own.

In many instances the architectural treatment

Figure 7. Cupar Station, Fife, a very fine example of an Italianate station. Its scale reflected Cupar's position as county town of Fife. The building included accommodation for station staff, as was common at the time. (John R Hume)

was only skin deep, and behind facades lay innovative iron and steel structures. St Enoch and Queen Street stations in Glasgow and the concourse in Aberdeen Joint station were built with arched overall roofs, and Central, Waverley and Perth had economically designed ridge and furrow roofs. Central's massive trusses are still timelessly impressive.

The designers of transport buildings were in some instances engineers. Thomas Telford, Blyth and Westland and their successors, Donald Matheson of the Caledonian, James Carsewell and his staff on the North British stand out as significant figures, often in partnership with architects. Of architects of recognised standing, Sir William Tite was perhaps the earliest, his Perth station still in part surviving. Sir Robert Rowand Anderson designed the buildings fronting Central Station in Glasgow, and Sir J J Burnet was responsible for

several stations on the Glasgow Central Railway. James Miller was the architect most extensively employed by railway companies, his partnership with Donald Mathieson in Central Station and Wemyss Bay being significant. Other Glasgow architects responsible for transport buildings included Robert Wemyss, Brand & Lithgow, W F McGibbon, and D V Wyllie. William Clark, engineer to Glasgow Corporation Tramways Department designed a series of horse and electric tramway depots of character. The number of transport buildings under construction at any one time could, however, not really justify a high level of specialisation outside the railway themselves, and only James Miller could be said to be a specialist, among the architects.

The impact of buildings for transport on urban communities was seldom dramatic; indeed the intention was generally to harmonise with existing

Figure 8. Oban Station, opened in 1880 by the Callander and Oban Railway. A timber building (originally varnished) with an iron-framed roof, the station was considered an ornament to the town when it was completed. It was demolished in the 1980s. (John R Hume)

patterns of urban building (see Figures 4 and 6). Railway hotels were the most insistent, their sheer bulk dominating both streetscapes and wider townscapes. The larger passenger and goods stations could also be impressive, as at High Street and College, Glasgow and in Perth, Dundee and Aberdeen, but their visual impact was often limited by out-of-centre locations. The sheer bulk and land area occupied by transport facilities of all kinds but especially of railways was seldom evident before aerial photography, the limited linear experience of individual travellers obscuring these enormous interventions in town and city plans. What these buildings lacked in streetscape statement, however, they often offered in distinctive, even dramatic, experiences: the gloomy gothic of Glasgow St Enoch was a never-to-be-forgotten experience. But the more modest, less assertive buildings make their contribution, too, adding significantly to the rich mix of architectural styles and building types which make up the Scottish urban experience. Their numbers are now sadly depleted: we should conserve the best, and add new ones of distinction – and distinctiveness – when opportunity offers. Why not architectural-award winning filling stations and car showrooms?

NOTES

1. References to individual buildings are in general taken from the author's *Industrial Archaeology of Glasgow* (Glasgow, 1974), from his two volume *Industrial Archaeology of Scotland* (London, 1976 and 1977), and from Colin Johnston and John R Hume, *Glasgow Stations* (Newton Abbot, 1979). Information has also been taken from the Buildings of Scotland and RIAS guides series. To footnote these in detail would not make reference significantly easier. The general context of transport in Victorian urban Scotland is discussed in the author's article 'Transport and Towns in Victorian Scotland', in George Gordon and Brian Dicks (eds), *Scottish Urban History* Aberdeen, 1983.

   This article contains in its references a fairly complete bibliography of books and articles in this general area. Perhaps the most important addition to the literature since 1983 is John Thomas and David Turnock, *A Regional History of the Railways of Great Britain*, Vol 15 (North of Scotland, Newton Abbot, 1989). Many of the railway stations mentioned are illustrated in the author's contribution to Gordon Biddle and O S Nock, *The Railway Heritage of Britain*, (London, 1983). Other, earlier, views appear in the extensive railway enthusiast literature of which O S Nock, *The Caledonian Railway* (London, circa 1961) and Peter Tatlow, *Highland Miscellany* (Poole, 1985) are particularly useful. The startling balloon roof of the first Princes Street Station, Edinburgh, is shown in a photograph in the possession of Eric Lomax.

2. Elizabeth Whitfeld, 'Victorian Mews in Edinburgh', in *Studies in Scottish Antiquity*, Ed D Breeze (Edinburgh, 1984).

15

MILES GLENDINNING

The Ballantyne Report:
A '1917 Revolution' in Scottish Housing

... the duty of the nation to undertake the great work of providing decent homes for the citizens of a great Empire. (Ballantyne Report, p 6)

AROUND the turn of the century, Western Europe was swept by a reaction away from unfettered capitalism, and towards State-directed discipline – a revolution in the nature of social and economic modernity, which transcended the social classes, uniting professional reformists and working-class activists. One of the key battlegrounds of this transformation was urban housing. The old, dense, mixed-together dwellings in which many lived, were now widely regarded as one of the sharpest indictments against laissez-faire society. In most countries, the State began to intervene, harnessing the previously unco-ordinated system of speculative provision by controlling rent levels, establishing production 'standards' in accordance with criteria of 'need', and encouraging construction of lower-density dwellings in which functions and occupants were more highly segregated. The resulting system, in most cases, proved highly stable, even through wars and political upheaval: the Netherlands' pioneering 1901 Housing Law, for example, stayed almost unchanged until the mid 1960s.

There were, however, wide variations between countries in the manner, and degree, of State intervention in housing. In most cases, the main State rôle was to subsidise and regulate, while actual provision remained with private agencies, co-operatives or societies. In a few cases, there was a much more forcefully interventionist policy, in which the State itself began to assume the lead rôle in actually building and owning social housing – something more popularly associated, today, with the post-1945 'communist bloc'. In the West, Scotland was the only country which adopted such a policy of revolutionary rather than evolutionary change in social housing.

The main driving force for this change in early twentieth-century Scotland lay at working-class level, in the unique passion, and political strength, of anti-landlordism – the result of a combination of harsh letting regulations in the cities, and the hatred of rural landowners by immigrants from the Highlands and Ireland. When brought to boiling point in the emergency climate of wartime, the pent-up force of anti-landlordism began to sweep away the foundations of the private housing system. In 1915, rent strikes by Clydeside munitions workers pressurised the Government into imposing crippling rent controls on the private housing market. After the war, the latter was gradually asphyxiated: by the 1940s and 50s, while less than 1% of new housing in Belgium or 3% in Denmark, for instance, was built by public agencies, in Scotland around 80% of new dwellings were built and owned by the state (largely in the form of local authorities), and subject to highly politicised policy-making, focused on demands for ever higher 'output'.

The Ballantyne Commission and the Ideology of Housing Reform

This radical policy change was not made possible solely by the political muscle of skilled workers. Its emergence was supported and legitimised by the ideological arguments of reformist, anti-capitalist factions *within* the ruling classes. What is most remarkable, and provides the reason for our title – the '1917 Revolution' of housing – is that both the key argumentation, and the policy thrust, of this ideological reformism were combined in one single document, issued in that year. A document which, even more remarkably, was an official Government publication: the Report of the Royal Commission on the Housing of the Industrial Population of Scotland (Cd 8731: hereafter referred to as the 'Ballantyne Report' after its chairman).

The Ballantyne Commission had been set up in 1912 to examine housing conditions in mining areas: already, even before the war, there had been official fears that Scottish housing could cause 'industrial unrest'.[1] But in the wartime climate of emergency and heady national 'community', its remit was expanded to that of a national survey. By the time it reported, in 1917, the rent strikers had already delivered their body-blow to the pre-war system, leaving Ballantyne in the role of executioner. The Report's influence on subsequent debate was so pervasive that it has traditionally been viewed by policy-makers and even historians in uncritical, even eulogistic terms. Only recently has this self-confirming argumentation become undermined, with the decline in the cohesion and legitimacy of State corporatism from the 1970s.

The purpose of this article is to sketch out a reassessment of the Ballantyne Report and its legacy – to try and pinpoint more precisely its social and political context, and its role, in the great battlefield of Scottish housing. In terms of social class, we will find that Ballantyne articulated the waxing power of a new class of professional officals dedicated to Utopian and 'social' ideals, skilfully deploying technical-hygienic arguments alongside moral and political appeals to 'national community', in order to defeat the localised, small-capitalist concerns of landlords and traditional urban property interests. And in these new arguments of 'national solidarity', the autonomous, but in some respects subsidiary position of Scottish society within the British state, was also expressed. This was an unprecedentedly daring bid to create an entirely new area of Scottish social policy, conceived in explicit terms of national community. Yet paradoxically, it was justified by an argument dependent on claims of Scottish housing's 'inferiority' in relation to English patterns.

'Standards', 'Shortages' and the Definition of the Scottish 'Housing Problem'

The central message of the Ballantyne Report was that Scottish working-class housing up to 1914 had comprehensively 'failed', in both its quantity and its quality. Qualitatively, because what had been provided fell below acceptable 'standards'; and quantitatively, because this deficiency had created a huge 'shortage' of satisfactory houses, which could not be remedied by the previously dominant agency of provision – private building. On this basis the Report concluded that the existing system, organisation and architecture alike, should be jettisoned, and replaced by radically different patterns.

What we are chiefly concerned with in this article is how the 'poor quality' of Scottish housing was defined, and what use was made of that definition. We begin with a broad generalisation, that contemporary European reformist debates about the physical form of housing claimed that there were three main types of qualitative deficiencies: dilapidation; lack of basic facilities; and cramped conditions. Of these, Ballantyne's analysis focused overwhelmingly on the third. Its argumentation comprised a mixture of reformist medical and moral arguments against dense housing, of a sort which were familiar all over Europe, with a highly specific polarisation between simplified 'recipes' of 'bad' Scottish and 'good' English housing, taking in not only room size and arrangement, but type and layout of dwelling-blocks as a whole.

'Life in One Room'

'Overcrowding' was identified as the *special* housing problem of Scotland, and its persistence, therefore, as the key qualitative 'failure' of Scottish private-enterprise provision. It was defined through a complex analysis, which closely integrated the general and scientific (in the form of statistical tabulations of the effects of 'crowding') with the particular and shocking (in the form of case studies grounded in the nineteenth-century reformist-journalistic tradition of slum reportage). Both statistics and case studies were characterised by a striking dichotomy of treatment. In the foreground were investigations into the medical/hygienic implications of housing density, and into the practical aspects of life in working-class dwellings. But in the background, pervading the slum tableaux, was a different concern: with the supposed risk of proletarian immorality and disorder, and its control through increased segregation and openness.

'Overcrowding' was defined in two related ways. The first was the 'crowding' of dwellings on a piece of urban land, or within a block. This was attributed chiefly to the building of dense tenement blocks, whose alleged social disadvantages the Report emphasised. For instance, in the area of housework, it was concluded that the awkwardness of living in an upstairs house outweighed the convenience of a dwelling all on one floor. And it was claimed that the tenement was a completely unsuitable place for children: piteous tableaux were related of their 'sad attempts to play' in the stairs and back courts.[2]

The emotional temperature rose noticeably when Ballantyne went on to consider the 'crowding' or lack of segregation of people *within* dwellings or particular parts of dwellings. Two linked issues arose here. The first was the question of how living space was to be measured.[3] Here Ballantyne advocated a move away from the system prevalent here (and on the Continent) – namely, measurement by undivided cubic volume or square area – towards a system used in England, of measurement by number of rooms. The latter seemed more attuned to a policy of increased segregation of activities: 'The question naturally occurs whether the ample cubic space allotted to a two room house might not have been redistributed so as to provide the additional privacy and convenience of ... three rooms.'

Then, there was the question of how space was used. Here, from the fact that the Report's overt argumentation concentrated on medical matters, one might have expected its detailed investigation to concentrate on cooking, plumbing, sanitation, and ventilation. But instead, for reasons we shall discuss in a minute, the focus was firmly on sleeping arrangements. The normal sleeping provision in new Scots working-class houses in the late nineteenth and early twentieth centuries – internal bed-closets or bed-recesses adjoining kitchen or living rooms – achieved a partial segregation of sleeping from living and cooking, while maximising the proportion of living to sleeping space. Ballantyne, however, branded the 'national partiality for the box bed'[4] as an extreme of communalism in living-arrangements, preferring 'warmth ... to floorspace and light'.

The Report's investigation of the special national malaise of 'overcrowding' reached its symbolic climax in chapter 11, entitled 'Life in One Room'. Here, the medical argumentation was rammed home through a potent mixture of disease statistics (especially regarding tuberculosis and phthisis) and declamatory statements about child mortality. For example: 'When the family passes into the one-roomed house, the children enter the valley of the shadow of death'. Ballantyne attacked the one-room house, or 'single-end', on two medical grounds: first, that it facilitated the spread of infection through sputum; and second (rather curiously, in view of its high ceiling), that it inhibited the 'open-air treatment' of pre-antibiotics days. There was no attempt to distinguish between old and new dwellings, or, for that matter, to systematically filter out other social-economic factors associated with disease. The difficulty of establishing any direct cause-effect link between disease and occupancy was noted in the evidence of several key Medical Officers, such as those of

Aberdeen, Dundee or Renfrewshire. But their unglamorous argumentation was overshadowed by the invective of Glasgow's Medical Officers, such as Dr Russell, who flatly stated that 'it is these small houses which produce the high death rate of Glasgow'.[5]

Despite the detail and passion of these medical set piece arguments, the biggest bogeyman in the Report's critique of 'Life in One Room' was not disease, but the middle-class fear of working-class social disorder and promiscuity, and above all of incest. Here, the emphasis on the role of class and the physical environment in encouraging deviant behaviour contrasts with the 1990s concept of 'child abuse', with its assumption of individual responsibility, and its reliance on criminal-law sanctions. 'The one-room house,' Ballantyne thundered, 'lies on the extreme margin of industrial civilisation ... life in one room is incompatible with family decency; it is incapable of affording conditions for a healthy or moral family life ... How can you live and preserve "the white flower of a blameless life" – in one room?' Some groups, such as single people, might find the single-end a 'wholesome' house, but, the Report insisted, 'these are the anomalies of life ... a home in the proper sense of the word, a place for the nurture of a family, it can never be.'[6] Moreover, these groups posed a further moral threat: that of vagrancy, encouraged by other dwelling types such as the subdivided 'farmed out' house, the common lodging house, and (in rural areas) the bothy.

'Value for Money': The Link Between 'Quality' and 'Quantity'

Having concluded that Scottish housing was badly deficient in quality, Ballantyne then went on to argue that it had also failed in quantity, through an inability to build enough houses. The starting-point of this argument was a deep slump in housing production that had occurred in the years before the war. Ballantyne claimed that this was a permanent, structural decline: private enterprise had become 'unable to house' the working classes – or, at any rate, to do so at affordable rents. But as there had not only been a glut of vacant houses,

and falling rents, as recently as 1910, but also substantial pre-1914 improvements in the very 'standards' emphasised by Ballantyne (eg, as we will see, a reduction in the proportion of one-roomed houses) the resulting formulation of private enterprise's 'failure' had to be rather complicated.[7] This had been a 'failure ... to keep pace with the steadily rising demand for more and better house room'. In other words, it had been not an absolute but a relative failure. The Report even went so far as to suggest that, as pre-war houses had been so comprehensively deficient, high pre-war output had in some ways actually been a bad thing!

What was the cause of this relative 'failure' of output? The key causes identified were the 'instability' of speculative building, and the 'rapacity' of property owners.[8] These, it was asserted, had inflated ground rents, and thus had pushed overall costs up and standards down. Evidence that the proportion of ground rents to total rents was frequently quite small, was countered by the distinctly circular argument of 'value for money':[9] 'The price paid and value received cannot be separated ... directly the working-class occupier has to pay such prices for the use of a site, he does not get anything like value for his money ... on the contrary, the high cost of land has resulted in him and his family living under congested and unhealthy conditions as to air, space and light'. Longer-term, structural deficiencies were also identified, including the legal framework of the feuing system. Ballantyne claimed (chapter 22) that this had caused people to build too densely and expensively – although a sideways glance at the even denser tenement patterns built under different legal systems on the Continent might have suggested a more cautious formulation of that claim.

Social Utopianism and Professional Power

As is clear from the extreme complexity of this definition of relative quantitative 'failure', this was not an argument about building economics and organisation, but another element in the social-Utopian assault on laissez-faire provision. In that context, its complex formulation would prove to be of great potency. It gave official backing to a concept of the cause-effect relationship between 'standards' and 'shortages', which would dominate Scottish housing discourses throughout most of the twentieth century, and would sustain the mass politicisation of the housing question. This startling Government endorsement of a radical social interventionist policy was made possible by an equally dramatic shift of power and ideology within the ruling classes concerning housing.

The demands for greater segregation and density-reduction in working-class dwellings ultimately stemmed from innovations of the rich, during the feudal era. For example, as far back as the palaces of James IV around 1500, monarchs and landowners had begun to reject communal, semi-public sleeping habits in favour of specialised bedchambers. But only with the development of urban mass society in the nineteenth century did the ruling classes become seriously concerned about controlling, or policing, the spread of those processes. In the turn-of-century years of revulsion against uncontrolled capitalism, the initiative was taken not by the 'old' rich but by the increasingly elaborate networks of professional groups and voluntary reformists, attempting to propagate bourgeois concepts of residential stability, domestic self-containedness, and hygiene among the working class, within an ideology of collective or 'national' social solidarity.

Within the burgh police (or, from the late nineteenth-century, municipal) framework, Dean of Guild building inspectors had long controlled the layout of tenements' surroundings, and the internal planning of the block or the dwelling. Their aim, like Ballantyne's, was to reduce densities of tenements on sites, and of houses within tenements, and to increase self-containment of, and within, dwellings. Hygienic initiatives inside dwellings focused on the conversion of enclosed bed-closets to ventilated recesses (a move which paradoxically, in some ways, diminished segregation) and provision of sanitary facilities.

By the turn of the century, the scope of Scottish municipal official intervention had begun to extend into large slum-clearance schemes, and even direct rehousing – a 'municipal socialism' which was unparalleled in the developed world. These increased municipal efforts were spurred on further by the lobbying of a new and more passionate kind of housing and urban reformist, who applied a fresh, declamatory language to social questions such as housing by lobbyists and officials alike. Across Europe, this rhetoric of Utopian 'national community' contrasted with the technical language of the old sanitary regulations, and anticipated the mass idealist doctrines of the twentieth century, such as Socialism and Nationalism. Often, in housing reform, it was bolstered by anti-tenement rhetoric. But what was unique about Scotland, and Ballantyne, was that this rhetoric was adopted wholesale as Government policy.

The Ballantyne Report, and especially the 'Life in One Room' chapter, represented an extreme of the endorsement of the new kind of socio-ethical argumentation by reform-minded public officials. People such as municipal officers, doctors and housing reformists were dominant in the Commission's membership and choice of witnesses, while speculative builders, landlords and local capitalists (as well as tenants themselves) were virtually excluded. By comparison with the reformists' powerful mixture of statistics and invective, the evidence of the few small capitalist contributors seemed dry and bumbling. Ballantyne's language suggested that, in the official view, the latter had already been written out of the script, to an extent unparalleled in Europe: the Committee stated flatly that 'housing is, in our view, primarily a department or section of public health administration'.[10]

'Scottish House' and 'English House'

The vehemence of the Report's Utopian polemic on Scottish housing was accentuated by the prominence given to an unfavourable comparison of Scottish and English housing patterns. This comparison, although presented as a simple, strong contrast, was in fact rather a complex and anomalous one.

The Scottish pole of the Ballantyne antithesis was provided chiefly by a simplified definition of the tenement: 'the deliberately erected tenement' ... 'so different from the two-storey self-contained cottages in English towns'.[11] In the density of building, the tenement was cast as an unrelieved human ant-hill. And the intermixing of slum vignettes with discussion of the attributes of new dwellings, had a subtle effect of stigmatising the latter along with the former. Defined as it was through polarisation and simplification, Ballantyne's picture of the Scottish House was a homogeneous one, devoid of significant chronological or geographical distinctions: 'the similarity, or even identity ... which marks the housing problem in the towns of Scotland'.[12]

Its counterpart, the English House, was defined through a corresponding process, which lumped together favourable statistics, derived from pre-1914 housing patterns which no-one was suggesting should be copied, with a new image, the Garden Suburb cottage, which no-one had worked out how to build cheaply here.

The first, chiefly statistical element in Ballantyne's 'English House' definition was provided by the pre-1914 'byelaw' working-class housing of England, Wales and Ireland. Dwellings were thinly and cheaply built in brick, and arranged in horizontal lines at a relatively low density, in a way which maximised privacy, with self-contained access and yard/garden. Internally, the four-roomed English 'two up two down', with its floor space of around 500 sq ft and its 8ft ceilings, often contained about the same cubic volume as the 2-apartment Scots tenement house, and necessitated an internal staircase; but its small rooms afforded greater privacy and specialisation. However, its cheap, self-regulating construction depended on a reversionary system of tenure ('leasehold') which neither Ballantyne nor previous commentators were prepared to countenance in Scotland.[13]

The other, far more visually prominent element in the 'English House' definition was the new 'garden suburb' pattern of detached cottages in a leafy setting. Although originally an English and American invention of the late nineteenth century, by 1912–17 the garden suburb had become an inter-national fashion among housing reformers. For example, Patrick Geddes toured German and English examples in 1909, and on his return predicted that 'the cottages of the coming garden suburbs' must gradually supersede the 'evil Continental tradition of walled cities and crowded population.'[14] But early examples showed that, if built in conformity with existing Scottish or Continental building standards, the rents of garden suburb cottages would be far too high for ordinary workers. Ballantyne deprecated the solidity of tenement-based standards, claiming that, as a result, tenants paid higher rents for poorer accommodation; but, in the end, they only recommended token adjustments (chapter 21). Nobody, now or later, would seriously contemplate dismantling the nation's building standards, and so the cottage suburb remained an expensive, rather than cheap form of housing.

Thus the Report seemed to suggest that the real choice facing the nation was between old, overcrowded Scottish slums and new, English garden suburbs – a simplified and in some ways mischevious comparison, based on the conflation of new dwellings occupied as intended, with old, sublet or in other ways outmoded types. In view of these anomalies, why was the Scottish-English small house comparison made a central feature of Ballantyne's argument? At a tactical level, there were obvious advantages in using arguments comprehensible in England, given that the two countries shared a common government, and that the main aim of the Report was a huge expansion of governmental activity. But even in the areas of the organisation and physical form of their housing, there were features which set both Scotland and England apart from that of the Continent. Some common features seemed to stem from the early and comprehensive adoption of capitalism by both countries: these included the building of specialised residential areas at high speed by speculative builders; and the use of materials (whether ashlar or brick), and architectural 'terrace' styles, which emphasised uniformity and an almost industrial modernity. Others seemed to be influenced by maritime climate, notably the (by

Continental standards) obsessive preoccupation with openness and ventilation: this emerged in features such as the external drainage systems, the sash windows, the retention of open fires rather than stoves (with consequent proliferation of chimney-pots), and the avoidance of deep-courtyard layouts. Even internally, the Scottish use of partitioned recesses and subdivisions within rooms was, in some ways, closer to small English rooms than to large, undifferentiated Continental rooms.

If Ballantyne had chosen to compare Scottish housing not with England but with prominent continental countries, what might have seemed remarkable was how far 'ahead' Scotland was in density reduction.[15] Before 1914, through normal capitalist processes, including a glut of vacant single-ends and two-apartments (and consequent falling rents), the emphasis of production was beginning to shift to larger dwellings. In Clydebank, the archetypal 'new tenement town', in 1911 17% of the burgh's 8,747 dwellings were one-roomed, 63% two-roomed and 15% three-roomed. In Glasgow, the average number of rooms was steadily rising, and the percentage of households living in single-ends had dropped from 26% in 1891 to 21% in 1901. By comparison, in 1910, 25% of Paris households lived in one room, as did 34% of those in Brussels. In Germany, with its deep, dense '*Mietskasernen*', the difference was even more marked: in 1901, the percentage of households living in one-room dwellings in Berlin (50%) was actually *higher* than that in 1861! By comparison to the high site coverage and small internal courts or lightwells of Berlin or New York tenements, the ribbon-like street-block perimeter layouts of Scotland seemed almost absurdly low in density. The closest overseas comparison to these 'row house' tenements (as well as to the use of bed recesses for internal subdivision) was probably the Netherlands, which also, interestingly, followed a similar path in the reduction of the proportion of one-roomed dwellings: from 28% in 1899 to 19% in 1909.

To us, today, a European comparison seems the natural approach in a cultural or social area such as housing. But for 'Imperial Scotland' during World War I, a comparison with England was arguably more straightforward and useful.

Recommendations

The Report's analysis led to a trenchant conclusion: that the prevalent system of provision should be abandoned, in favour of local authorities taking direct responsibility for production and, where necessary, building directly on a large scale.[16]

A dissentient minority's report (the 'Lovat Report') warned that such 'an attack upon the largest source of supply, the one which ... has supplied 99 per cent of the total houses built ... can only be recommended by those who see no objection to municipal building of small houses becoming a monopoly'.[17] They warned the majority not to become carried away, on a wartime wave of communitarian excitement, into recommending 'forms of State action, which might have the result of stereotyping the conditions of an abnormal period'. But the majority insisted that the present system was not only morally suspect but inefficient and unreliable: 'the nation cannot afford to act on anything but a certainty.'

In the physical form of housing, too, the Commission majority group saw the wartime emergency as a catharsis: 'It is only now that the nation has had the means of discovering how far Scotland has been left behind, and by what poor standards the housing of her working classes has been measured'.[18] Here, there was also to be revolution, with new 'standards' to reduce 'overcrowding' of both dwellings and sites. Reform of the 'small dwelling' was crucial: 'the policy adopted for dealing with the one-room house will determine, in large measure, the general housing policy of the country.'[19] Ballantyne demanded that the building of new single-ends should be forbidden, as should that of even two-roomed houses, other than 'in exceptional circumstances'. Statutory room size minima should be adjusted to encourage more but smaller rooms – a recommendation to which we shall return later. New flats should only be built in two or three storey form, or, better still, phased out in favour of cottages. Likewise, the land law system should be altered, and town planning restrictions introduced, to make available suburban building land for low-density cottage development.

The Ballantyne Legacy: Housing Finance and Organisation

Thus the Ballantyne Report demanded a revolution in the organisation, and in the form, of Scottish housing. As it turned out, however, the two areas saw different outcomes. Within housing organisation and tenure, the results were revolutionary. The private market, already disorientated by rent control, was further undermined by the beginning of a national programme of direct municipal building in 1919 – a programme at first directed towards better-off workers and the middle class (previously catered for by new private building), but which within four years had begun to include building of new dwellings for slum 'displacees' (previously housed in old, 'filtered down' dwellings). The entire structure of private provision, from 'top' to 'bottom', was shadowed and increasingly replaced by new municipal building.

This was not, however, a revolution that happened overnight. At first, large-scale building was confined to the cities and large burghs, and, even there, there were counter-trends, notably Edinburgh Corporation's vigorous inter-war attempts to promote private building; rural public housing did not begin in earnest until the 1930s. Within urban building, the rise of the Labour Party to municipal power in Glasgow and elsewhere added the factor of local political patronage and (through 'direct labour' building) employment to the equation. By the 1940s and 50s, the revolution was complete: urban working-class housing had been converted from a fragmented product of cumulative small decisions into a co-ordinated, aggressively politicised programme, driven by concepts such as 'needs' or 'standards' and fuelled by mounting demands for higher 'output' of new dwellings.

Over these decades, the Ballantyne ideology of Scottish housing 'inferiority', and supporting demands for 'special treatment', proved to be a very effective way of persuading English politicians to acquiesce in this huge expansion of Scottish state activity. And, in a quirk of history, the emergency conditions of war ensured not only that this strategy of state intervention in housing would enjoy success in Scotland, but that, in the chaotic aftermath of the rent strikes, it would be grasped at by the Government as a short-term vehicle for housing reform in England as well. From the 1920s onwards, English housing saw repeated attempts to return to 'normal conditions' of private building, creating in effect a new Scottish-English divergence in social policy.

Within Scotland, Ballantyne's formulation of the 'problem' of Scottish housing had more pervasive ideological effects. It inspired several generations of housing research and propaganda grounded in constantly shifting 'league table' statistical comparisons with England and resultant, ever-rising estimates of 'shortage'. The highly politicised structure of Scottish social housing policy was supported by two stout columns erected by Ballantyne, one above the other. At the base, the concept of Scottish 'bad housing'; above, the demand for higher subsidies and escalating State action. This ideology was shared and understood across the whole social housing system, from the slum-dweller lobbying her councillor for rehousing, to the government minister formulating state policy. In 1971, for example, the Labour politician William Ross, speaking of 'the tradition of Scottish housing finance', argued that 'one of the great responsibilities of a Secretary of State for Scotland is to convince his Cabinet colleagues that the Scottish housing position is very much worse than the English one and that the whole position is different'. (*Hansard*, 16–12–71) By those charged with safeguarding this 'tradition', the Ballantyne Report itself came to be viewed with increasing veneration. To them, it was *the* key legitimatory text – a great beacon which had signalled the way to 'better housing'.

The Ballantyne Legacy: Housing Architecture

Considering Ballantyne's trenchant criticisms of the physical patterns of Scottish housing, its impact on those patterns was surprisingly complex, even

expectations of the vast majority of the Dundee working population.[12]

The mild controversy this argument provoked when it was aired at the 1916 Scottish National Housing Congress[13] seems, however, to have unnerved Thomson, whose assertion that Dundee Town Council would have 'nothing to do' with cottages undoubtedly overstated Corporation hostility to the format.[14] Whatever the reason, his stance was modified less than a year later when, in a paper to the Incorporated Sanitary Association of Scotland, he took care to distance himself from an outright rejection of cottage accommodation, which was now conceded as offering an 'almost ideal mode of living', leading to the recommendation that the aim of the Scottish local authorities should not lie in the 'erection of cottages alone or of tenements alone', but in 'the provision of both'.[15]

Thomson's earlier experiments in tenement design had included plans for an 'experimental block of Model-Dwelling houses' in the Blackscroft area,

drawn up on behalf of the Corporation in March 1907. He explained its arrangement as follows:

The proposed block ... would be four storeys in height. On each floor there would be 6 houses, making in all 24 dwellings. Each house would consist of a Living Room 14 feet by 11 feet, in connection with which, and without encroachment on the floor space of the room, there would be a small bedchamber screened off from the Living Room by a partition 7 feet high, and sufficiently large to accommodate a full-sized and smaller bed or cot for children ... On each floor, ie, for every six tenants, there would be provided one washing house, one bathroom, and two water-closets. The bathrooms would each be fitted with an instantaneous water heater connected up and gas supply through a halfpenny-in-the-slot meter, and thus any tenant would be able to obtain a hot bath for a halfpenny, that being the value of the gas required to heat water for one bath. The houses would be

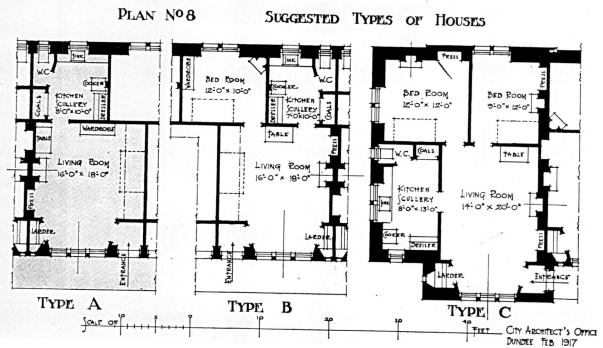

Figure 2. Specimen one, two and three apartment house plans for the Logie, Springhill and Stirling Park schemes, Dundee, contained on James Thomson's Report on the 'selection of land suitable for the Housing of the Working Classes' (1917), Dundee City Archives.

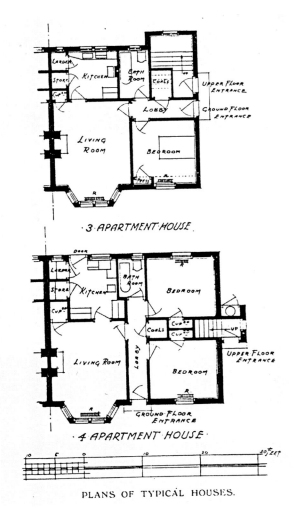

· 3 · APARTMENT · HOUSE ·

· 4 · APARTMENT · HOUSE ·

PLANS OF TYPICAL HOUSES.

Figure 3. 'Typical' plans, adopted in the final Logie scheme. The standard of accommodation provided has been exaggerated in both cases, by the inclusion of the kitchen in the 'apartment' count. From Dundee Town Council's Souvenir of the Opening of the Logie Scheme *(1920, Dundee Central Library).*

erected substantially, furnished internally in the plainest possible way, lighted by exceptionally large windows and ventilated automatically.[16]

The level of accommodation aimed at in 1917 similarly promised all 'proper facilities and con-veniences', which now extended to the provision, in individual dwellings, of an internal water-closet, and the supply of hot water and central heating from a communal boiler. In contrast to the 1907

proposals, the 1917 blocks were to be restricted to a height of two storeys, and arranged in 'short lengths' with a generous provision of shared ground to front, side and rear, and so aligned 'that the sun will reach during a part of every day, the windows of all habitable rooms'. Similarly, 'the erection of wash houses and cellars, usual in the back space of tenements', was to be entirely omit-ted', and the intervening areas 'kept free from outbuildings [and] boundary walls', thereby en-hancing a 'free flow of air and admission of sunlight'.[17]

These proposals paraphrased qualifications placed on the provision of tenement accommoda-tion in the Royal Commission Report on the *Housing of the Industrial Population of Scotland, Rural and Urban* (1917),[18] to which Thomson had contributed,[19] again suggesting that his concern now lay in reaching a workable compromise with mainstream reformist experiments. Still further evidence in this respect is provided by his descrip-tion of the 'modified' blocks, as a 'happy mean' between the 'former barrack-like Tenement' and 'modern Cottage', and his contention that these could be supplied with 'all the qualities and equip-ment' of their cottage counterparts:

Tenements of this description are essential in most industrial communities ... The tenant may in many instances be a single woman, or two sisters, or a widow, or an elderly couple; and it surely could not be suggested that any one of this class of tenant should be placed in a cottage which could neither be furnished nor used by the occupier. Yet there is no reason why these persons should not enjoy most of the advantages of cottage dwellings in their tenement houses, and it is with that object in view that the housing problem is being dealt with in Dundee. The disadvantages and dangers of the old style of tenement will disappear, and the advantages and pleasures of the new type of tenement will, it is hoped, be provided by the erection of houses of a size for which the workers can afford to pay and which they can enjoy equally well as though they were housed in cottage dwellings.[20]

Further concessions followed, prompted by Thomson's consultations with the Tudor Walters Committee and, more directly, the pressures brought to bear on the Council by an increasingly assertive Local Government Board for Scotland. The decision (April 1917) to erect a full scale model of one of the proposed two apartment units in Dudhope Park contributed to the same process. Public interest was such that the model attracted more than 64,000 visitors, a significant number of whom were prepared to highlight the deficiencies of an arrangement (see Figure 2) that made no provision for a bathroom or lobby,[21] omissions that ran counter to Local Government Board guidelines and which were rectified in the designs as finally executed (see Figure 3).

A further and scarcely less radical revision of the 1917 arrangement involved a reduction in the number of houses provided, which was finally set at two hundred and fifty units,[22] to square almost exactly with the ratio of twelve houses to an acre recommended by the Local Government Board, having been afforded currency by Raymond Unwin's Garden City tract *Nothing Gained by Overcrowding*

(1912). The revised plan (see Figure 4) continued to be bisected by a tree lined avenue that was overlooked by an impressively proportioned viewing platform and flanked by curving side streets, a juxtaposition of formal and informal elements that is again suggestive of Unwin's influence, mirroring the shift in planning conventions that had determined the lay-outs of Letchworth Garden City and Hampstead Garden suburb.[23]

Although still described as 'tenements', the Logie flats were accessed independently rather than by a close (see Figures 5 and 6). The arrangement had probably underpinned Thomson's 1917 proposals and, afforded additional credibility by the recommendations contained in the Local Government Board's *Special Report on the Design, Construction and Materials of Various Types of Small Dwelling-Houses in Scotland* (1917),[24] would rapidly assume a wider national significance, as a source for the four flats-to-a-block format adopted by so many Scottish local authorities throughout the inter war period. Reaffirming the importance of his contribution to this process, Thomson gave the arrangement additional exposure in December

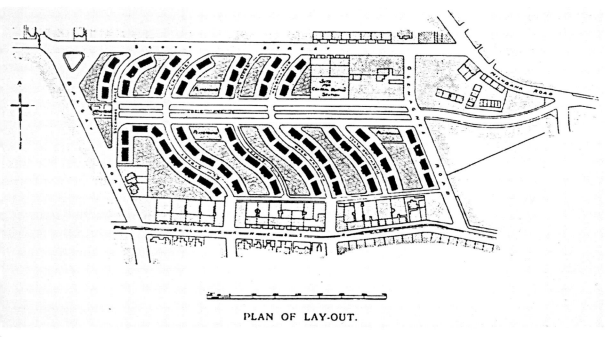

PLAN OF LAY-OUT.

Figure 4. Lay-out of the Logie estate, as finally adopted (1919). From Dundee Town Council's Souvenir of the Opening of the Logie Scheme *(1920, Dundee Central Library).*

Figure 5. Elm Street, Logie, viewed from Logie Avenue.

Figure 6. 5–8 Sycamore Place, Logie, viewed from Balgay Road.

1918, when he identified it as an appropriate response to the 'intermediate' zones described in his first Dundee Town Planning Report, in which it was once again presented in terms of architectural compromise, this time between the cottages and villas projected for the development of Dundee's outer ring area, and the thinned out eighteenth and nineteenth-century 'barracks' tenements that would continue (by implication) to occupy the old town centre.[25]

No one-apartment units were included in the final scheme, thereby ignoring Thomson's advice that the provision of this level of accommodation was necessary to meet the housing requirements of single women mill workers.[26] The two and three apartment mix nevertheless fell well short of the Local Government ideal of 50% × three apartment, 40% × four apartment and 10% × five apartment units, suggesting that the spirit of compromise that surrounded the evolution of the Dundee plans was far from one sided, and that in its determination

to secure early tangible evidence of the Government's municipal house building efforts, the Board made significant concessions in the direction of what it would describe, wryly, as Thomson's 'practical idealism'.[27]

Corporation confidence in Thomson's negotiating skills was indeed such that the roads and sewers had already been laid before the Logie plans received Local Government Board approval in June 1919.[28] The ceremony of cutting the first sod, by the Vice-President of the Local Government Board for Scotland, Sir George McCrae, took place on the 4th July 1919, more than a month before the official passing of the Housing and Town Planning (Scotland) Act, encouraging the Corporation claim that the scheme was 'the first in Scotland to be proceeded with by a Local Authority in partnership with the State', enjoying an 'easy first position of the Municipal Housing Derby'.[29] Building was well underway by 1st September 1919 when two blocks had 'reached the level of the window sill on the

Figure 7. Three-storey tenement blocks, Glenagnes Road, Logie. Erected to Thomson's designs 1922–23.

Figure 8. General view of the Logie estate, taken in circa 1922 to celebrate the completion of the scheme, which the caption claims to be the earliest of its type in Scotland (University of St Andrews Muniments Collection). Note the provision of a viewing platform, overlooking the central avenue.

ground floor'. Two months later one hundred and ninety-six men were registered as working on the site, and five blocks were 'roofed and ready for plastering work and slating' and a further nineteen in the course of construction.[30] Work on what was arguably the estate's most 'advanced' feature, the communal wash-house and boiler, supplying every house with hot water and central heating, began slightly later, in December 1919. Proposals for public baths, intended to service the Logie and Blackness areas, were never proceeded with.[31]

The wash-house complex was designed by Thomson [32] who, having submitted outline plans for the estate, assumed the rôle of 'controlling architect', co-ordinating the contributions of five local architectural firms, each of whom was assigned responsibility for a separate group of houses,[33] a largely cosmetic delegation of design responsibility that accounted for modest variations in house plan and elevation. The naming of the thoroughfares (Logie Avenue, Elm Street, Sycamore Place, Lime Street, Ashbank Road and Beechwood Place) [34] reaffirmed the estate's 'Garden Village' aspirations and preceded its official opening, by Lord Provost William Don on 27th May 1920, when eleven blocks were ready for occupation.[35] Don's celebratory speech lauded the pioneering importance of the scheme and drew attention to the 'revolutionary' significance of the houses, a theme that was developed further in the Council's accompanying souvenir pamphlet which emphasised the novelty of brick as opposed to stone construction, falsified the standard of accommodation provided (which it presented in terms of three and four apartment units (see Figure 3) and affirmed the Town Council's calculated rejection of the 'tenement system', which was now identified as a 'defective' tradition inextricably linked with 'congestion' and 'degradation'.[36]

The irony of this last assessment could scarcely

have been lost on Thomson who continued to mount a dogged defence on behalf of the provision of tenement accommodation until his dismissal, under controversial circumstances, from the combined posts of City Engineer and Director of Housing in 1924.[37] The widespread support his efforts in this respect attracted reflected a growing recognition that, whatever else it had achieved, the 1919 Act had failed to deliver 'cheap' housing, evidenced, for example, by the eventual cost of the Logie estate (over £200,000)[38] and the level of rents charged, which were set above working class norms, with the result that few, if any, of the new houses were occupied by tenants drawn from the 'poorer' sector originally targeted by post War legislation.[39]

When permission to resume tenement building was granted in 1922 it was therefore the result of special pleading, and signalled a significant shift in Dundee Corporation housing policy, which would henceforth make provision for accommodation aimed at populations displaced by slum clearances.[40] Appropriately, the first tenements to be completed in the process of this renewed phase of house building were erected at Logie, in the shape of two blocks overlooking the estate's easternmost boundary, Glenagnes Road (see Figure 7), which comprised the final post World War I additions to a scheme that had otherwise moved steadily towards completion in the summer of 1921 (see Figure 8).[41]

Departing from the example of Thomson's 1917–21 experiments, each of the Glenagnes Road blocks was three storeys in height, faced in stone and entered by a communal close, testifying to a quite calculated revival of traditional tenement features that also combined with a perpetuation of accommodation levels (ie a two and three apartment mix, with individual units supplied with bathroom, scullery and internal water-closet) afforded in the first phase houses. It proved to be a highly influential arrangement that, with modifications, would be adapted to meet low cost housing requirements in Dundee throughout the remainder of the 1920s and 1930s, providing a final vindication of Thomson's faith in the flexibility of the tenement format and its enduring relevance to the evolving Scottish townscape.

NOTES

1. See, for example, I Adams, *The Making of Urban Scotland* (London, 1978), p 178: B Lenman and D Carroll, 'Council Housing in Dundee', *Town Planning Review*, vol 43, July 1972, pp 275–85.
2. Reported in *Dundee Town Council Minutes* (hereafter *DTCM*), 1916–17, pp 515–34.
3. *DTCM*, pp 513–14. The purchase price was £4,500, as detailed in Dundee Town Council, *Housing of the Working Classes: Souvenir of the Opening of the Logie Scheme* (Dundee, 1920), p 11.
4. *DTCM*, 1916–17, p 1226.
5. *DTCM*, 1906/7, p 244.
6. First contact was on the 8th August 1905, when the Public Health Committee was invited to send delegates to the Letchworth Garden City 'cheap cottages' exhibition. The committee 'saw no cause to send any Representatives' (*DTCM*, 1904/5, p 905).
7. P Geddes, *Cities in Evolution: An Introduction to the Town Planning Movement and to the Study of Civics*, (London, 1915), pp 132–60.
8. Lenman and Carroll, 'Council Housing in Dundee', p 280. Geddes' request that the Town Council should bring his town Planning Exhibition 'at present in Chelsea and shortly to be brought to Edinburgh' to Dundee, 'as likely to be of educative value', was not, however, supported (*DTCM*, 1910/11, pp 416–17).
9. For the Law Hill proposals see *DTCM*, 1907/8, pp 1313, 1343; 1908/9, p 1190; 1909/10, pp 732, 1306–11; 1910/11, pp 193–4, 996. Details of Thomson's architectural tours (both of which were undertaken in the company of Walsh) are contained in *DTCM*, 1908/9, pp 1190, 1294–5.
10. *DTCM*, 1908/9, p 84.
11. Dated 10th December 1914, and submitted in the names of Thomson and A W Paton, Convenor of the Housing and Town Planning Committee (*DTCM*, 1914/15, pp 191–5).
12. See below footnote 6. The profile of Dundee's turn of the century working population (including the impact of the predominantly female workforce employed in the jute mills) is examined by C A Whatley in *The Remaking of Juteopolis, Dundee circa*

1891–1991 (Ed C A Whatley, Dundee, 1992), pp 7–19.

13. Reported in *Dundee Courier*, 29 November 1916, p 5; *DTCM*, 1916/17, pp 174–8.

14. Hence, for example, the (never implemented) proposal to promote an 'open' competition for 'cottages ... for the working classes', (*DTCM*, 1914/15, p 190).

15. The full text is contained in *DTCM*, 1916/17, pp 1150–3.

16. *DTCM*, 1906/7, pp 455–6. Although the scheme was never implemented it provided a focus for subsequent discussion, see for example, *DTCM*, 1908/9, p 370; 1913/14, p 1389.

17. *DTCM*, 1916/17, pp 521, 525–6.

18. Cd 8731. *Report on the Housing of the Industrial Population of Scotland, Rural and Urban*, (Edinburgh, 1917), p 71.

19. *DTCM*, 1912/13, p 465.

20. *DTCM*, 1916/17, p 525, 1152.

21. *DTCM*, 1916/17, pp 789–90.

22. A figure first reported in *DTCM*, 1918/19, pp 846–8.

23. W L Creese, *The Search for Environment*, (New Haven, 1966), p 244.

24. Cd 8760. By the Architectural Inspector of the Local Government Board of Scotland, John Wilson. See especially plates F, G and H.

25. J Thomson, *Town Planning – Comprehensive Plan and Report*, December 1918, 35pp. (*DTCM*, 1918/19, p 224).

26. *DTCM*, 1917/18, pp 781–2. For the objections of the Dundee Women Citizens' Association to the provision of one apartment dwellings, see *DTCM*, 1918/19, p 423.

27. Reported in Dundee Town Council, *Housing of the Working Classes. Souvenir of the Opening of the Logie Scheme*, (Dundee, 1920), p 14.

28. *DTCM*, 1918/19, pp 346–8.

29. Reported in *Souvenir Opening of the Logie Scheme*, p 14.

30. *DTCM*, 1918/19, pp 1146, 1358.

31. *DTCM*, 1918/19, p 1143; 1919/20, pp 887, 1336; 1920/21, pp 655, 748, 1456; 1921/22, pp 961–2.

32. *DTCM*, 1918/19, p 1138.

33. *DTCM*, 1918/19, pp 223–4, 505. The firms involved were MacLaren and Soutar, Bruce and Morton, H Thomson, W D B Keith and Thoms and Wilkie (*Souvenir Opening of the Logie Scheme*, p 4).

34. *DTCM*, 1919/20, p 615. The original proposals had been for Victoria Avenue, Haig Street, Beatty Street, Allenby Street, Rawlinson Street and Kitchiner Street (*DTCM*, 1919/20, p 545).

35. *DTCM*, 1919/20, pp 867–72.

36. *Souvenir Opening of the Logie Scheme*, pp 7, 10–11.

37. For the circumstances of his dismissal, see J Frew, 'James McLellan Brown, 1886–1967', in *100 Years: Town Planning in Dundee* (Ed H Begg, Dundee, 1992), pp 16–17. Thomson's subsequent arguments on behalf of tenement accommodation, and the support these received from the Convenor of the Housing and Town planning Committee. John Reid, are examined in J Frew, 'Rehousing the Slum Dwellers; Tenement Design in Inter-War Dundee', in Whatley, *The Remaking of Juteopolis*, pp 56–7.

38. *DTCM*, 1918/19, pp 846–8; 1920/21, pp 873–9.

39. The annual rents ('exclusive of rates') were set at £16.18.0d (for a two apartment house) and £22.2.0d (three apartment), with an additional charge (2s and 2s 6d per week) for the supply of hot water (*Souvenir Opening of the Logie Scheme*, p 23). Tenants of the Elm Street houses, recorded in 1921, thus included an insurance inspector, electrical engineer, ship's purser, joiner and journalist, as well as a finance officer, teacher and lecturer in engineering, but no mill workers (*Dundee Directory 1920–21*). Thomson's Chief Assistant, Vernon Constable, is listed as an occupant of 5 Sycamore Place in 1922 (*Dundee Directory 1922–23*).

40. Frew, 'Rehousing the Slum Dwellers', pp 59–67.

41. *DTCM*, 1920/22, pp 735–9. For the Glenagnes Road tenements, see *DTCM*, 1921/22, pp 852–3, 1194, 1631; 1922/23, pp 264, 648, 798.

David Morrison Walker OBE: A Select Bibliography

THE vast majority of Professor David Walker's ever-increasing knowledge has yet to reach the paper, but there follows a reasonably comprehensive list of his *published* works to January 1996. Students and academics, architects and planners have benefited from his generous, selfless assistance and guidance, to an immeasurable and often unrecorded degree, the extent of his contribution often at best revealed in the acknowledgements. This select bibliography may only be considered as an indication of the nature and breadth of his contribution to architectural history and conservation: it does not include any of the unpublished lectures and seminar papers.

Books and Booklets

Architects and Architecture in Dundee 1770–1914, Abertay Historical Society Paper No 3 (AHSP, 1954). Reprinted/revised as *Dundee Architects and Architecture,* Abertay Historical Society, Paper No 18 (Dundee University, 1977).

Nineteenth Century Mansions in Dundee Area (Dundee College of Art, 1958). Text and lithographed illustrations.

Mains Castle and the Grahams of Fintry with Sir Francis Mudie, Abertay Historical Society Paper (AHSP, 1964).

Glasgow at a Glance: an architectural handbook, Andrew MacLaren Young and A M Doak, Eds (Hale, 1965). Text to majority of pre-1939 entries: further editions 1971, 1977, 1983.

The Architecture of Glasgow with Andor Gomme (Lund Humphries, 1968, revised and enlarged edition, 1987).

Broughty Castle and the Defence of Tay with Sir Francis Mudie and Iain MacIvor, Abertay Historical Society Paper (AHSP, 1970 and 1979).

Royal Incorporation of Architects in Scotland (RIAS) Architectural Guides:

Edinburgh: an illustrated Guide with Charles McKean (RIAS, 1982).

Buildings of Scotland, Edinburgh with John Gifford and Colin McWilliam (Penguin, 1984). Contribution particularly to the inner city.

Dundee: an illustrated introduction with Charles McKean (RIAS, 1984).

St Andrew's House: An Edinburgh Controversy 1912–1939 (HMSO, 1989).

Central Glasgow with Charles McKean and Frank Walker (Mainstream/RIAS, 1990).

Contributions to Books

'The Architecture of Dundee' in *Dundee and District,* British Association for the Advancement of Science, Handbook, S J Jones, Ed (1968).

'Scone Palace, Perthshire', in *The Country Seat,* John Harris and H M Colvin, Eds (Allen Lane, 1970), pp 210–14.

Extensive revision, with additional text, of Ian G Lindsay *Georgian Edinburgh* (Scottish Academic Press, Chatto & Windus, distributors, 1973).

'Scotland at the End of the Century' in *Edwardian Architecture and its Origins,* Alastair Service, Ed (Architectural Press, 1975), chapters on 'Sir John James Burnet', pp 192–215, 'Charles Rennie Mackintosh', pp 216–35, and 'The Partnership of James Salmon and John Gaff Gillespie', pp 236–49.

'William Burn: the Country House in Transition', in *Seven Victorian Architects,* Jane Fawcett, Ed (Thames & Hudson, 1976), chp 1, pp 8–31.

'Burn and Bryce' in V Fiddes and A Rowan, Eds, *Mr David Bryce 1803–1876,* chapter on (University of Edinburgh, 1976), Introduction, pp 23–30.

'The Revival Styles' in A A Tait, Ed, *Treasures in Trust,* in association with National Trust for Scotland (HMSO, 1981), pp 40–9.

Macmillan Encyclopaedia of Architects, entries on William Burn, David Hamilton, James Thomson and others (Macmillan, 1982).

'The Architecture of MacGibbon and Ross: the background to the books' in D J Breeze, Ed, *Studies in Scottish Antiquity,* presented to Stewart Cruden (John Donald, 1984), pp 391–449.

'William Burn and the influence of Sir Robert Smirke

and William Wilkins on Scottish Greek Revival Design 1810–1840', in N Allen, Ed, *Scottish Pioneers of the Greek Revival* (Scottish Georgian Society, 1984), pp 3–36.

'Mackintosh's Scottish Antecedents', in P Nuttgens, Ed, *Mackintosh and His Contemporaries* (John Murray, 1988), pp 32–8.

Scottish entries in Peter Howell and Ian Sutton, Eds, *The Faber Guide to Victorian Churches* (Faber, 1989).

'Mackintosh on Architecture', Introduction to two lectures, in P Robertson, Ed, *Charles Rennie Mackintosh: the Architectural Papers* (White Cockade, 1990), pp 153–79.

'Scotland and Paris', The University of St Andrews: *Studies in the History of Architecture and Design,* number 2, *Scotland and Europe* (St Andrews University Press, 1991), pp 15–40.

Introduction to *The Rudiments of Architecture* (Black & Harris, 1778 edition, 1992 reprint).

Dictionary of National Biography, Missing Persons Supplement, C S Nicholls, Ed (OUP, 1993), entry on William Stark, pp 631–2.

'The Development of Thomson's Style', G Stamp and S McKinstry, Eds, *Greek Thomson* (EUP, 1994), pp 23–50.

'The Country Houses, Larger Villas and Related Hotel Designs of Sir John James Burnet', A J Rowan and I Gow, Eds, *Scottish Country Houses 1600–1914,* essays presented to Catherine Cruft (EUP, 1995), 298–324.

Macmillan Dictionary of Art (Macmillan, 1996), entries on G W Browne; William Burn; J J Burnet; the Mackenzie Family; William Leiper; Peddie and Kinnear; F T Pilkington; James Salmon; William Stark; T S Tait; Charles Wilson.

'The Glasgow Years', in W Kaplan, Ed, *Charles Rennie Mackintosh* (Abbeville Press, 1996).

'A History of the Scottish Architectural Profession' with Charles McKean, in Rebecca M Bailey, Ed, *Scottish Architects' Papers: a source book* (Rutland Press, 1996), pp 18–61.

Periodicals

'Lamond of Dundee' (William Gillespie), *Architectural Review*, Vol 123, April 1958, pp 269–71.

'Duddingston House', *Country Life*, Vol 126, 24 September 1959, pp 358–61.

'Chatelherault, Lanarkshire: Threat to a Ducal Dog Kennel', *Country Life*, Vol 136, 17 December 1964, pp 1716–19.

'Glasgow Old' (2-part guide to central area), *Glasgow Institute of Architects Year Book*, Glasgow, 1965 and 1966 issues.

'Ian Gordon Lindsay 1906–1966', a memoir, *Architectural Review*, Vol 141, January 1966, pp 5–6.

'Salmon, Son, Grandson and Gillespie', *The Scottish Art Review*, Vol X, No 3, 1966, pp 17–21.

'James Sellars, Architect, Glasgow', *The Scottish Art Review*, Vol XI, No 1, 1967, pp 16–19.

'The Buildings of the Commercial College, Dundee', *Ecco*, Bulletin of Dundee Commercial College, Vol 1, 1966–67.

'Glendoick, Perthshire', *Country Life*, Vol 141, 30 March 1967, pp 708–12.

'Lost Splendours of the Fair City of Perth: part I', *Country Life*, 3 October 1968, pp 804–7.

'Completion of the Nineteenth Century Facade: Perth II', *Country Life*, Vol 144, 10 October 1968, pp 916–19.

'Charles Rennie Mackintosh', *Architectural Review*, Vol 144, November 1968. pp 355–63. Reprinted in J M Richards and N Pevsner, Eds, *The Anti Rationalists* (1973), and A Service, Ed, *Edwardian Architecture and its Origins* (1975).

'Fortress Palace of the North: Stirling I', *Country Life*, Vol 146, 14 August 1969, pp 372–4.

'Exploring the Old Burgh: Stirling II', *Country Life*, Vol 146, 21 August 1969, pp 452–4.

'Era of Banks and Churches: Stirling III', *Country Life*, Vol 146, 28 August 1969, pp 502–4.

'Architecture of Glasgow', *Times Literary Supplement*, 1969, p 191.

'From High Street to Gilmorehill', centenary article on the buildings of the University of Glasgow, *Scottish Field*, Vol 117, No 814, October 1970, pp 18–27, part with Anne Ross.

'Cairness, Aberdeenshire', *Country Life*, Vol 149, 28 January and 4 February 1971, with Colin McWilliam, p 184f, p 284f.

'Brechin Castle, Angus', *Country Life*, Vol 150, 12 and 19 August 1971, with J G Dunbar, p 378f, p 436f.

'Haddington, East Lothian: The Saving of a Scots Burgh', *Country Life*, Vol 152, 10 August 1972, pp 318–21.

'Haddington, East Lothian: Restoration on a Heroic Scale' *Country Life*, Vol 152, 17 August 1972, pp 402–4.

'The Stirlings of Dunblane and Falkirk, fragments of five architectural biographies', *Bulletin of the Scottish Georgian Society*, Vol 1, 1972, pp 40–59.

'Restoring Tower Houses in Scotland – I', with Alistair Rowan, *Country Life*, Vol 155, 14 February 1974, pp 289–301.

'Restoring Tower Houses in Scotland – II', with Alistair Rowan, *Country Life*, Vol 155, 21 February 1974, pp 358–61.

'Master of the Grand Manner: David Bryce 1803–1876', *Country Life*, Vol 160, 28 October 1976, pp 1210–11.

'A Fife Burgh Restored: St Monans, *Country Life*, Vol 161, 6 January 1977, pp 6–8.

'The Donaldson's Hospital Competition and the Palace

of Westminster, *Architectural History*, Vol 27, Studies in Architectural History presented to H M Colvin (Maneys, 1984), pp 488–97.

'Glasgow', *Werk: Bauen + Wohnen* (Zurich), September 1985.

'House of Dun: Unique in Scottish Architecture', *Heritage Scotland*, Vol 6, Part 1, 1989.

'William Burn', *Journal of the Royal Institute of British Architects*, June 1990.

'Thomas Tait', *Journal of the Royal Institute of British Architects*, August 1991, pp 20–5.

'The Rebuilding of Kings and Marischal Colleges', *Aberdeen University Review*, Vol 55, No 190, autumn 1993.

'Govan Old: its place in nineteenth and early twentieth century church design', in *Society of Friends of Govan Old*, Third Annual Report, 1993, pp 4–20.

'The Honeymans', *Charles Rennie Mackintosh Society Newsletter*, No 64, Spring 1994, pp 5–8.

'Listing in Scotland: Origins, Survey and Resurvey' *Transactions of the Ancient Monuments Society*, Vol 38, 1994, pp 31–94.

Reviews

Review of Thomas Howarth, *Charles Rennie Mackintosh*, in *Times Literary Supplement*, 1977, p 1450.

Review of Colin McWilliam, *Scottish Townscape*, in *Times Literary Supplement*, 1976, p 893.

Review of reprint of William Adam, *Vitruvius Scoticus*, in *Times Literary Supplement*, 1980, p 988.

Review of A A Tait, *Landscape Garden in Scotland*, in *Times Literary Supplement*, 1981, p 294.

Review of Peter Savage, *Lorimer and the Edinburgh Craft Designers*, in *Times Literary Supplement*, 1981, p 387.

Review of Roger Billcliffe, *Charles Rennie Mackintosh*, in *Times Literary Supplement*, 1981, p 445.

Review of A Fenton and B Walker *The Rural Architecture of Scotland*, in *Times Literary* Supplement, 1981, p 964.

Review of D G Campbell, *Scotland's Story in her Monuments*, in *Times Literary Supplement*, 1982, p 1373.

Review of Thomas Markus, Ed, *Order in Space and Society*, 1983, p 410.

Review of Katharine Sim, *David Robert RA 1796–1864*, in *Times Literary Supplement*, 1984, p 701.

Review of John Martin Robinson, *Georgian Model Farms*, in *Times Literary Supplement*, 1984, p 409.

Review of P Crowl, *The Intelligent Traveller's Guide to Historic Scotland*, in *Times Literary Supplement*, 1986, p 1199.

Newspapers

'Charles Rennie Mackintosh 1868–1968: an assessment', centenary tribute, *The Glasgow Herald*, 7 June 1968.

Departmental Publications

Guidelines for the Detailed Consideration of Listed Building Consent Cases, *Memorandum of Guidance on Listed Buildings and Conservation Areas* (1987), Appendix 1.

Book Illustrations

The Forests of North East Scotland, for H L Edlin of the Forestry Commission (HMSO, 1963, 1976).

In addition to the above, Professor Walker had advisory responsibilities in relation to Ian G Lindsay and Mary Cosh *Inveraray and the Dukes of Argyll* (EUP, 1973) as a result of the death of Ian Lindsay in 1966 while the writing of the book was in progress.

He also contributed research information on the architects practising in Edinburgh, Glasgow, Dundee, Aberdeen, Elgin, Perth and Stirling to H M Colvin *Dictionary of British Architects 1600–1840* (Yale, 1978, 1995) in which due acknowledgement is found. He assisted Geoffrey Beard with *Decorative Plasterwork in Great Britain* (Phaidon, 1975) and John Martin Robinson with the gazetteer of *Georgian Model Farms* (Clarendon, 1983).

Index